CHAUCER

A BIBLIOGRAPHICAL INTRODUCTION

TORONTO MEDIEVAL BIBLIOGRAPHIES 10

General Editor: John Leyerle

Published in association with
the Centre for Medieval Studies, University of Toronto

JOHN LEYERLE and ANNE QUICK

Chaucer

A BIBLIOGRAPHICAL INTRODUCTION

UNIVERSITY OF TORONTO PRESS
Toronto   Buffalo   London

© University of Toronto Press 1986
Toronto   Buffalo   London
Printed in Canada

ISBN 0-8020-2375-4 (cloth)
ISBN 0-8020-6408-6 (paper)

Canadian Cataloguing in Publication Data

Leyerle, John.
   Chaucer, a bibliographical introduction
   (Toronto medieval bibliographies ; 10)
   "Published in association with the Centre for
   Medieval Studies, University of Toronto."
   Includes index.
   ISBN 0-8020-2375-4 (bound) – ISBN 0-8020-6408-6 (pbk.)
   1. Chaucer, Geoffrey, d. 1400 – Bibliography.
   I. Quick, Anne Wenley, 1949-   II. University of
   Toronto. Centre for Medieval Studies. III. Title.
   IV. Series.
   Z8164.L49 1986   016.821'1   C86-093265-6

To the memory of
George Stern Quick, Jr
1941–1985

Editor's Preface

The study of the Middle Ages has been developed chiefly within university departments such as English or History. This pattern is increasingly being supplemented by an interdisciplinary approach in which the plan of work is shaped to fit the subject studied. The difference of approach is between Chaucer the English poet and Chaucer the civil servant of London attached to the court of Richard II, a man interested in the Ptolemaic universe and widely read in Latin, French, and Italian. Interdisciplinary programs tend to lead readers into areas relatively unfamiliar to them where critical bibliographies prepared with careful selectivity by an expert are essential. The Centre for Medieval Studies at the University of Toronto takes such an interdisciplinary approach to the Middle Ages, and the need for selective bibliographies has become apparent in our work. The Centre has undertaken to meet this need by sponsoring the Toronto Medieval Bibliographies.

In his valuable guide, *Serial Bibliographies for Medieval Studies*,* Richard H. Rouse describes 283 bibliographies; the number is surprisingly large and indicates the considerable effort now being made to provide inclusive lists of items relevant to medieval studies. The total amount in print is already vast; for one unfamiliar with a subject, significant work is difficult to locate and the problem grows worse with each year's output. The reader may well say, like the throng in *Piers Plowman* seeking the way to *Treuthe*, 'This were a wikked way but who-so hadde a gyde' (B.vi.I). The Toronto

*Publications of the Center for Medieval and Renaissance Studies 3, University of California, Los Angeles (Berkeley and Los Angeles 1969)

Medieval Bibliographies are meant to be such guides; each title is prepared by an expert and gives directions to important work in the subject.

Each volume gives a list of works selected with three specific aims. One is to aid students who are relatively new to the area of study, for example Medieval Latin Palaeography. Another is to guide more advanced readers in a subject where they have had little formal training, for example Medieval Rhetoric or Chaucer; and the third is to assist new libraries in forming a basic collection in the subject presented. Individual compilers are given scope to organize a presentation that they judge will best suit their subject and also to make brief critical comments as they think fit. Clarity and usefulness of a volume are preferred over any demand for exact uniformity from one volume to another.

Toronto, September 1985
JL

Contents

Chaucer's Sources and Influences 31

II
Chaucer's Works 99

General Critical Studies (CrS) 101

Abbreviations

Titles of Journals and Series

CE	*College English*
CFMA	*Les Classiques français du moyen âge*
ChauR	*Chaucer Review*
EETS	Early English Text Society
ELH	*English Literary History*
ELN	*English Language Notes*
E&S	*Essays and Studies* (English Association)
ES	*English Studies*
JEGP	*Journal of English and Germanic Philology*
MÆ	*Medium Ævum*
MLN	*Modern Language Notes*
MLQ	*Modern Language Quarterly*
MLR	*Modern Language Review*
MP	*Modern Philology*
MS	*Mediaeval Studies*
NM	*Neuphilologische Mitteilungen*
PL	Patrologiae cursus completus, series Latina, ed. J.-P. Migne
PMLA	*Publications of the Modern Language Association*
PQ	*Philological Quarterly*
RES	*Review of English Studies*
SATF	Société des anciens textes français
SP	*Studies in Philology*
TSLL	*Texas Studies in Literature and Language*
UTQ	*University of Toronto Quarterly*

Titles of Chaucer's Works as used by Robinson **M30**

Anel	*Anelida and Arcite*
Astr	*A Treatise on the Astrolabe*
BD	*The Book of the Duchess*
Bo	*Boece*
CkT	*The Cook's Tale*
ClT	*The Clerk's Tale*
CT	*The Canterbury Tales*
CYT	*The Canon's Yeoman's Tale*
Eq	*The Equatorie of the Planetis*

FranklT	*The Franklin's Tale*	*ParsT*	*The Parson's Tale*
FrT	*The Friar's Tale*	*PF*	*The Parliament of Fowls*
GenProl	*The General Prologue*	*PhysT*	*The Physician's Tale*
HF	*The House of Fame*	*Prol*	*Prologue*
KnT	*The Knight's Tale*	*PrT*	*The Prioress's Tale*
LGW	*The Legend of Good*	*Rom*	*The Romaunt of the Rose*
	Women	*RvT*	*The Reeve's Tale*
MancT	*The Manciple's Tale*	*SecNT*	*The Second Nun's Tale*
Mel	*The Tale of Melibee*	*ShipT*	*The Shipman's Tale*
MerchT	*The Merchant's Tale*	*SqT*	*The Squire's Tale*
MillT	*The Miller's Tale*	*SumT*	*The Summoner's Tale*
MkT	*The Monk's Tale*	*Thop*	*Sir Thopas*
MLT	*The Man of Law's Tale*	*Tr*	*Troilus and Criseyde*
NPT	*The Nun's Priest's Tale*	*WBT*	*The Wife of Bath's Tale*
PardT	*The Pardoner's Tale*		

Authors' Preface

Chaucer: A Bibliographical Introduction was compiled primarily for readers relatively unfamiliar with the works of Chaucer and their context. For those well-acquainted with Chaucer's writing, the compilers hope that this bibliography may have value as a convenient finding list, but we make no claim to inform our learned colleagues on a subject where we judge ourselves more apt to receive than give instruction. The aim of the volume accounts for its three-part division.

The first part concerns materials for the study of Chaucer's work and corresponds to the contents of an introduction to an edition of Chaucer. There are sections on bibliographical guides to Chaucer, on the texts and canon of his works, on his language and versification, on his life records, and, finally, on his literary sources and influences. The final section is subdivided under four headings by language of the texts cited: English, French, Italian, and Latin. No hard and fast line can be drawn between texts that Chaucer evidently knew at first hand and others that he knew only from excerpts in *florilegia* or cited so sparingly as to leave his degree of indebtedness uncertain. Our point here is to indicate that the list of texts cited in this section is limited to those that scholars have identified as having been direct sources or influences on his work as shown by verbal echoes extending over several lines of Chaucer's works.

The second part of the bibliography, and by far the longest, is devoted to Chaucer's works, beginning with general critical studies that concern several or all of his works. Each of the major works has a section on its own; the sequence of works follows the order of texts in Robinson's edition (**M30**). The abbreviations of Chaucer's works used here and summarized on pages xv-xvi are those employed by Robinson, set out on page 647 of his edition. In choosing items to be included, we paid particular attention to the needs of those unfamiliar with Chaucer's works. This principle of selection accounts for the inclusion of some items that may seem superseded by later works in the eyes of experts.

The third part, on the backgrounds to Chaucer's works, requires special explanation because it contains items over a wide range of topics in some of which we have no specialized competence. The range of topics appears in the table of contents and needs no repetition here. We were guided by advice from colleagues expert in these topics, but made the selection of works cited on the basis of what items seemed to us to be most helpful for a reader of Chaucer relatively unfamiliar with his work and almost completely unfamiliar with English society and life in the second half of the fourteenth century. This part of the bibliography is offered, then, in a provisional way, with the caution that it will likely require substantial modification in the next edition.

The treatment of names in the bibliography needs some explanation. The names of classical and medieval authors appear in the forms used in the National Union Catalogue of the Library of Congress, because those are the forms widely used in other library systems. Some oddities result. Saint Jerome, for example, appears in the Latin form of his name as Hieronymus. Nigel Longchamps is listed as Nigellus Wireker, although the latter name has little historical foundation, as the headnote to the entry makes evident. The names of modern authors appear in the form used by the author in the work being cited, even though some authors sign their works in various forms. In the index, the full first names of authors are given as an aid in consulting catalogues. Where initials only appear in the index, they are, as Richard Pfaff put the matter, in his preface to *Medieval Latin Liturgy* (volume 8 in this series), those of 'a few who resist all attempts to pry beyond their initials.'

The entries are cross-referenced somewhat more fully than is usual in a bibliography for those expert in the subject. The reason is the one already given: the work is directed mainly to those unfamiliar with Chaucer's works and their context.

A similar comment should be made about headnotes and, to some degree, about the annotations after each title cited. If a reader expert in Chaucer wonders why he or she is being informed repeatedly about commonplaces, the reason is that the volume is directed to those not yet at such a stage of understanding, but hoping to reach it.

In compiling this bibliography an effort was made to survey all material published on Chaucer to the end of 1979. When we completed our work of selecting and annotating this material in 1981, we found the results wanting in both accuracy and selection of titles. The manuscript was reworked from the originals in an effort to correct inaccuracies and reduce omissions of essential items. The reworking of the manuscript turned out to be a protracted task. To ignore all works published after 1979 seemed an artificial constraint as the decade of the 1980s progressed. We managed to squeeze in some important works, if by no means all, published in this decade, but the basis of selection remains material published up to the end of 1979. The blurring of the cut-off date and the remaining inaccuracies and omissions that have eluded us illustrate the wry observation that bibliographies are not so much completed as abandoned if they are to appear at all. A systematic sifting of all items published after 1979 will have to wait for the next edition.

Many colleagues and friends have assisted us in compiling this bibliography. Students in John Leyerle's graduate Chaucer seminars in 1972-3 and 1973-4 read extensively in assigned areas of Chaucer criticism and evaluated what they read from their point of view: that of graduate students who began the task relatively unfamiliar with the subject. Their reaction was valuable in reminding us steadily of the needs and outlook of our primary audience. Reginald Berry, Malcolm Burson, Helen Hoy, Allison Kingsmill, and Kathy Martindale were particularly helpful in doing this work, and we thank them most warmly. William Stoneman compiled the index in its first version and checked many points with patience and thoroughness. Brenda Missen checked the manuscript entries against title pages with care and steady attention to details. The late Angus Cameron gave us good advice and warm support. George Rigg read the manuscript with acute attention to details and made many helpful comments and suggestions, as did the several readers for the University of Toronto Press who remain unknown to us but who deserve our thanks here. Stephen Barney suggested many improvements to the section on *Troilus*. Our largest debt, by far, is to Patricia Eberle, who worked over the manuscript with immense attention, care, and energy. Her contribution to the project has been greater than we have any right to ask of even the most generous and helpful of colleagues, and we are very grateful that she was willing to make it.

Anna Burko scrutinized the final draft of the manuscript and worked as copy-editor on it. Her care and experience with this task clarified ambiguities and saved us from many errors. Prudence Tracy kept an eye, sometimes friendly, sometimes wary, on the project during its long history and saw the manuscript into print. To all of these people go our deep thanks and acknowledgement that the number of errors still here are our own and would have been much larger without the dedicated skill and effort of all those who assisted us in the project. We don't even have an Adam Scrivener to blame for the remaining faults.

This introduction mainly concerns the limits of this bibliography. Our purpose is not to disclaim final responsibility for them but, in making them clear, to make clearer the audience for whom the work is intended, and also to indicate how it has been prepared to help that audience in reading the works of the incomparable Geoffrey Chaucer.

Toronto, September 1985
JL and AQ

I
Materials for the Study of Chaucer's Works

Part I of this bibliography has five major sections. They provide guidance in approaching Chaucer's work taken as a whole. The first section lists bibliographies of work on Chaucer, including bibliographical handbooks and indices. The second section provides information on Chaucer's texts and canon. Included here are listings of facsimiles, editions, textual studies, studies of the Chaucerian canon and its dating, texts wrongly attributed to Chaucer, and his lost works. The third section covers language and versification and starts with some items on Middle English to provide a context for the specific studies on Chaucer's language. The fourth section covers the life-records of Chaucer, dealing mainly with his legal and financial situation; surprisingly, not one allusion in the life-records is made to his poetry. The final section is by far the longest and covers Chaucer's sources and influences, which have been studied with great energy, perseverance, and skill by generations of scholars. As their work has shown very clearly, Chaucer was a bookish poet, and his writing can be understood fully only when placed in the literary context that influenced him so deeply. Because of the importance of this section, it has its own headnote (pp. 31–3).

BIBLIOGRAPHIES

Comprehensive Bibliographies of Works on Chaucer

These are listed chronologically. For an edition which includes a full bibliography for 1964-74 see Fisher **M29**.

M1
Hammond, Eleanor Prescott. *Chaucer: A Bibliographical Manual* (New York 1908, repr. 1933)
Hammond's work is the standard guide up to 1908. The introduction summarizes the development of critical views of special problems, and a long section on works known to Chaucer, with its notes for his knowledge of them, is an excellent starting-point for the study of Chaucer's learning. Hammond includes descriptions of MSS and early editions.

M2
Griffith, Dudley David. *Bibliography of Chaucer, 1908-53* (Seattle 1955)
In supplementing Hammond **M1**, Griffith revises somewhat the arrangement of items, lists many reviews, and provides some annotations and a good index.

M3
Crawford, William R. *Bibliography of Chaucer, 1954-63* (Seattle and London 1967)
Crawford continues the work of Griffith **M2** and adds a bibliographical essay, 'New Directions in Chaucer Criticism.'

M4
Baird, Lorrayne Y. *A Bibliography of Chaucer, 1964-73* (Boston 1977)
Baird continues the work of Crawford **M3**.

Annual Bibliographies

M5
English Association. *The Year's Work in English Studies* (London 1921-   )

Each volume gives, in essay format, summaries of the year's books
and articles in English studies; the emphasis is on works published
in England. The series begins with listings from 1919.
M6
Modern Language Association, Committee on Chaucer Research
and Bibliography. 'Chaucer Research,' *ChauR* 1- (1966/7-)
This annual bibliography includes work in progress, work com-
pleted but unpublished, and work published by the time of the
report. Beginning with Report No. 27 (for 1966), by T.A. Kirby, it is
published in the *Chaucer Review;* for Reports 1-26, see **M10**.
M7
Modern Humanities Research Association. *Annual Bibliography of
English Language and Literature* (Cambridge 1921-)
Beginning with listings from 1920, this bibliography contains an
annual listing of work on Chaucer with particular reference to titles
published in England.
M8
_____ *The Year's Work in Modern Language Studies* (London
1931-)
Beginning with listings from 1929-30, this series gives short
descriptions of work in such broad areas as Celtic, Germanic,
Latin, and Romance; most of the material is peripheral to Chaucer,
but some items are useful for Chaucer's background.
M9
Modern Language Association of America. *Publications of the
Modern Language Association (PMLA)*
An annual bibliography has been printed each year since 1921.
Each bibliography includes all Chaucer items that have come to the
attention of the Association in a given year; the aim is completeness, and there are no annotations. The bibliographies from 1921-50
have been reprinted as *MLA American Bibliography of Books and
Articles on the Modern Languages and Literatures,* 6 vols. (New York
1964). In 1957-63, the bibliography was expanded to include works
not of American authorship and publication, and the title was
changed from *American Bibliography* to *Annual Bibliography.* In
1964 the title was changed to *MLA International Bibliography* to
emphasize the international scope of the work.
M10
_____ The Chaucer Group: Committee on Bibliographical and

Research Projects. *Chaucer Research,* Reports 1-26 ([Baton Rouge, La.] 1937-65)
This annual bibliography includes work in progress and work completed but not yet published, as well as published work. For Reports 27ff. see **M6**.
M11
New Chaucer Society. 'An Annotated Chaucer Bibliography,' compiled by John H. Fisher et al., in *Studies in the Age of Chaucer.* Publications of the New Chaucer Society 1-   (1979-   )
Each volume contains a selective, annotated bibliography based primarily on **M9** and classified according to Chaucer's works and related subjects. Vol. 1 (1979) contains entries for 1975 and 1976, vol. 2 (1980) for 1977 and 1978. Starting with vol. 3, coverage is on an annual basis for the second year back; thus 1981 covers 1979, etc.
M12
Rzepecki, Arnold N., intro. and comp. of index. *Literature and Language Bibliographies from the American Year Book, 1910-1919.* Cumulated Bibliography Series 1 (Ann Arbor 1970)
This collected bibliography is reprinted from the *American Year Book* annuals, 1910-19; when the *American Year Book* suspended publication in 1920, the Modern Language Association of America took over the publication of this annual bibliography, which eventually became the *MLA International Bibliography* (see **M9**).

Selective Bibliographies

The essays printed in Rowland **CrS13** include selective bibliographies.

M13
Baugh, Albert C. *Chaucer.* Goldentree Bibliographies in Language and Literature, gen. ed. O.B. Hardison, Jr. (New York 1968; 2nd ed. Arlington Heights, Ill. 1977)
Baugh includes a full selection of recent works dealing directly with Chaucer; the selection of background and related studies is limited. There are no annotations.
M14
Benson, L.D. 'A Reader's Guide to Writings on Chaucer' and

'Chaucer: A Select Bibliography' in Brewer **B8**, 321-72
Benson gives a selected, briefly-annotated bibliography arranged by
topics and prefaced by a bibliographical essay.
M15
The New Cambridge Bibliography of English Literature, ed. George
Watson (Cambridge 1974) I, 557-628
This bibliography is based on and replaces *The Cambridge
Bibliography of English Literature*, 4 vols. ed. F.W. Bateson
(Cambridge 1940), and its *Supplement*, vol. V (Cambridge 1957) ed.
George Watson. The pages cited provide a concise guide to
Chaucer studies.

Handbooks

M16
Wells, John Edwin. *A Manual of the Writings in Middle English
1050-1400* (New Haven and London 1916; many reprints) and
Supplements 1-9 (New Haven and London 1919-51)
The manual is organized by literary genres; each chapter is a work-
by-work commentary on the literature of the genre, followed by full
bibliographical notes. The supplements cover material published up
to 1945. Wells is being superseded by the Severs-Hartung revised
Manual, of which several volumes have already apeared; see **M17**.
The Chaucer section of Wells (pp. 599-747 and 866-81) was
designed as a supplement to Hammond **M1**.
M17
Severs, J. Burke and Albert E. Hartung, gen. eds. *A Manual of the
Writings in Middle English 1050-1500: By Members of the Middle
English Group of the Modern Language Association of America*
(New Haven 1967-   )
Basing their manual on Wells's **M16** and following a similar format,
Severs and Hartung extend the work to 1500. To date six volumes
have appeared; the only material of directly Chaucerian interest is
Rossell Hope Robbins' 'The Chaucerian Apocrypha' in vol. IV.

Indices

From the viewpoint of the Chaucerian, the four books listed below are useful primarily for their lists of MSS containing the works of Chaucer. Much of this information is available in the editions and bibliographical guides listed elsewhere in this bibliography, but it is especially accessible in these indices, which give a sense of the literary context of some of Chaucer's poems; thus *WBT* appears among feminist and antifeminist works listed in Utley **M21**, and *SecNT* appears among the numerous devotional poems cited in Brown **M18**. In addition to serving as guides to important areas of Middle English literature, these works provide valuable information on such topics as the literature of Chaucer's predecessors and contemporaries, the relative popularity of various Middle English works, and the Chaucerian apocrypha.

M18
Brown, Carleton. *A Register of Middle English Religious and Didactic Verse.* 2 vols. (Oxford 1916, 1920)
The first volume is a list of MSS containing religious and didactic poems; the second lists the poems, alphabetized by first line, with MS information for each entry.

M19
Brown, Carleton and Rossell Hope Robbins. *The Index of Middle English Verse* (New York 1943)
This index supplements Brown **M18**. It includes secular verse, alphabetized by first line, and a conversion table for the numbers in Brown.

M20
Robbins, Rossell Hope and John L. Cutler. *Supplement to the Index of Middle English Verse* (Lexington, Ky. 1965)
The volume is designed to update Brown and Robbins **M19**.

M21
Utley, Francis Lee. *The Crooked Rib: An Analytical Index to the Argument about Women in English and Scots Literature to the End of the Year 1568.* Ohio State University Contributions in Languages and Literature 10 (Columbus 1944)
Utley includes an introduction on satires and defences of women in English literature, and indices to poems about women by first line, title, and MS or print; among those indexed are *WBT, ClT, MerchT, FranklT, LGW,* and some of the short poems. The work is useful for study of analogues to the Marriage Group.

TEXTS AND CANON OF CHAUCER'S WORKS

Facsimiles

M22
The Ellesmere Chaucer: Reproduced in Facsimile. 2 vols. (Manchester 1911)
The Ellesmere MS is used as the basis for most editions of *CT*, such as Robinson **M30**. The MS is noted for its fine illustrations of the pilgrims.
M23
Geoffrey Chaucer. *The Canterbury Tales: A Facsimile and Transcription of the Hengwrt Manuscript, with Variants from the Ellesmere Manuscript,* ed. Paul G. Ruggiers, intro. Donald C. Baker, with 'A Paleographical Introduction' by A.I. Doyle and M.B. Parkes. Variorum Edition of the Works of Geoffrey Chaucer 1 (Norman, Okla. and Folkestone 1979)
This first volume of the Variorum Chaucer is designed to provide reference texts of the two most valuable *CT* MSS, Hengwrt and Ellesmere; Hengwrt, supplemented by Ellesmere where Hengwrt is wanting, is the base text in the Variorum edition of *CT*. Facsimile and transcription appear on facing pages; the Ellesmere variants are printed line by line beside the Hengwrt transcription. The paleographical introduction by Doyle and Parkes is thorough and valuable.
M24
_____ *Troilus and Criseyde: A Facsimile of Corpus Christi College, Cambridge, MS. 61,* intro. M.B. Parkes and Elizabeth Salter (Cambridge 1978)
This MS, dated by the editors no later than 1415, was evidently planned as a deluxe copy; it contains the famous full-colour frontispiece showing Chaucer declaiming from a rostrum to a courtly audience. M.B. Parkes provides a paleographical description (pp. 1-13). Salter, in an essay on the frontispiece (pp. 15-23), argues (against Galway **M117** and in agreement with Pearsall **M127**) that the picture of Chaucer is adapted from the tradition of preaching miniatures and cannot provide evidence for any historical occasion, but she notes that the deluxe quality of the MS does imply a high level of appreciation for *Tr* by its contemporary audience.

M25

_____ *The Works, 1532 with Supplementary Material from the Editions of 1542, 1561, 1598, and 1602,* ed. D.S. Brewer (Menston, Eng. 1969; repr. 1974, 1976)
Brewer's edition is a composite facsimile which provides a conspectus of Chaucer's works as they appeared to readers in the 16th and early 17th centuries, a textual tradition which included many works wrongly ascribed to Chaucer. Thynne's edition of 1532 is the nucleus, to which material from later editions is added. The resulting facsimile makes available all that appeared under Chaucer's name from 1532 to 1602. Brewer includes a bibliographical introduction.

M26
The Works of Geoffrey Chaucer and Others: Being a Reproduction in Facsimile of the First Collected Edition 1532 from the Copy in the British Museum, ed. Walter W. Skeat (London 1905)
The work includes a biographical account of William Thynne, who produced the 1532 edition, and a list of the first eight printed editions of the works of Chaucer.

Editions

This section lists editions of Chaucer's works as a whole; for editions of individual works, such as *CT* and *Tr,* see the relevant sections of this bibliography. For a comprehensive list of the early editions of Chaucer's works, see Hammond **M1**, 114-49.

M27
Baugh, Albert C., ed. *Chaucer's Major Poetry* (New York 1963)
Baugh omits *Rom, Anel,* much of *LGW,* some of the short lyrics, and all of the prose; the linguistic apparatus and glossary are full and helpful.

M28
Donaldson, E.T., ed. *Chaucer's Poetry: An Anthology for the Modern Reader* (New York 1958, 2nd ed. 1975)
This edition, aimed at the general reader, has slightly modernized spelling and generous glossing at the foot of the page. The prose *Tales* and some short poems are omitted; the short critical essays on

each poem are excellent introductions to Chaucer's work. Donaldson uses the Hengwrt MS as the base text for *CT* and the Corpus MS at the base text for *Tr.*

M29
Fisher, John H., ed. *The Complete Poetry and Prose of Geoffrey Chaucer* (New York 1977)
Fisher's useful edition includes an introduction to each work, explanatory notes and glosses at the foot of each page, and a long bibliography, including a complete bibliography for 1964-74. It is the only edition of Chaucer's works which includes *Eq.* The text of each work derives from a base MS, 'conservatively emended,' except that Fisher prints a composite version of *LGWProl.*

M30
Robinson, F.N., ed. *The Works of Geoffrey Chaucer* (Boston 1933, 2nd ed. 1957)
Robinson's is the standard one-volume edition. His text is good, and his explanatory notes are excellent and exhaustive, if overly spare in bibliographical details. The main weaknesses of this edition are the very brief glossary and the section on language. See Skeat **M31**. A new edition is underway under the general editorship of L.D. Benson and R.A. Pratt.

M31
Skeat, Walter W., ed. *The Complete Works of Geoffrey Chaucer.* 6 vols. (Oxford 1894, 2nd ed. 1899; many reprints, including a 1-vol. abridged ed.)
The first scholarly edition of Chaucer, this remains a standard reference work. Skeat's notes are often fuller than Robinson's; he also lists variant readings at the foot of each page and includes material not found in Robinson, such as descriptions of MSS and a full glossary. Although Skeat's edition is nearly a century old, it remains of major importance in studies of Chaucer. A supplementary volume includes works falsely ascribed to Chaucer; see Skeat **M43**.

Textual Studies

This section includes textual studies of Chaucer's work in general; for studies of specific works, see the sections on those works. See

Manly and Rickert **CT1** and Root **Tr2** for important textual studies
that are models of their kind. See Dempster **CT18** for the state of
CT MSS at Chaucer's death and in the 15th century; see Doyle and
Pace **SP2** for a description of a recently-discovered MS containing
several of the short poems; see Doyle and Parkes, 'A Paleographical
Introduction' in **M23** for a detailed description and discussion of the
Hengwrt MS of *CT;* for a discussion of the linguistic characteristics
of MSS of Chaucer's works see Wild **M105**.

M32
Caie, Graham D. 'The Significance of the Early Chaucer
Manuscript Glosses (with Special Reference to the *Wife of Bath's
Prologue*),' *ChauR* 10 (1975-6) 350-60
Caie shows that early MS glosses are valuable as witnesses to
contemporary understanding of Chaucer's poetry.
M33
Donaldson, E.T. 'Chaucer, *Canterbury Tales* D117: A Critical
Edition,' *Speculum* 40 (1965) 626-33; repr. in Donaldson **CrS7**,
119-30
This analysis of a single line from *CT* provides a good introduction
to the problems of editing Chaucer.
M34
_____ 'The Manuscripts of Chaucer's Works and their Use' in
Brewer **B8**, 85-108
Donaldson gives a clear introduction to the problems of editing and
discusses the limitations inherent in any single edition of Chaucer.
M35
_____ 'The Psychology of Editors of Middle English Texts' in
English Studies Today, 4th ser.: *Lectures and Papers Read at the Sixth
Conference of the International Association of University Professors
of English, held at Venice August 1965,* ed. Ilva Cellini and Giorgio
Melchiori (Rome 1966) 45-62; repr. in Donaldson **CrS7**, 102-18
Donaldson takes a critical view of the principles of editing as
practised by Manly and Rickert **CT1** and proposes new principles
for the editing of Middle English works.
M36
Doyle, A.I. and M.B. Parkes. 'The Production of Copies of the
Canterbury Tales and the *Confessio amantis* in the Early Fifteenth
Century' in *Medieval Scribes, Manuscripts, and Libraries: Essays*

Presented to N.R. Ker, ed. M.B. Parkes and Andrew G. Watson
(London 1978) 163-210
Doyle and Parkes provide an important account of the earliest
scribal treatments of Chaucer's works.
M37
Hammond, Eleanor Prescott. 'The Nine-Syllabled Pentameter Line
in Some Post-Chaucerian Manuscripts,' *MP* 23 (1925-6) 129-52
Hammond surveys methods of transcription in several different
poems, and shows that personalities of scribes affected their
transcriptions; for comparisons she uses only the headless or
broken-backed nine-syllable lines from rhyme-royal stanzas in *PF,
SecNT,* Hoccleve's *Letter of Cupid,* and Lydgate's *Complaint of the
Black Knight.*
M38
Thynne, Francis. *Animaduersions uppon the Annotacions and
Corrections of some imperfections of impressiones of Chaucer's
workes (sett downe before tyme, and nowe) reprinted in the yere of
our lorde 1598; sett downe by Francis Thynne,* ed. G.H. Kingsley
from the MS in the Bridgewater Library; rev. Frederick J. Furnivall,
with many additions including *The Pilgrim's Tale.* EETS o.s. 9
(London 1865) and Chaucer Society 2nd ser. 13 (London 1876; repr.
1891, 1898)
Thynne's *Animadversions* are a review of the 1598 edition of
Chaucer's works by Thomas Speght; they offer insight into the
editorial methods and principles of the time. A revised edition of
Speght, incorporating many of Thynne's corrections, appeared in
1602.
M39
Windeatt, B.A. 'The Scribes as Chaucer's Early Critics,' *Studies in
the Age of Chaucer* 1 (1979) 119-41
Taking most of his examples from the *Tr* MSS, Windeatt argues that
MS variants are valuable as evidence for what Chaucer's contem-
poraries found difficult and unusual in his work.

Canon and Dating

This section includes discussions of the canon and general studies
on dating; for the dates of individual works see the appropriate

sections. For an important early discussion of the canon, see Tyrwhitt **CT3**. For a possible addition to the canon, see Price **Eq1**.

M40

Brusendorff, Aage. *The Chaucer Tradition* (London and Copenhagen 1925)
Brusendorff's book is a stimulating and controversial discussion of the MS tradition of Chaucer's works; the first chapter, which deals with the Chaucer tradition in general, is particularly useful to the beginner.

M41

Skeat, Walter W. *The Chaucer Canon: With a Discussion of the Works Associated with the Name of Geoffrey Chaucer* (Oxford 1900)
Skeat's is still the standard work on the canon.

M42

Tatlock, John S.P. *The Development and Chronology of Chaucer's Works.* Chaucer Society 2nd ser. 37 (London 1907; repr. Gloucester, Mass. 1963)
Although somewhat out of date, Tatlock's study is still important, and is a good starting place for work on the topic.

Works Formerly Attributed to Chaucer

Some of the works listed below were not actually attributed to Chaucer but were included, along with others thought to be his, in early printed editions of his works. For a complete, annotated list of all the verse and prose printed with the works of Chaucer, see Hammond **M1**, 406-63. For facsimiles of the works attributed to Chaucer in the 16th and early 17th centuries, see **M25**.

TEXTS

M43

Skeat, Walter W., ed. *Chaucerian and Other Pieces: Being a Supplement to the Complete Works of Geoffrey Chaucer* (Oxford 1897)
This supplement to Skeat **M31** gathers in one place many of the works formerly attributed to Chaucer. Many of these have since

been re-edited (for some of these editions see **B191-210**), but
Skeat's volume is still extremely useful as a survey of the
Chaucerian apocrypha. The works included in the volume are:
- Anonymous, *Envoy to Alison* (pp. 359-60), *The Flower and the Leaf*
  (361-79), *The Assembly of Ladies* (380-404), *The Court of Love*
  (409-47), *Jack Upland* (191-204), *The Plowman's Tale* (= *The
  Complaint of the Plowman* 147-90), and several other short
  poems;
- Clanvowe, Sir John, *The Cuckoo and the Nightingale* (= *The Book of
  Cupid* 347-58);
- Gower, John, *The Praise of Peace* (205-16);
- Henryson, Robert, *The Testament of Cresseid* (327-46);
- Hoccleve, Thomas, *The Letter of Cupid* (217-32) and *To the Kinges
  Most Noble Grace* [and] *To the Lordes and Knightes of the Garter*
  (233-6);
- Lydgate, John, *The Complaint of the Black Knight* (= *The Complaint
  of a Loveres Lyfe* 245-65), *The Floure of Curtesye* (266-74), *A
  Goodly Balade* (405-8), and several other short poems, including
  three no longer attributed to Lydgate (275-98);
- Roos, Sir Richard, *La Belle Dame sans merci* (299-326);
- Scogan, Henry, *A Moral Balade* (237-44);
- Usk, Thomas, *The Testament of Love* (1-146).

SPURIOUS *CANTERBURY TALES*

The Chaucerian apocrypha include a sub-group of spurious
Canterbury Tales. One of these, *The Tale of Gamelyn,* appears in
many *CT* MSS following the *Cook's Prologue* or his fragmentary
Tale; it is printed in Skeat **M31**, IV, 645-67 and V, 477-89, and in
French and Hale **B196**, 207-35. *The Plowman's Tale,* also called *The
Complaint of the Ploughman,* is printed in Skeat **M43**, 147-90.
Lydgate's *Siege of Thebes,* **B206**, was designed by its author as an
addition to *CT* and it opens with a conversation between Chaucer's
Host and Lydgate, as a newly arrived Canterbury pilgrim. *The
Pilgrim's Tale,* an attack on the corruption of the clergy which
quotes and adapts a number of lines from Chaucer's works (and
twice explicitly names Chaucer as its source), was mistakenly
attributed to Chaucer by Francis Thynne, who claimed that his
father William had originally intended to publish it in his first
edition of Chaucer's works (see **M38**, 7-10); Furnivall gives an

edition of the *Tale* in **M38** and Fraser gives a diplomatic text in **M44**.

M44
The Court of Venus, ed. and intro. Russell A. Fraser (Durham, N.C. 1955)
The Court of Venus is the title Fraser assigns to three fragments from poetic miscellanies printed in the 16th century. Two of the works are attributed to Chaucer in John Bale's *Illustrium maioris Britanniae* (1548; quoted in Spurgeon **CrS16**, III, 19): one is a *Prologue* describing the poet's encounter with Genius, the priest of Venus, one day in May when he found himself alone in the woods after following the sounds of a hunt (pp. 115-18); the other is *The Pilgrim's Tale,* an account of the poet's anti-clerical reflections while on pilgrimage (pp. 82-110). In his later *Index Britanniae scriptorum* (ed. Reginald Lane Poole [Oxford 1902], 389), Bale changed the ascription of the first work to [Robert] Shyngleton, a dissenting priest of the 16th century; Fraser (pp. 32-3) argues that Shyngleton wrote *The Pilgrim's Tale* as well.

M45
The Tale of Beryn, with A Prologue of the Merry Adventure of the Pardoner with a Tapster at Canterbury, re-ed. F.J. Furnivall and W.G. Stone from the Duke of Northumberland's unique MS, with English abstract by W.A. Clouston of the French original and Asiatic versions of the tale. EETS e.s. 105 (London 1909; repr. Millwood, N.Y. 1973)
This work is a 15th-century continuation of *CT.*

STUDIES

M46
Bonner, Francis W. 'The Genesis of the Chaucer Apocrypha,' *SP* 48 (1951) 461-81
Bonner points out that the lists of Chaucer's works made by himself and his contemporaries, which helped to establish the canon of his works, were also a stimulus to false attributions because they listed as Chaucer's a number of works now lost; see the next section.

M47
Swart, Felix. 'Chaucer and the English Reformation,' *Neophilologus* 62 (1978) 616-19

Swart discusses how the apocryphal *Pilgrim's Tale* and *Plowman's Tale* were printed in order to make Chaucer seem to be an early supporter of the English Reformation.

Lost Works

Lists of Chaucer's works, compiled by his contemporaries as well as by Chaucer himself, contain a number of items of which no copies, apparently, survive. Among those mentioned by the poet himself are *The Book of the Leoun* (*CT* V.1087), *Origenes upon the Maudelayne* (*LGW* F428, G418), *Of the Wreched Engendrynge of Mankynde* (*LGW* G414-15), and various untitled songs, lays, 'ympnes,' balades, roundels, virelais, and stories about love which cannot be identified with any of his known works. On the lost works in general see Skeat **M41** and Hammond **M1**; on the lost early works see Robbins **CrS64**.

The title *Of the Wreched Engendrynge of Mankynde* (*LGW* G414-15) is generally assumed to refer to a translation of the *De miseria condicionis humane* or *De contemptu mundi* of Pope Innocent III. For a text and translation of Innocent's work, together with a study of Chaucer's authorship, see Lewis **M259**; for the use of Innocent in *CT*, see Lewis **CT151**.

M48
Lewis, Robert Enzer. 'What Did Chaucer Mean by *Of the Wreched Engendrynge of Mankynde?*' *ChauR* 2 (1967-8) 139-58
Lewis elucidates Chaucer's reference (*LGW* G414-15) to Innocent III's *De miseria condicionis humane* and shows how the Latin and English titles can be reconciled; he concludes that Chaucer had a translator's knowledge of the Latin text.
M49
McCall, John P. 'Chaucer and the Pseudo Origen *De Maria Magdalena:* A Preliminary Study,' *Speculum* 46 (1971) 491-509
Chaucer states (*LGW* F428, G418) that he translated this work long before; McCall notes the homily's wide appeal, indicated by its survival in over 150 MSS (listed at the end), and argues that its affective style influenced Chaucer early in his career.
M50
Moore, Arthur K. 'Chaucer's Lost Songs,' *JEGP* 48 (1949) 196-208

Moore examines the evidence of Chaucer's works and of contemporary references and argues that no lost works need to be hypothesized in order to support Chaucer's reputation among his contemporaries.

LANGUAGE AND VERSIFICATION

Middle English

This section includes a selection of reference works on Middle English.

M51
Brunner, Karl. *Abriss der mittelenglischen Grammatik,* 5th ed.
(Tübingen 1962); *An Outline of Middle English Grammar,* trans.
Grahame Johnston (Cambridge, Mass. 1963)
Brunner's study is a concise handbook; it includes an index to words that receive special discussion.

M52
Chambers, R.W. and Marjorie Daunt, eds. *A Book of London English, 1384-1425* (Oxford 1931)
The volume provides selections from 14th-century English documents produced in London.

M53
Middle English Dictionary, ed. Hans Kurath, Sherman Kuhn, John Reidy, et al. (Ann Arbor 1952-)
This valuable work is complete through the letter P; it should be supplemented, even for the letters A-P, by reference to entries in the *OED* **M56**. The *MED* gives a full range of variant spellings.

M54
Mossé, Fernand. *A Handbook of Middle English,* trans. James A.
Walker (Baltimore 1952); originally published as vol. II of *Manuel de l'anglais du moyen âge des origines au XIVe siècle* (Paris 1949)
Mossé's work is written for the student; it contains a sketch of the grammar and an extensive selection of annotated Middle English texts.

M55
Mustanoja, Tauno F. *A Middle-English Syntax,* Part I: *Parts of*

Speech. Mémoires de la Société néophilologique de Helsinki 23 (Helsinki 1960)

Mustanoja's study is the standard work; it includes an index of words discussed, a general bibliography, and separate bibliographies for each part of speech; variant spellings are given for each headword.

M56

The Oxford English Dictionary, ed. J.A.H. Murray et al. 13 vols. (Oxford 1933, repr. 1961)

The single indispensable reference work for students of the English language, the *OED* lists meanings in the order of their historical appearance, supplies examples for each meaning, and includes a large number of Middle English words and usages; variant spellings are given for each headword. A number of the dates given for Middle English works, however, are no longer accepted.

M57

Visser, F.Th. *An Historical Syntax of the English Language.* 3 vols. (Leiden 1963-73)

Visser's comprehensive study gives examples of English syntactical constructions from the Old English period to the late 19th century.

M58

Whiting, Bartlett Jere, with the collaboration of Helen Wescott Whiting. *Proverbs, Sentences, and Proverbial Phrases: From English Writings mainly before 1500* (Cambridge, Mass. 1968)

Whiting lists a large number of Middle English proverbs according to key word; see Whiting **M104** for Chaucer's use of proverbs.

M59

Wyld, Henry Cecil. *A Short History of English with a Bibliography of Recent Books on the Subject, and Lists of Texts and Editions* (London 1914; 3rd ed. rev. and enlarged 1927, repr. 1929)

Wyld includes a thorough study of historical morphology and phonology.

Chaucer's Language and Versification

The studies listed here deal with Chaucer's language in general, or with specific topics such as prosody, wordplay, and the use of dialect forms. For studies of Chaucer's language and versification in specific works, see Brodie **CT405**, Donaldson **CT136**, Green **Anel2**, Keiser **CT316**, Manly **CT338**, Stanley **Tr63**, and Tolkien **CT144**.

M60
Baum, Paull F. 'Chaucer's Puns,' *PMLA* 71 (1956) 225-46
Baum gives an alphabetically-organized list of Chaucer's puns.
M61
_____ *Chaucer's Verse* (Durham, N.C. 1961)
Baum presents a full discussion of Chaucer's metre and prosody.
M62
Benson, L.D. 'Chaucer's Historical Present, its Meaning and Uses,' *ES* 42 (1961) 65-77
Benson suggests that Chaucer uses the historical present chiefly for stylistic reasons.
M63
Ten Brink, Bernhard. *Chaucers Sprache und Verskunst.* 2nd ed., rev. Friedrich Kluge (Leipzig 1899); trans. as *The Language and Metre of Chaucer* by M. Bentinck Smith (London 1901, repr. 1920; repr. New York 1968)
Ten Brink's standard work includes chapters on phonology, accidence, and the structure of the verse line and stanza.
M64
Burnley, J.D. *Chaucer's Language and the Philosophers' Tradition.* Chaucer Studies 2 (Cambridge and Totowa, N.J. 1979)
Burnley analyses semantic fields that are related to moral and psychological themes important in Chaucer's works.
M65
Child, Francis J. 'Observations on the Language of Chaucer,' *Memoirs of the American Academy of Arts and Sciences* n.s. 8, 2 (1863) 445-502
Although long out of date, Child's work is the starting point for most later studies.
M66
Corson, Hiram. *Index of Proper Names and Subjects to Chaucer's Canterbury Tales: Together with Comparisons and Similes, Metaphors and Proverbs, Maxims, etc. in the Same.* Chaucer Society 1st ser. 72 (London and New York 1911, for the issue of 1884; repr. Philadelphia 1977)
Corson's index (based on the Manly-Rickert ed. **CT1**) includes

scriptural quotations and allusions.
M67
Davis, N. 'Chaucer and Fourteenth-Century English' in Brewer **B8**, 58-84.
Davis analyses Chaucer's language in its contemporary context; he surveys work done in the field and offers suggestions for further research.
M68
Davis, Norman et al., comp. *A Chaucer Glossary* (Oxford 1979)
The work is in dictionary format and concentrates on meanings of words not familiar to modern readers of Chaucer; the spelling of words is based on Skeat's text **M31**, and the order of references to works is based on the Tatlock-Kennedy concordance, **M103**.
M69
Dillon, Bert. *A Chaucer Dictionary: Proper Names and Allusions, Excluding Place Names* (Boston 1974)
Dillon identifies many references, allusions, and borrowings in Chaucer's works; each entry cites relevant scholarship and lists the occurrences of the item in Chaucer's works. For place names in Chaucer, see Magoun **M82**.
M70
Donaldson, E. Talbot. 'Chaucer's Final -*e*,' *PMLA* 63 (1948) 1101-24
Donaldson argues that final -*e* in Chaucer's verse was pronounced.
M71
Donner, Morton. 'Derived Words in Chaucer's Language,' *ChauR* 13 (1978-9) 1-15
Basing his account on derived words that are first recorded in Chaucer's works, Donner discusses Chaucer's use of word formation as a means of creating syntactic parallelism and economy of expression.
M72
Elliott, Ralph W.V. *Chaucer's English* (London 1974)
Elliott covers a wide range of topics, such as grammar and pronunciation, slang, technical language, literary terms, proper names, and oaths; he includes extensive notes on recent scholarship in the field.
M73
Everett, Dorothy. 'Chaucer's "Good Ear",' *RES* 23 (1947) 201-8; repr. in Everett, *Essays on Middle English Literature,* ed. Patricia

Kean (London 1955, repr. 1959) 139-48
Everett discusses briefly a variety of evidence of Chaucer's sensitivity to the rhythms of speech and to borrowed rhythms from such literary sources as Dante, tail-rhyme romances, and alliterative verse.

M74
Fisiak, Jacek. *Morphemic Structure of Chaucer's English* (University, Ala. 1965)
Fisiak's highly technical study uses the methodology of descriptive linguistics.

M75
Gaylord, Alan T. 'Scanning the Prosodists: An Essay in Metacriticism,' *ChauR* 11 (1976-7) 22-82
Gaylord's lengthy review article on studies of Chaucer's prosody discusses Baum **M60**, Ten Brink **M63**, Halle and Keyser **M76**, Robinson **M90**, and Southworth **M99-100**, among others.

M76
Halle, Morris and Samuel Jay Keyser. 'Chaucer and the Study of Prosody,' *CE* 28 (1966) 187-219
Halle and Keyser discuss Chaucer's line as iambic pentameter.

M77
Héraucourt, Will. *Die Wertwelt Chaucers, die Wertwelt einer Zeitwende* (Heidelberg 1939)
Héraucourt studies the vocabulary of Chaucer in relation to the value system of the period.

M78
Kerkhof, J. *Studies in the Language of Geoffrey Chaucer.* Leidse Germanistische en Anglistische Reeks van de Rijksuniversiteit te Leiden, dl. 5 (Leiden 1966, 2nd ed. rev. and enlarged 1982)
Kerkhof offers a detailed study of Chaucer's syntax, organized by parts of speech, and includes bibliographical notes.

M79
Kittredge, George Lyman. *Observations on the Language of Chaucer's 'Troilus.'* Chaucer Society 2nd ser. 28 (London 1891)
Classifying words ending in -e according to part of speech, Kittredge uses grammatical form and word derivation in an attempt to find a basis for determining when final -e is pronounced.

M80
Kökeritz, Helge. *A Guide to Chaucer's Pronunciation* (New Haven

and Stockholm 1954; repr. New York 1961, 1962) repr. as Medieval Academy of America Reprints for Teaching 3 (Toronto, Buffalo, London 1978)

Kökeritz's standard guide presents a conservative pronunciation.
M81

——— 'Rhetorical Word-Play in Chaucer,' *PMLA* 69 (1954) 937-52

Kökeritz lists some of Chaucer's puns and discusses his use of *traductio, adnominatio,* and *significatio.*
M82

Magoun, Francis P., Jr. *A Chaucer Gazetteer* (Chicago 1961)

Magoun gives an alphabetical index and brief discussion of all the geographical names and names of geographical origin used by Chaucer.
M83

Manly, John M. 'Observations on the Language of Chaucer's *Legend of Good Women,*' [Harvard] *Studies and Notes in Philology and Literature* 2 (1893) 1-120

Manly follows the work of Kittredge **M79** on *Tr,* and examines nouns, pronouns, verbs, and adverbs with a view to discovering when final *-e* is to be pronounced.
M84

Marshall, Isabel and Lela Porter. *Ryme-Index to the Manuscript Texts of Chaucer's Minor Poems.* Chaucer Society 1st ser. 78 (London 1887; repr. as vol. 80, London 1889)

The poems indexed are *BD, Complaint to Pity, PF, Complaint of Mars, An ABC, Anel, HF, LGW, Truth, Complaint of Venus, Scogan, Bukton, Gentilesse, Proverbs, Lak of Stedfastnesse, Fortune, Purse,* and Hoccleve's *Mother of God.* An appendix by W.W. Skeat includes indices to *The Owl and the Nightingale, The Flower and the Leaf,* and *The Assembly of Ladies.*
M85

Masui, Michio. *The Structure of Chaucer's Rime Words: An Exploration into the Poetic Language of Chaucer* (Tokyo 1964)

In pt. I, Masui discusses the influence of rhyme on syntax and word-formation; in pt. II, he discusses some of the semantic and stylistic effects of rhyme; and in pt. III, he gives complete indices of rhyme-words for *CT* (Manly-Rickert ed. **CT1**) and for *Tr* (Root ed. **Tr1**).

M86
Mersand, Joseph. *Chaucer's Romance Vocabulary* (New York 1937, 2nd ed. 1939)
Mersand's is the only study of this subject, but it overstates Chaucer's romance innovations, partly because it did not have the benefit of the *MED* (**M53**), partly because it follows the *OED* (**M56**) in assigning an early date to *Tr.* See also **Eq3**.
M87
Mustanoja, Tauno F. 'Chaucer's Prosody' in Rowland **CrS13**, 65-94
Mustanoja gives a critical survey, with bibliography, of studies of Chaucer's language and versification.
M88
Owen, Charles A., Jr. ' "Thy drasty rymyng …",' *SP* 63 (1966) 533-64
Owen discusses *Anel* as an experiment in rhyming and shows how Chaucer used rhyme to good artistic effect in *Thop, Tr,* and *GenProl.*
M89
Phelan, Walter S. 'The Study of Chaucer's Vocabulary,' *Computers and the Humanities* 12 (1978) 61-9
Phelan describes a system for the analysis of Chaucer's vocabulary with the aid of a computer.
M90
Robinson, Ian. *Chaucer's Prosody: A Study of the Middle English Verse Tradition* (Cambridge 1971)
Robinson proposes a new and controversial theory of Chaucer's prosody.
M91
Ross, Thomas W. *Chaucer's Bawdy* (New York 1972)
This glossary of bawdy and indecorous words in Chaucer is accompanied by a short introduction. There is some critical discussion in the glossary entries.
M92
Schlauch, Margaret. 'The Art of Chaucer's Prose' in Brewer **CrS4**, 140-63
Schlauch examines the language and style of *Mel, ParsT,* and *Astr.*
M93
_____ 'Chaucer's Prose Rhythms,' *PMLA* 65 (1950) 568-89

Schlauch discusses Chaucer's possible adaptation of the *cursus* and cadenced classical prose.
M94
_____ 'Chaucer's Colloquial English: Its Structural Traits,' *PMLA* 67 (1952) 1103-16
Schlauch examines some of the structural characteristics of informal English, especially in passages of dialogue, which are used by Chaucer to create a sense of immediacy and of social and psychological appropriateness.
M95
Shannon, Edgar F. 'Chaucer's Use of the Octosyllabic Verse in the *Book of the Duchess* and the *House of Fame,*' *JEGP* 12 (1913) 277-94
Shannon suggests that Chaucer's metrical skill improved from *BD* to *HF* and that Chaucer allowed himself artistic license to vary the metre.
M96
Skeat, W.W. *Rime-Index to Chaucer's 'Troilus and Criseyde.'*
Chaucer Society 1st ser. 84 (London 1892)
Skeat gives an alphabetized list of final syllables of rhyme-words and records their occurrence; in an appendix he offers explanations for his principle that final -*e* in rhyme position was always pronounced.
M97
_____ 'On Chaucer's Use of the Kentish Dialect' in *Essays on Chaucer, his Words and Works,* ed. F.J. Furnivall. Chaucer Society 2nd ser. 29, pt. VI, no. 20 (London n.d., for 1892) 657-71
Skeat shows that Chaucer uses a number of Kentish forms to provide himself with a variety of rhymes.
M98
Smyser, H.M. 'Chaucer's Use of *gin* and *do,*' *Speculum* 42 (1967) 68-83
Smyser shows that the periphrastic preterite form *gan* plus an infinitive does not convey aspect, but is merely an alternative to the simple preterite which is convenient in poetry because the infinitives of many verbs rhyme more easily than the preterites; Chaucer's use of *do,* by contrast, is always causative.
M99
Southworth, James G. *Verses of Cadence: An Introduction to the*

Prosody of Chaucer and his Followers (Oxford 1954)
Assuming that final -*e* was not pronounced in Chaucer's verse and
that the iambic-decasyllabic hypothesis about Chaucer's prosody is
thus invalid, Southworth offers a critical survey of previous work on
phonology and prosody and argues for a new theory of Chaucer's
prosody based on MS evidence.
M100
_____ *The Prosody of Chaucer and his Followers: Supplementary
Chapters to 'Verses of Cadence'* (Oxford 1962)
Southworth argues that theories of Chaucer's prosody should be
based on MS evidence of spelling and pointing; he offers a hypoth-
esis based on the assumptions that final -*e* was silent and that MS
pointing signalled intonation. He concludes that a large number of
Chaucer's lines do not fit the iambic pentameter model because
Chaucer's prosody was 'essentially a rhythmic rather than a metri-
cal line.'
M101
Spearing, A.C. 'Chaucer's Language' in Hussey et al. **CrS45**, 89-114
Spearing provides a brief and clear introduction for beginning
students.
M102
Stevens, Martin. 'The Royal Stanza in Early English Literature,'
PMLA 94 (1979) 62-76
Stevens discusses Chaucer's use of the rhyme-royal stanza, for royal
address in *PF* and *Tr* and as a characterizing device in *CT;* he
argues that the term 'prose' as used for *MLT* refers to formal
stanzas of equal length.
M103
Tatlock, John S.P. and Arthur Kennedy. *A Concordance to the
Complete Works of Geoffrey Chaucer and to the 'Romaunt of the
Rose'* (Washington 1927; repr. Gloucester, Mass. 1963)
The concordance gives full line contexts for each word and is based
on the Globe edition of Chaucer, *The Works of Geoffrey Chaucer,*
ed. Alfred W. Pollard et al. (London 1898). The organization is by
headwords in modern English, where modern forms exist, a plan
which is sometimes misleading or inaccurate.
M104
Whiting, Bartlett Jere. *Chaucer's Use of Proverbs.* Harvard Studies
in Comparative Literature 11 (Cambridge, Mass. 1934; repr. New

York 1973)

By examining the full range of proverbs, proverbial phrases, and sententious expressions in their context in Chaucer's work, and by comparing the use of proverbs by Deschamps, by John Gower, and by authors in the French fabliau tradition with Chaucer's use, Whiting shows that the use of proverbs is a distinctive and important feature of Chaucer's style. See Whiting **M58** for a compilation of Middle English proverbs, and Lumiansky **Tr47** for a study of Chaucer's proverbs in *Tr.*

M105

Wild, Friedrich. *Die sprachlichen Eigentümlichkeiten der wichtigeren Chaucer-Handschriften und die Sprache Chaucers.* Wiener Beiträge zur englischen Philologie 44 (Vienna and Leipzig 1915)

Wild discusses the linguistic characteristics of important Chaucer MSS; the study is divided into phonological and grammatical sections and includes a glossary.

LIFE-RECORDS

Editions of Documents

M106

Crow, Martin M. and Clair C. Olson, eds., from materials compiled by John M. Manly and Edith Rickert, with the assistance of Lilian J. Redstone et al. *Chaucer Life-Records* (Oxford 1966)

This single indispensable tool for students of Chaucer's life includes all the known documents in which Chaucer is mentioned, as well as collateral documents that do not mention him directly. A commentary, originally compiled by Lilian Redstone and condensed and supplemented by Crow and Olson, accompanies many of the documents, which are arranged by subject in chapters, each devoted to an episode in Chaucer's life.

M107

Selby, W.D., F.J. Furnivall, et al., eds. *Life-Records of Chaucer.* 4 vols. Chaucer Society 2nd ser. 12, 14, 21, 32 (London 1875-1900, repr. 1967)

This work is now largely superseded by Crow and Olson **M106**, but it contains some documents on tangential matters and fuller versions of some documents printed there; unlike Crow and Olson's work, it is in single chronological order, and is thus useful as a supplement to their work.

M108
Kuhl, Ernest P. 'Index to *The Life-Records of Chaucer*,' *MP* 10 (1912-13) 527-52
Kuhl provides an index of the names of Selby et al. **M107**; he includes all contemporary names cited except those of kings and queens and of Chaucer himself.

Biographical Studies

The studies listed below are based wholly or in part on documentary evidence, including the portraits of Chaucer. They do not include studies of Chaucer's ancestors or descendants, or biographical speculations based solely on the poet's writings; for the difficulties involved in such speculations see Kane **CrS48**. For Chaucer's knowledge of and possible connections with Oxford and Cambridge see Bennett **CT13**. For an entertainingly acerbic account of legendary elements in the biography of Chaucer, see Lounsbury **M138**, I, 127-224. For an account of portraits of Chaucer, see Brusendorff **M40**, 13-27.

M109
Baugh, Albert C. 'The Background of Chaucer's Mission to Spain' in Esch **CrS9**, 55-69
Baugh argues that in 1366 Chaucer was in Spain on a diplomatic mission for the King.

M110
_____ 'Chaucer the Man' in Rowland **CrS13**, 1-20
Baugh reviews the bibliography pertaining to Chaucer's life and discusses the relevance of the life-records to his poetry.

M111
Bland, D.S. 'Chaucer and the Inns of Court: A Re-examination,' *ES* 33 (1952) 145-55
Bland reviews the evidence that Chaucer studied at the Inns of Court and concludes that it is only a plausible theory.

M112
Brewer, D.S. *Chaucer* (London 1953, 2nd ed. 1960; 3rd ed. rev. with supplement 1973)

Brewer provides a readable, brief account of Chaucer's life, times, and works. The 3rd edition includes a long critical essay not found in earlier editions.

M113

——— *Chaucer and his World* (London and New York 1978) Written for the non-specialist but based on the documentary evidence for the poet's life, this study sets him in the context of his age; it contains many well-chosen illustrations.

M114

Call, Reginald. 'The Plimpton Chaucer and Other Problems of Chaucerian Portraiture,' *Speculum* 22 (1947) 135-44 Call suggests that the portrait which hangs in the Plimpton Library at Columbia University may have passed from the 'Chaucer House' at Woodstock to Thomas Warton to the Reverend I. Tyson to the Baroness Burdett-Coutts to Mr. Plimpton; he also discusses the significance of the other portraits of Chaucer.

M115

Chute, Marchette. *Geoffrey Chaucer of England* (New York 1946, many reprints) In this readable and entertaining introduction to Chaucer's life and works, Chute cautions readers against accepting the narrator of *CT* as a full and accurate self-portrait of Chaucer the man.

M116

Du Boulay, F.R.H. 'The Historical Chaucer' in Brewer **B8**, 33-57 Du Boulay presents an able discussion of Chaucer's place in the aristocratic society of his day.

M117

Galway, Margaret. 'The *Troilus* Frontispiece,' *MLR* 44 (1949) 161-77 Galway discusses the full-page illumination at the beginning of Cambridge, Corpus Christi College, MS. 61, a copy of *Tr,* suggesting identifications for some of the figures depicted.

M118

Garbáty, Thomas Jay. 'Chaucer in Spain, 1366: Soldier of Fortune or Agent of the Crown?' *ELN* (1967-8) 81-7 Garbáty interprets the documentary evidence that Chaucer went to Spain in 1366.

M119

Gardner, John. *The Life and Times of Chaucer* (New York 1977) Gardner's lively, iconoclastic biography is aimed at the general reader; because he borrows techniques from the historical novel, his speculative re-creations of events are sometimes fictional, and obligations to previous work are not fully acknowledged. Reviewed by Sumner Ferris, *Speculum* 52 (1977) 970-74 and Janet M. Cowan, *RES* n.s. 29 (1978) 471-2.

M120
Honoré-Duvergé, Suzanne. 'Chaucer en Espagne? (1366)' in *Recueil de travaux offerts à M. Clovis Brunel.* 2 vols. Mémoires et documents publiés par la Société de l'Ecole des chartes 12 (Paris 1955) II, 9-13
Honoré-Duvergé shows that the document of 1366 offering safe-conduct to 'Geoffroy de Chauserre' refers to Chaucer, and she speculates on the nature of his mission to Spain.

M121
Kittredge, G.L. 'Chaucer and Some of his Friends,' *MP* 1 (1903-4) 1-18
Kittredge identifies Sir Lewis Clifford and Sir John Clanvowe as friends of Chaucer and suggests that biographical details from their lives be used to date and elaborate on details of Chaucer's life.

M122
Kuhl, Ernest P. 'Some Friends of Chaucer,' *PMLA* 29 (1914) 270-76
Kuhl discusses Chaucer's relationship with three of his contemporaries: Richard Morel, Ralph Strode, and John Gower.

M123
McCall, John P. and George Rudisill, Jr. 'The Parliament of 1386 and Chaucer's Trojan Parliament,' *JEGP* 58 (1959) 276-88
This study describes the parliament Chaucer attended in 1386 and suggests that it might have influenced the depiction of the Trojan parliament in *Tr.*

M124
McFarlane, K.B. 'Part II: Lollard Knights' in McFarlane, *Lancastrian Kings and Lollard Knights* (Oxford 1972) 137-226
McFarlane evaluates the evidence for the existence of Lollard beliefs and practices among the lesser aristrocracy and discusses the proven connections between Chaucer and some of the Lollard knights.

M125
McGregor, James H. 'The Iconography of Chaucer in Hoccleve's *De regimine principum* and in the *Troilus* Frontispiece,' *ChauR* 11

(1976-7) 338-50

McGregor suggests that in both portraits Chaucer is depicted as a teacher-philosopher.

M126

Manly, John M. 'Chaucer's Mission to Lombardy,' *MLN* 49 (1934) 209-16

Manly cites documents which clarify the details of Chaucer's mission to Italy in 1378.

M127

Pearsall, Derek. 'The *Troilus* Frontispiece and Chaucer's Audience,' *Yearbook of English Studies* 7 (1977) 68-74, 4 pls.

Using iconographic parallels from 14th-century French miniatures, Pearsall shows that the famous *Troilus* frontispiece in Cambridge, Corpus Christi College, MS. 61 does not provide evidence that Chaucer ever read his works to a court audience; he also points out that there is no other positive evidence on this point.

M128

Plucknett, T.F.T. 'Chaucer's Escapade,' *Law Quarterly Review* 64 (1948) 33-6

Plucknett disputes the interpretation by Watts **M133** of the *raptus* of Cecilia Chaumpaigne, of which Chaucer was accused and released in 1380, arguing that, while *raptus* refers to rape, no evidence was offered for the charge and Chaucer was released from it.

M129

Pratt, Robert A. 'Geoffrey Chaucer, Esq., and Sir John Hawkwood,' *ELH* 16 (1949) 188-93

Pratt offers new documentary evidence for Chaucer's mission to Italy in 1378 and discusses his possible relationship with Sir John Hawkwood, the famous English free-lance captain in Italy.

M130

Rickert, Edith, 'Chaucer at School,' *MP* 29 (1931-2) 257-74

Rickert suggests that Chaucer might have attended St. Paul's Almonry School as a boy; the school possessed many of the books that Chaucer is known to have read.

M131

―――― 'Was Chaucer a Student at the Inner Temple?' in *The Manly Anniversary Studies in Language and Literature* [no ed.] (Chicago 1923) 20-31

Rickert argues that the reported testimony of Master Buckley that Chaucer was named in a record of the Inner Temple is probably trustworthy.

M132

Spielmann, M.H. *The Portraits of Geoffrey Chaucer.* Chaucer Society 2nd ser. 31 (London 1900)

Spielmann reproduces and describes ten of the portraits and miniatures of Chaucer.

M133

Watts, P.R. 'The Strange Case of Geoffrey Chaucer and Cecilia Chaumpaigne,' *Law Quarterly Review* 63 (1947) 491-515

Reading the records in the context of the legal language of the late fourteenth century, Watts argues that *raptus* can only mean rape and that Cecilia's release of Chaucer in 1380 from this charge indicates payment by him of indemnification to avoid a trial.

CHAUCER'S SOURCES AND INFLUENCES

Chaucer was a learned poet, and his works make use of literary sources of remarkable range and variety. This section lists the texts which Chaucer used in one or more of his works, in specific borrowings or in translated passages.

The list may err on the side of inclusiveness because of the value the compilers see in having a relatively complete list of Chaucer's sources. Where to draw the line excluding a source from this list is sometimes hard to know; for example, should 'Satire X' by Juvenal (**M267**) be listed here or under *Tr*, where a few lines from it are translated? Possible sources for which specific borrowings have not been identified are listed in Part II under the relevant work, together with analogues and parallels. One category of analogues, the fabliaux, is included here, however, because discrimination between specific sources and mere analogues is notoriously difficult for this genre.

The distinction between sources listed here and possible sources listed in Part II can thus be only an approximation. Some of the works listed in this section were probably known to Chaucer only through excerpts in florilegia. Some of the works listed as possible sources in Part II may well have been known to Chaucer in more

detail than is apparent from his written works. A further compli-
cation of the issue arises because Chaucer occasionally lists authors
that he probably had not read, as in the catalogue of medical
authors that occurs in the portrait of the Physician in *GenProl.*
Consequently, the material on Chaucer's learning presented in this
section should be used in conjunction with the information on
sources presented in Part II; cross-references are given in both Part
I and Part II. In both parts, the lists of Chaucer's sources reflect the
results of scholarly research to date and do not pretend to
completeness.

The items in this section include the best modern edition of each
source and a translation if one is available. For two sources that had
very great influence on several of Chaucer's works, the *Consolatio
philosophiae* and the *Roman de la rose,* a selection of the secondary
works most useful to readers of Chaucer is included. This section
gives the modern reader advantages that Chaucer himself did not
enjoy, because he read his sources in MS form. MSS often came with
false or confused attributions of authors, and the text was often in a
corrupt or truncated form. There was, indeed, no 'received' text, so
a reader had to rely on what MS he could see or what he could
remember. Many MSS included marginal or interlinear glosses and
accessus, or introductions, which would affect a medieval reader's
understanding of the text. And medieval readers did not have
modern reference tools such as concordances, dictionaries,
bibliographies, and handbooks — all the aids to study that modern
scholars now regard as vital for their work. Under these circumstances Chaucer deserves our admiration for the range and
sensitivity of his reading, not blame for the occasional errors or
obscurities in his use and treatment of sources.

See Hammond **M1**, 73-105 for a full list of all literary sources
that had been posited by 1908; Dillon **M69** suggests a number of
additional titles. See the notes in Skeat **M31** and Robinson **M30** for
discussions and bibliographies of the sources of individual works of
Chaucer and for exact references to the sources of individual
passages. For texts and discussions of the sources of *CT,* see also
Bryan and Dempster **CT8**.

Studies of Chaucer's knowledge and use of the medieval
rhetorical tradition are listed under **B158-72**; see also Payne **CrS62**.
For studies of non-literary influences on Chaucer's work and for his

learning in such fields as science and philosophy, see Part III, Backgrounds.

This section is divided alphabetically by language of the source and, under each language, alphabetically by author of the source, or, if the source is anonymous, by title. Authors like Boccaccio, who wrote in more than one language, are listed under their native language; those, like Māshā' allāh, who were known to Chaucer only in Latin translation, are listed under Latin. Authors' names are in the forms used by the Library of Congress *Catalogue*, because very many libraries follow those forms in their own catalogues; common alternative forms of the name are also included. Comments under the first bibliographical item for each source (that is, the best modern edition) include a discussion of the use Chaucer made of that source.

Studies of Sources and Influences in More than One Language

See Benson and Andersson **M156** for texts and translations of the *CT* fabliau analogues.

M134
Brewer, D.S. 'The Relationship of Chaucer to the English and European Traditions' in Brewer **CrS4**, 1-38
Using the opening lines of *BD* as his point of departure, Brewer assesses the relative influences of French and English poetry, as represented here by Froissart and by popular English romance, on the poetic diction of Chaucer.
M135
Brown, Emerson, Jr. 'Chaucer and the European Literary Tradition' in Economou **CrS8**, 37-54
Brown discusses in general terms the influence of Latin, French, and Italian literature on Chaucer; he sets specific passages from Chaucer's works against their sources in order to illustrate the variety of Chaucer's techniques of literary allusion.
M136
Callan, Norman. 'Thyn Owne Book: A Note on Chaucer, Gower, and Ovid,' *RES* 22 (1946) 269-81

Callan compares Chaucer's and Gower's versions of Ovid's tale of Pyramus and Thisbe in order to distinguish two different kinds of literary borrowing.

M137
Elliott, R.W.V. 'Chaucer's Reading' in Cawley **CrS6**, 46-68
Elliott explores the kinds of influence Chaucer's reading had on his own composition and discusses Chaucer's view of the rival claims to authority of books and experience.

M138
Lounsbury, Thomas R. *Studies in Chaucer.* 3 vols. (New York 1892, repr. 1962)
In a long chapter, 'The Learning of Chaucer' (II, 169-426), Lounsbury discusses the nature and extent of Chaucer's use of sources, both in florilegia and at first hand; his comprehensive essay provided the starting point for much later work on the subject, and is still a basic guide to Chaucer's learning.

M139
Plimpton, George A. *The Education of Chaucer: Illustrated from the School Books in Use in his Time* (London and New York 1935)
Plimpton's study is useful primarily for its beautiful reproductions from late medieval school books, such as primers, Cato's *Disticha,* and arithmetical treatises.

M140
Pratt, Robert A. 'The Importance of Manuscripts for the Study of Medieval Education, as Revealed by the Learning of Chaucer,' *Progress of Medieval and Renaissance Studies in the United States and Canada,* ed. S. Harrison Thomson, Bulletin 20 (Boulder, Colo. 1949) 43-51
Pratt discusses the transmission of classical texts and of information culled from classical texts in medieval school readers, commentaries, and glosses; he points out the importance of such books for source studies. See also Pratt **M249** and **M253**.

M141
Schaar, Claes. *The Golden Mirror: Studies in Chaucer's Descriptive Technique and its Literary Background.* Skrifter utgivna av kungl. humanistiska Vetenskapssamfundet i Lund 54 (Lund 1955, repr. 1967)
This rich and detailed work provides careful analysis of Chaucer's

descriptions and close comparisons of Chaucer's works with his sources.

M142

Wetherbee, Winthrop P. 'Some Intellectual Themes in Chaucer's Poetry' in Economou **CrS8**, 75-91
Wetherbee argues that the forms and major themes of Chaucer's early poetry derive not only from Boethius but also from the Latin philosophical allegories and love lyrics of the 12th-century schools, and from their vernacular counterpart in Jean de Meun's work.

English Sources and Influences

Chaucer did not borrow from English works in quite the way that he borrowed from French, Italian, and Latin ones, but there is no doubt that he knew and was influenced by contemporary English literary works. For the argument that Chaucer knew and used the Auchinleck MS (Edinburgh, National Library, Advocates MS. 19.2.1), a collection of Middle English romances, see Loomis **CT268** and **CT330**. For the argument that Chaucer knew *Sir Gawain and the Green Knight,* see Whiting **CT256**. See Donaldson **CT136** for the influence of popular poetry on *MillT* and Davis **M67** for general parallels between Chaucer and contemporary English writings. For an important study of Chaucer's poetry in relation to the poetry of his contemporaries, see Burrow **CrS31**. For editions of works by Chaucer's contemporaries see **M43-5** and **B191-210**. For Chaucer's knowledge of English theatre, see Fifield **CrS41**, Harder **CT130**, and Lancashire **CT283**.

GENERAL STUDIES

M143

Kirk, Elizabeth D. 'Chaucer and his English Contemporaries' in Economou **CrS8**, 111-27
After briefly comparing Chaucer's work to that of Gower, Langland, and the *Pearl* poet, Kirk argues that his greatest debt, among English works, is to anonymous popular poetry.

M144

Robinson, Ian. *Chaucer and the English Tradition* (London and New York 1972, repr. 1975)
Robinson assesses Chaucer's native English qualities, comparing him to his contemporaries.

GOWER, JOHN (ca. 1330-1408)

Gower and Chaucer apparently had a close personal as well as literary relationship; in 1378 Gower was entrusted with power of attorney for Chaucer, and Chaucer invoked him by name as a moral authority at the end of *Tr* (V.1856). Exact lines of indebtedness between Chaucer and Gower are often difficult to establish because they treated a number of the same themes and tales, but Chaucer apparently knew the *Confessio amantis*, the *Vox clamantis,* and the *Mirour de l'omme* and perhaps some of the shorter poems as well.

Confessio amantis

Edition

M145

John Gower. *Confessio amantis* in *The English Works of John Gower,* ed. G.C. Macaulay. 2 vols. EETS e.s. 81-2 (London, New York, Toronto 1900; repr. 1957)
The *Confessio* includes versions of a number of the tales in *CT* and *LGW: WBT* (*Conf.* 1.1407-1861), *MLT* (*Conf.* 2.587-1598), *PhysT* (*Conf.* 7.5131-5306), *MancT* (*Conf.* 3.783-817), Thisbe (*Conf.* 3.1331-1494), Medea (*Conf.* 5.3247-4229), Lucrece (*Conf.* 7.4754-5130), Ariadne (*Conf.* 5.5231-5495), Phyllis (*Conf.* 4.731-878). In addition, the visions that frame *LGW* and the *Confessio* are similar in a number of ways; see Fisher **M149**, 235-50. The tale of Ceyx and Alcyone, which Chaucer used in *BD* (62-220) is also in the *Confessio* (4.2927-3123). Macaulay's edition includes extensive notes on Gower's sources and on parallels with Chaucer.

Mirour de l'omme

Edition

M146

John Gower. *Mirour de l'omme* in *The Complete Works of John Gower,* vol. I: *The French Works,* ed. G.C. Macaulay (Oxford 1899) 1-334

Chaucer's knowledge of the *Mirour* is not certain. See Mann **CT53**, 207-8 and passim for the argument that Gower's critique of the estates influenced the portraits in *GenProl;* see Fisher **M149**, 204-42 passim for the suggested influence of the work on a number of Chaucer's early works, including *PF* and *HF.*

Vox clamantis

Edition

M147

John Gower. *Vox clamantis* in *The Complete Works of John Gower,* vol. IV: *The Latin Works,* ed. G.C. Macaulay (Oxford 1902) 3-313

See Mann **CT53**, 207-8 and passim for the argument that Gower's critique of the estates influenced the portraits in *GenProl;* see Fisher **M149**, 204-42 passim for echoes of the *Vox* in a variety of Chaucer's works.

Translation

M148

The Major Latin Works of John Gower: The Voice of One Crying and The Tripartite Chronicle, trans. and intro. Eric W. Stockton (Seattle, Wash. 1962) 47-288

Stockton's translation is annotated with detailed references to echoes of the *Vox clamantis* in Chaucer's works, and it includes an introduction discussing the influence of the work on Chaucer.

Studies

See Burrow **CrS31** for a discussion of Gower and Chaucer as poets of a common literary school.

M149
Fisher, John H. *John Gower: Moral Philosopher and Friend of Chaucer* (New York 1964)
Fisher discusses the influences of Gower and Chaucer on each other and tries to reconstruct a history of their relationship; of most direct relevance here is the chapter 'Gower and Chaucer' (pp. 204-302), which gives an extensive account of parallel passages in their works.

French Sources and Influences

See Muscatine **CrS57** and Clemen **CrS32** for general critical studies of Chaucer's works that discuss the French sources and influences in detail. See Wimsatt **BD4** for the French sources of *BD*, and Lowes **LGW5** for the French sources of *LGWProl*. For studies of Chaucer's use of fabliaux see **M156-7**.

GENERAL STUDIES

M150
Braddy, Haldeen. 'The French Influence on Chaucer' in Rowland **CrS13**, 143-59
Braddy gives a brief survey of studies of the French sources for Chaucer's works, with a selected bibliography.
M151
Wimsatt, J.I. 'Chaucer and French Poetry' in Brewer **B8**, 109-36
Wimsatt focusses on Guillaume de Lorris, Jean de Meun, and Guillaume de Machaut, discussing their influence on Chaucer.

BEAUVEAU, SENESCHAL OF ANJOU

Le Roman de Troyle et de Criseida — see Pratt **Tr9**.

BENOIT DE SAINTE-MORE [Benoît de Sainte-Maure] (fl. 1160)

Le Roman de Troie

Edition

M152
Le Roman de Troie par Benoît de Sainte-Maure, ed. Léopold Constans. 6 vols. SATF (Paris 1904-12)
The *Roman* includes the first appearance of the Troilus and Criseyde story in vernacular literature and was one of the sources for *Tr.* See Lumiansky **CT52** for the argument that the portraits in the *Roman* influenced the portraits in *GenProl.*

Translation

For a translation of some portions of the *Roman* which parallel *Tr,* see Gordon **Tr4**. The parallels between the *Roman* and *Tr* are more extensive, as Mieszkowski **Tr6** has shown.

DESCHAMPS, EUSTACHE (ca. 1346-ca. 1406)

See Olson **B171** for the suggestion that the *Art de dictier* (Deschamps VII, 266-92 — see **M153**) represents a non-Augustinian theory of poetry that Chaucer may have known.

Miroir de mariage

Edition

M153
Eustache Deschamps. *Miroir de mariage,* vol. IX in *Oeuvres complètes de Eustache Deschamps,* ed. Le Marquis de Queux de Saint-Hilaire and Gaston Raynaud. 11 vols. SATF (Paris 1878-1903)
The *Miroir* was the source for much of the antifeminist material in *WBT* and *MerchT.*

Studies

M154

Lowes, John Livingston. 'Chaucer and the *Miroir de mariage*,'
MP 8 (1910-11) 165-86, 305-34
Lowes discusses the influence of the *Miroir* on *MerchT*, on *WBT*,
and on the character of the Wife of Bath.

M155

_____ 'Illustrations of Chaucer, drawn chiefly from
Deschamps,' *Romanic Review* 2 (1911) 113-28
Lowes quotes parallel passages in the poetry of Deschamps and
Chaucer to illustrate the intellectual milieu they shared.

FABLIAUX

See Bédier **B130**, Muscatine **B147**, and Nykrog **B148** for studies of
the fabliaux and their intended audience; see Richardson **CT36** for
Chaucer's innovative use of the fabliau form.

Edition and Translation

M156

Benson, Larry D. and Theodore M. Andersson, eds. and trans. *The
Literary Context of Chaucer's Fabliaux: Texts and Translations*
(Indianapolis and New York 1971)
The volume includes texts and translations of analogues to
Chaucer's fabliaux: *MillT, RvT, MerchT, ShipT*. Analogues to the
fabliau elements in other tales (*SumT, MancT,* and *FrT*) are also
included.

Study

M157

Economou, George D. 'Introduction: Chaucer the Innovator'
in Economou **CrS8**, 1-14
Economou argues that studies of sources and influences bring to
light Chaucer's distinctive innovations; he illustrates his argument
by a comparison of *MillT* and *RvT* with the French fabliau tradition.

FROISSART, JEAN (ca. 1337-ca. 1410)

Complete Works

M158
Oeuvres de Froissart: Poésies, ed. Aug. Scheler. 3 vols. (Brussels 1870-72)
This collected edition includes all of the texts known to be sources for Chaucer. Scheler provides brief comments on each text, and a glossary, III, 307-417.

Le Dittié de la flour de la Margherite

Edition

In **M158**, II, 209-15
Lowes **LGW5** shows that this was one of the *marguerite* poems that served as sources for *LGWProl.*

Paradys d'amours

Edition

In **M158**, I, 1-52
Wimsatt **BD4** discusses the importance of this poem as a source for *BD.*

Trésor amoureux

Edition

In **M158**, III, 54-281
This poem is an important source for the visit to Morpheus in *HF* (66ff.); see the notes to the passage in Robinson **M30**.

GRANSON, OTON DE [Othon de Graunson, Grandson] (ob. 1397)

Edition

M159
Piaget, Arthur. *Oton de Grandson, sa vie et ses poésies.* Mémoires et documents publiées par la Société d'histoire de la Suisse romande 3rd ser. 1 (Lausanne 1941)
Chaucer's *Complaint of Venus* is based on three balades by Granson; see the notes in Robinson **M30**. The balades appear here under Item VI, 'Les Cinq Balades ensuivans,' as I (pp. 209-10), IV (211-12), and V (212-13); the three balades are also printed in Skeat **M31**, I, 400-09.

Study

M160
Braddy, Haldeen. *Chaucer and the French Poet Graunson* (Baton Rouge, La. 1947; repr. Port Washington, N.Y. 1968) 54-70
Braddy presents evidence for the influence of Granson on Chaucer's short poems.

GUILLAUME DE DEGUILLEVILLE [Deguileville] (fl. 1320)

Le Pèlerinage de vie humaine

Edition

M161
Le Pèlerinage de vie humaine de Guillaume de Deguileville, ed. J.J. Stürzinger. Roxburghe Club (London 1893)
Chaucer's *An ABC* is a close translation of part of the *Pèlerinage;* the relevant sections of the French text are also printed side by side with Chaucer's poem in Skeat **M31**, I, 261-71. This edition is based on the first version (ca. 1330); the second version has not appeared in a modern edition.

Translations

M162
*The Pilgrimage of the Lyf of the Manhode from the French of
Guillaume de Deguileville,* ed. William Aldis Wright. Roxburghe
Club (London 1869)
This is an edition of an early 14th-century Middle English prose
translation, based on the first French version.
M163
*The Pilgrimage of the Life of Man Englisht by John Lydgate, A.D.
1426, from the French of Guillaume de Deguileville, A.D. 1330,
1335,* ed. F.J. Furnivall, with introduction, notes, glossary, and
indices by Katharine B. Locock. 3 vols. EETS e.s. 77, 83, 92
(London 1899, 1901, 1904; repr. in 1 vol. Millwood, N.Y. 1973)
Lydgate's verse translation is based on the second French version
(ca. 1355).

GUILLAUME DE LORRIS (fl. 1230) — see *ROMAN DE LA ROSE.*

GUILLAUME DE MACHAUT (ca. 1300-ca. 1377)

Editions

M164
Oeuvres de Guillaume de Machaut, ed. Ernest Hoepffner. 3 vols.
SATF (Paris 1908-21)
Three of the works printed here are important influences on *BD: Dit
de la Fonteinne amoureuse* (III, 143-244), *Jugement dou Roy de
Behaigne* (I, 57-136), and *Remede de Fortune* (II, 1-158); see
Wimsatt **BD4** for discussion of these and other influences of
Machaut.
M165
Guillaume de Machaut: Poésies lyriques, ed. V. Chichmaref. 2 vols.
(Paris 1909)

This edition includes a large number of lyrics not included in **M164**. See Wimsatt **SP9** for the influence of Machaut's lyric poetry on Chaucer. See Wimsatt **Tr19** for the argument that Machaut's lay 'Mireoir amoureux' (II, 362-70) was a source for Antigone's song, *Tr* II.827-75; Robinson **M30** states that Machaut's 'Paradis d'amour' (II, 345-62) is the source.

JEAN DE MEUN (ca. 1260-ca. 1305)

See *ROMAN DE LA ROSE* below; see also **M237** for Jean's translation of the *Consolatio philosophiae*.

Li testament

Edition

M166
Li testament de maistre Jehan de Meung in *Le Roman de la rose,* ed. Dominique Martin Méon. 4 vols. (Paris 1814; repr. with intro. by D. Poirion, 1973) IV, 1-121
The *Testament* may have been a source for *WBProl* (483) and *RvT* (3883ff.); see the notes in Robinson **M30**.

MACHAUT — see GUILLAUME DE MACHAUT above.

MARIE DE FRANCE (fl. late 12th c.)

Chaucer refers to the Breton *lai*, the literary form for which Marie is best known, in *FranklT* (709-15), but he does not cite her by name; no extant work by Marie is a source for *FranklT*. For the possibility that her fable *Del cok et del gupil* is one of the sources for *NPT*, see Pratt **CT371**.

NICOLE DE MARGIVAL (13th c.) [supposed author]

La Panthère d'amours

Edition

M167
Le Dit de la Panthère d'amours par Nicole de Margival, ed. Henry
A. Todd. SATF (Paris 1883)
The attribution of the *Panthère* to Nicole de Margival is now
regarded as uncertain. It is an important source for *HF*; see the
notes in Robinson **M30** and Patch **HF3**.

RENAUD DE LOUHANS (fl. 1336)

For an edition of his adaptation of the *Liber consolationis* of
Albertano of Brescia, see **CT344**, 568-614; for a translation into
modern English, see **M221**.

ROMAN DE LA ROSE (1230 and 1275-80)

Probably no single work, with the exception of the *Consolatio
philosophiae* of Boethius, exercised greater influence on Chaucer
than the *Roman de la rose*, begun by Guillaume de Lorris about
1230 and completed by Jean de Meun about 1275-80. Chaucer
unquestionably knew the *Roman* well, because he translated it,
borrowed passages from it throughout his career, and made use of
material from it in many different poems. Because the *Roman* was
a pervasive influence on Chaucer a relatively full selection of
editions, translations, and studies of the work is given here.
   See Muscatine **CrS57**, 30-41 and 71-97 for a detailed analysis of
tradition and innovation in the literary techniques of the two parts
of the *Roman*. Muscatine regards Guillaume as a conventional poet
writing within a stylized tradition of courtly poetry and Jean as an
innovator writing with originality and using dramatic monologues
for characterization. For studies of the allegorical tradition from the
Psychomachia of Prudentius to the *Roman*, see Jauss **B141-2**,

Jung **B143**, and Tuve **B156**. See Lewis **B181**, 1-156 for an
influential study of courtly love in the *Roman;* he discusses the
origins of the allegorical love-vision and points out that Guillaume
extended the tradition of allegory in the *Psychomachia* by
allegorizing the internal aspects of the lady's personality. For the
tradition of Nature in Jean's part of the poem, see Economou **B137**,
104-24. See Robertson **CrS65** for a controversial interpretation of
the garden of the *Roman.*

Chaucer states that he translated the *Roman* (*LGW* F329 and
G255); both Deschamps and Lydgate attribute such a translation to
him. Only an incomplete translation in Middle English now
survives, however, and only the first section, lines 1-1704, can be
attributed to Chaucer; see Brusendorff **M40**, Kittredge **Rom2**, and
Sutherland **Rom1**. For editions and studies of the Middle English
translation see **Rom1-2**.

Bibliography

Useful bibliographical material is given in Barney **M177**, Dahlberg
M171, Fleming **M182**, Jauss **B142**, II, 203-80, Muscatine **CrS57**,
Robinson **M30**, and Sutherland **Rom1**.

M168
Jung, Marc-René. 'Der *Rosenroman* in der Kritik seit dem 18.
Jahrhundert,' *Romanische Forschungen* 78 (1966) 203-52
This very thorough review of criticism of the *Roman* from 1700 to
1966 contains much valuable bibliographical information as well as
a bibliography of 20th-century criticism which includes many
important studies by European scholars.

Editions

M169
Langlois, Ernest, ed. *Le Roman de la rose*. 5 vols. SATF (Paris
1914-24, repr. New York 1965)
This is the standard scholarly edition of the text, with notes on MS
variations below the text and a glossary in vol. V; for Langlois'
method of recension, see **M175**. The notes at the back of each

volume are based on **M176** and are particularly helpful in identifying the sources of the poem.
M170
Lecoy, Félix, ed. *Le Roman de la rose.* 3 vols. CFMA 92, 95, 98
(Paris 1965-70)
This edition is based on Paris, Bibliothèque nationale, MS. fr. 1573, with textual variants from four control MSS in each volume and a glossary in vol. III; notes at the back of each volume cite Langlois' identifications of sources as well as additional sources that have since been discovered. A full introduction offers a summary of scholarship on the poem.

Modern Translations

M171
Dahlberg, Charles, trans. *The Romance of the Rose* (Princeton 1971)
This prose translation includes an introduction, notes, bibliography, and reproductions of sixty-four MS illustrations.
M172
Robbins, Harry W., trans. *The Romance of the Rose,* ed. and intro.
Charles W. Dunn (New York 1962)
This verse translation is not always reliable in details; it has a brief introduction.

Textual and Source Studies

M173
Bourdillon, F.W. *The Early Editions of the 'Roman de la rose'*
(London 1906)
Bourdillon gives descriptions of twenty-one editions of the *Roman,* including information on the texts of various editions and the facsimiles they contain.
M174
Kuhn, Alfred. 'Die Illustration des *Rosenromans,' Jahrbuch der kunsthistorischen Sammlungen des allerhöchsten Kaiserhauses* 31
(1913-14) 1-66
Kuhn provides a guide to illumination of MSS of the *Roman,* many of which were lavishly illustrated.

M175
Langlois, Ernest. *Les Manuscrits du 'Roman de la rose': Description et classement* (Lille and Paris 1910, repr. Geneva 1974)
Langlois describes the MSS of the *Roman* and provides lists of their owners and of MS contents. He designates different families of MSS and classifies all variants, but the classification is not fully worked out; consequently, the pattern of textual recension used in his subsequent edition, **M169**, is not clear.

M176
_____ *Origines et sources du 'Roman de la rose'* (Paris 1891)
Langlois documents the sources of a large number of selected passages in the *Roman* and sets the first part of the poem in the traditions of the dream-vision and the art of love; still the basic study, it should be supplemented by Paré **M184-5**.

Critical Studies

M177
Barney, Stephen A. *Allegories of History, Allegories of Love* (Hamden, Conn. 1979) 179-215
Barney discusses the nature of the allegory in the *Roman* and offers a guide to reading the two parts of the poem; he includes a detailed bibliographical essay.

M178
Cipriani, Lisi. 'Studies in the Influence of the *Romance of the Rose* upon Chaucer,' *PMLA* 22 (1907) 552-95
Cipriani describes resemblances between the *Roman* and Chaucer's works, notably *BD, PF, LGW,* and *Tr,* suggesting that the influence of the *Roman* is found most distinctly in philosophical, psychological, and ethical reflections, especially in *Tr.*

M179
Eberle, Patricia J. ' "The Lovers' Glass": Nature's Discourse on Optics and the Optical Design of the *Romance of the Rose*' in *The Language of Love and the Visual Imagination in the High Middle Ages,* ed. John Leyerle, *UTQ* 46 (1976-77) 241-62
Eberle demonstrates that the *Roman* is, as Jean de Meun calls it, a 'mirouer aus amoureus,' an optical glass of poetry that gives a reader multiple perspectives on love.

M180

Fansler, Dean Spruill. *Chaucer and the 'Roman de la rose'* (New York 1914; repr. Gloucester, Mass. 1965)
Fansler discusses at length the influence of both parts of the French poem on Chaucer's works. He summarizes previous work, adds his own material, and concludes that Chaucer borrowed a proportionately equal number of lines from each of the two authors of the *Roman.*

M181

Faral, Edmond. 'Le *Roman de la rose* et la pensée française au XIIIe siècle,' *Revue des deux mondes* 35 (1926) 430-57
Faral sees the source of Guillaume's portion of the *Roman* as the poet's own experience; he points out that Jean de Meun borrowed much of his own material from earlier authors and was an important link in the transmission of that material to late medieval and Renaissance authors.

M182

Fleming, John V. *The 'Roman de la rose': A Study in Allegory and Iconography* (Princeton 1969)
Fleming uses iconography as an aid to understanding the *Roman,* arguing that the illustrations produced many years later provide a gloss to the allegorical meaning of the original text; the method and conclusions are influenced by Robertson **CrS66**.

M183

Gunn, Alan M.F. *The Mirror of Love: A Reinterpretation of 'The Romance of the Rose.'* Texas Technological College Research Publication in Literature (Lubbock, Tex. 1951; repr. 1952)
Gunn discusses the abundance of apparently unrelated topics in Jean's part of the *Roman* and suggests that it is the result of uncommon enthusiasm for applying the rhetorical device of *amplificatio.*

M184

Paré, G. *'Le Roman de la rose' et la scolastique courtoise* (Paris and Ottawa 1941)
Paré argues that the vocabulary employed and the ideas expressed in Jean's philosophical and theological discussions are derived from scholastic tradition.

M185

—— *Les Idées et les lettres au XIIIe siècle: 'Le Roman de la rose.'*
Publications de l'Institut d'études médiévales Albert-le-Grand
(Montreal 1947)
Paré expands his earlier study of the *Roman,* **M184,** focussing his
attention on the second part of the poem.

M186

Poirion, Daniel. 'Narcisse et Pygmalion dans *Le Roman de la rose'*
in *Essays in Honor of Louis Francis Solano,* ed. Raymond J. Cormier
and Urban T. Holmes. University of North Carolina Studies in the
Romance Languages and Literatures 92 (Chapel Hill 1970) 153-65
Poirion uses a study of the stories of Narcissus and Pygmalion as a
means of exploring the poem's allegorical method.

M187

Strohm, Paul. 'Guillaume as Narrator and Lover in the *Roman de la
rose,*' *Romanic Review* 59 (1968) 3-9
Strohm suggests that there is an important distinction between lover
and narrator in Guillaume's part of the *Roman.*

M188

Wetherbee, Winthrop. 'The Literal and the Allegorical: Jean de
Meun and the *De planctu naturae,*' *MS* 33 (1971) 264-91; repr. in
rev. and shortened form as 'Jean de Meun and the Chartrians' in
Wetherbee, *Platonism and Poetry in the Twelfth Century* (Princeton
1972) 255-66
Wetherbee makes an enlightening comparison between the poetic
methods of Jean de Meun and Alan of Lille.

ROMAN DE RENART (late 12th-14th c.)

M189

Le Roman de Renart, ed. Mario Roques. CFMA 78, 79, 81, 85, 88,
90, etc. (Paris 1948-   )
See Hulbert **CT367,** Petersen **CT370,** and Pratt **CT371,** for
Chaucer's use of this work; Pratt argues that the sources of *NPT*
also include material related to *Renart,* such as *Renart le contrefait*
and Marie de France's fable, *Del cok et del gupil.*

TRIVET, NICHOLAS (ca. 1258-1328)

[Life of Constance in] *Chroniques écrites pour Marie d'Angleterre, fille d'Edward I*

Edition and Translation

M190

'The Life of Constance (the source of Chaucer's *Man of Law's Tale*) from the Anglo-Norman Chronicle of Nicholas Trivet (after A.D. 1334) copied from the Arundel MS. 56, collated with a MS in the Royal Library at Stockholm,' ed. and trans. Edmund Brock, and 'The Story of Constance (for Chaucer's *Man of Law's Tale*), Englisht in a MS of about 1430-1440 A.D., belonging to Sir A. Acland-Hood, Bart., from the French Chronicle of Nicholas Trivet, after 1334 A.D.,' in pts. I and III of *Originals and Analogues of Some of Chaucer's Canterbury Tales,* ed. F.J. Furnivall, Edmund Brock, and W.A. Clouston. Chaucer Society 2nd ser. 7, 10, 15, 20, 22 [paged as 1 vol.] (London 1872-87), pp. 1-53, 221-50 Trivet's version of the Life of Constance served as the principal source for *MLT;* see Schlauch **CT155** for another edition of Trivet's text with marginal summaries in English and a general account of its influence on Chaucer. For a detailed comparison of Trivet's and Chaucer's versions see Block **CT149**; for a brief summary of Trivet's version, see French **CrS42**, 224-30. The only indication brought forward to date that Chaucer knew and used other sections of the *Chroniques* is the suggestion that he read the section on the later career of Maurice and derived from it the reference to 'Mahoun' (Mohammed) in *MLT* 224; see Robert A. Pratt, 'Chaucer and *Les Cronicles* of Nicholas Trevet' in *Studies in the Language and Culture of the Middle Ages and Later,* ed. E. Bagby Atwood and Archibald A. Hill (Austin, Tex. 1969) 303-11. The full text of the *Chroniques* has not been edited. The Chaucer Society edition of Trivet includes a 15th-century English translation as well as a translation in modern English.

Explanatio librorum Boetii de consolatione philosophiae

Chaucer used Trivet's as yet unedited commentary on Boethius'

Consolatio philosophiae when preparing his own translation of the work; see Petersen **Bo2**. On Trivet's commentary, see Jourdain **M238** and Courcelle **M240**, 318-19; an incomplete list of MSS of this widely circulated commentary may be found in Courcelle **M240**, 412-13.

Italian Sources and Influences

GENERAL STUDIES

M191
Pratt, Robert A. 'Chaucer and the Visconti Libraries,' *ELH* 6 (1939) 191-9
Pratt argues that most of the poems indebted to Boccaccio, Petrarch, and Dante's *Convivio* were written after Chaucer's second trip to Italy in 1378; in the earlier works, the chief Italian influence is Dante's *Divina commedia*.
M192
Praz, Mario. 'Chaucer and the Great Italian Writers of the Trecento,' *Monthly Criterion* 6 (1927) 18-39, 131-57, 238-42; repr. in rev. form in Praz, *The Flaming Heart* (Garden City, N.Y. 1958) 29-89
In the course of his general discussion of Chaucer's debt to Dante and Boccaccio, Praz suggests that the influence of the *Divina commedia* was more pervasive than the number of actual verbal parallels indicates.
M193
Ruggiers, Paul G. 'The Italian Influence on Chaucer' in Rowland **CrS13**, 160-84
Ruggiers discusses the nature and extent of Italian influences on Chaucer and includes a selected survey and bibliography of research.
M194
Schless, Howard. 'Transformations: Chaucer's Use of Italian' in Brewer **B8**, 184-223
Schless discusses the disputed question of Dante's influence on Chaucer and examines Chaucer's transformations of his borrowings from Boccaccio, focussing on passages from *PF* and the *Teseida* and from *Tr* and the *Filostrato*.

BOCCACCIO, GIOVANNI (1313-1375)

Complete Works

M195
Tutte le opere di Giovanni Boccaccio, ed. Vittore Branca. 12 vols.
I classici mondadori (Milan 1964-74)
The standard edition, this includes the Latin works.

General Studies

M196
Cummings, Hubertis M. *The Indebtedness of Chaucer's Works to the Italian Works of Boccaccio (a Review and Summary).* University of Cincinnati Studies 10, pt. 2 (Cincinnati 1916, repr. New York 1965)
Cummings examines the evidence to date for Chaucer's use of Boccaccio's major works and argues that no firm evidence exists for Chaucer's knowledge of any of his Italian works, with the exception of the *Filostrato* and *Teseida,* and that no good evidence exists that Chaucer knew these two works as works of Boccaccio; he lists parallel passages in *Tr* and *KnT* with the two Italian sources.
M197
Wright, Herbert C. *Boccaccio in England from Chaucer to Tennyson* (London 1957), pp. 45-58 [*KnT*], 59-101 [*Tr*], 116-22 [*ClT*], and passim
Wright sets Chaucer's translations from Boccaccio in the context of contemporary translations into a variety of vernaculars and gives a detailed discussion of Boccaccio's influence in *ClT, KnT,* and *Tr.*

Decameron

Edition

In **M195**, vol. IV
Whether Chaucer knew the *Decameron* or not is a matter of dispute; see Cummings **M196**, Farnham **M199**, and McGrady **M200**.

Translation

M198
Giovanni Boccaccio. *The Decameron,* trans. with intro. G.H.
MacWilliam. Penguin Classics (Harmondsworth and New York
1972, many reprints)
The translation includes all the tales as well as the Proemium,
the Preface to the Ladies, and the rubrics included in the MSS of
the work; the introduction gives a brief account of previous
English translations.

Studies

M199
Farnham, Willard. 'England's Discovery of the *Decameron,*'
PMLA 39 (1924) 123-39
After a study of the slow spread of knowledge of the *Decameron*
through Europe to England, Farnham argues that Chaucer
probably did not know the work.
M200
McGrady, Donald. 'Chaucer and the *Decameron* Reconsidered,'
ChauR 12 (1977-8) 1-26
McGrady provides a detailed and careful refutation of the con-
clusions of Cummings **M196** and Farnham **M199**, that Chaucer
could not have known the *Decameron.*

De casibus virorum illustrium

Edition

In **M195**, vol. IX
This work was an important source for *MkT* and also influenced
LGW; see Root **CT356**.

Translation

M201
Giovanni Boccaccio. *The Fates of Illustrious Men,* trans. and

abridged Louis Brewer Hall. *Milestones of Thought* (New York 1965)
Hall translates approximately half of the Latin text; he gives a brief discussion of Boccaccio's text and its sources and a selected bibliography.

De mulieribus claris

Edition

In **M195**, vol. X
This work was a source for much of *LGW* and part of *MkT*.

Translation

M202
Giovanni Boccaccio. *Concerning Famous Women,* trans. Guido A. Guarino (New Brunswick, N.J. 1963; repr. London 1964)
The translation is complete and includes a full introduction and notes on Boccaccio's sources.

Il filocolo

Edition

In **M195**, vol. I
This work was probably the major source for *FranklT;* see Dempster and Tatlock **CT265**, and Lowes **CT269**. It was also used in *Tr*; see the notes in Robinson **M30**.

Il filostrato

Edition

In **M195**, vol. II
This is the main source for *Tr*. For a detailed study of Chaucer's use of it, see Meech **Tr11**; see also Lewis **Tr10**, Rossetti **Tr12**, and Young **Tr8** for studies of Chaucer's alterations of his source.

Translation

M203
The Filostrato of Giovanni Boccaccio, trans. Nathaniel Edward
Griffin and Arthur Beckwith Myrick (Philadelphia 1929, repr.
New York 1967)
This close prose translation, printed in parallel columns with the
Italian text of Moutier, is accompanied by an introduction by
Myrick on the relations among the various sources for *Tr.*

Il teseida

Edition

In **M195**, vol. II
This work is a main source for *KnT;* see Boitani **CT102** and Pratt
CT106.

Translation

M204
Giovanni Boccaccio. *The Book of Theseus,* trans. Bernadette
Marie McCoy (New York 1974)
McCoy's translation includes the glosses found in some early MSS
of the *Teseida.*

DANTE ALIGHIERI (1265-1321)

General Studies

M205
Lowes, John Livingston. 'Chaucer and Dante,' *MP* 14 (1916-17)
705-35
Arguing that Dante's influence was more extensive than had been
previously supposed, Lowes demonstrates that Chaucer frequently
draws on several sources at one time.
M206
Schless, Howard. 'Chaucer and Dante' in Bethurum **CrS1**, 134-54

Schless reviews previous criticism on the influence of Dante and discusses the theory and methodology of these source studies.

M207

Tatlock, John S.P. 'Chaucer and Dante,' *MP* 3 (1905-6) 367-72
Tatlock discusses the influence on Chaucer of Dante's discussions of fortune and fate.

Il convivio

Edition

M208

Dante Alighieri. *Il convivio,* ed. Maria Simonelli. Testi e saggi di letterature moderne, Testi 2 (Bologna 1966)
The *Convivio* is the source for the discussion of *gentilesse* in *WBT* (1109ff.), where Dante is cited as the source; see Lowes **CT190**. For a convenient reprinting of the relevant passages from the *Convivio,* see Whiting **CT192**. This edition includes notes and an index of names.

Translation

M209

Dante's Convivio Translated into English, trans. William Walrond Jackson (Oxford 1909)
This prose translation includes an analytical summary of the work, a subject index, and brief textual notes.

La divina commedia

Edition

M210

Dante Alighieri. *The Divine Comedy,* ed. and trans. with commentary Charles S. Singleton. 6 vols. Bollingen Series 80 (Princeton 1970-75)
The *Divina commedia* was an important influence on *HF;* see ,the notes in Robinson **M30**. Chaucer's translation of the prayer of St. Bernard from Canto 33 of *Paradiso* appears as the Invocation to

Mary in *SecNT;* see Gerould, **CT382**. On the general influence of the work on Chaucer, see Praz **M192**, Schless **M194**, and Lowes **M205**. The edition is presented in facing-page format, with an Italian text based on the edition of Giorgio Petrocchi ([Milan] 1966-8). The notes are valuable as a synthesis of criticism and scholarship.

PETRARCA, FRANCESCO [Petrarch] (1304-1374)

Chaucer's *ClT* is based on Petrarch's adaptation and expansion of a story he found in Boccaccio's *Decameron;* Petrarch's version, which takes the form of a letter to Boccaccio (*Epistolae seniles* bk. 17, lr. 3), is printed in Severs **CT219**, together with an anonymous French translation of it which Chaucer also used. For an English translation of the letter, see French **CrS42**, 291-311. Petrarch's sonnet, 'S'amor non è,' is the source for the 'Canticus Troili' in *Tr*; see Thomson **Tr24** for a text of the poem and a study of its relation to Chaucer's version.

SERCAMBI, GIOVANNI (1348-1424)

Sercambi's *Novelle* may have been a source for the framing device of *CT;* see Pratt and Young **CT11** for a discussion and for the relevant extracts from the *Novelle*.

Latin Sources and Influences

See McCall **CrS54** for the influence of classical myth and medieval mythographers. For Chaucer's use of Medieval Latin rhetorical treatises see **B158-72**. See Eisner **CT9** for Chaucer's use of the *Kalendarium* of Nicholas of Lynn; for his knowledge of Latin alchemical treatises see Aiken **CT389**, Duncan **CT390**, and Spargo **CT391**. See Mann **CT53** for Chaucer's use of medieval estates satire and Pratt **M253** on some Medieval Latin MSS probably known to him. See Bennett **HF1** and **PF2**, and Wetherbee **M188** for Chaucer's use of philosophical poetry in Latin.

GENERAL STUDIES

M211

Dronke, Peter and Jill Mann. 'Chaucer and the Medieval Latin Poets' in Brewer **B8**, 154-83

In pt. I, Dronke discusses Chaucer's knowledge of the *Cosmographia* of Bernard Silvestris and the *Planctus naturae* and *Anticlaudianus* of Alan of Lille; he mentions the possible influence of the *Ilias* of Simon Chèvre d'Or and discusses the known influence of 'Dares,' the epic *Frigii Daretis Ilias* of Joseph of Exeter; and he discusses the pervasive influence of the *Poetria nova* of Geoffrey of Vinsauf. In pt. II, Mann discusses Chaucer's knowledge of Medieval Latin satire: the *Speculum stultorum* of Nigel Wireker (Nigel de Longchamps), the *Vox clamantis* of John Gower, and Goliardic satire such as the *Apocalypsis Goliae* and the songs of Walter of Châtillon.

M212

Harbert, Bruce. 'Chaucer and the Latin Classics' in Brewer **B8**, 137-53

Harbert discusses the kinds of MSS in which Chaucer would have read the Latin classics and reviews the evidence for his knowledge of Cicero, Livy, the medieval 'Cato' (*Catonis disticha*), Statius, Claudian, Virgil, and Ovid. He emphasizes the point that Chaucer's knowledge of classical authors need not imply first-hand reading of their works, and he discusses the medieval translations and commentaries which could have shaped Chaucer's view of the classics.

M213

Hoffman, Richard L. 'The Influence of the Classics on Chaucer' in Rowland **CrS13**, 185-201

Hoffman discusses the extent of Chaucer's knowledge of classical Latin authors and surveys scholarship on their influence on Chaucer.

M214

Shannon, Edgar Finley. *Chaucer and the Roman Poets.* Harvard Studies in Comparative Literature 7 (Cambridge, Mass. 1929; repr. New York 1964)

Shannon examines the direct and indirect influence of the Roman poets, particularly Ovid; he also discusses intermediary sources, verbal echoes, and adaptations.

ALANUS DE INSULIS [Alan of Lille, Alain de Lille] (ca. 1116-1202)

Anticlaudianus

Edition

M215
Alain de Lille. *Anticlaudianus: Texte critique avec une introduction et des tables,* ed. R. Bossuat (Paris 1955)
Chaucer's description of Fame's tidings (*HF* 1029) is based on Alan's description of *Fama* in *Anticlaudianus,* mentioned in *HF* 986; see the notes in Robinson **M30** and Skeat **M31** for other parallels, and see Fyler **M282**, 30-31, 47-9, 50 for a discussion of Chaucer's adaptation of the work. See Gerould **CT382** for its use in *SecNT.* This edition supersedes the one in *PL* 210: 481-576.

Translation

M216
Alan of Lille. *Anticlaudianus or the Good and Perfect Man,* trans. with commentary James J. Sheridan. Medieval Sources in Translation 14 (Toronto 1973)
The translation is based on the edition by Bossuat **M215** and includes an introduction discussing the sources and summarizing the argument.

De planctu naturae [*Planctus naturae*]

Edition

M217
Häring, Nikolaus M. 'Alan of Lille, *De planctu naturae,*' *Studi medievali* 3rd ser. 19 (1978) 797-879
Chaucer refers to the work by name and author in *PF* (316), and it is a main source for the portrait of Nature in the poem; see Bennett **PF2**. This edition supersedes the inferior one in *PL* 210: 431A-482C.

Translation

M218
Alan of Lille. *The Plaint of Nature*, trans. with commentary James J. Sheridan. Mediaeval Sources in Translation 26 (Toronto 1980)
Sheridan's translation is based on the edition of Häring **M217**.

ALBERTANO DA BRESCIA (fl. 1238-1246)

De arte loquendi et tacendi

Edition

M219
Albertano da Brescia. *De arte loquendi et tacendi* in Thor Sundby, *Brunetto Latinos Levnet og Skrifter* (Copenhagen 1869); trans. by Rodolfo Renier as *Della vita e delle opere di Brunetto Latini* (Florence 1884), Appendix III, pp. 475-506
This work is one of the sources of *MancT;* see the notes in Robinson **M30**.

Liber consolationis et consilii

Edition

M220
Albertani Brixiensis liber consolationis et consilii ex quo hausta est fabula Gallica de Melibeo et Prudentia, ed. Thor Sundby. Chaucer Society 2nd ser. 8 (London 1873)
This work is the ultimate source of *Mel;* Chaucer did not know Albertano's text at first hand, but used the redaction of Renaud de Louhans.

Redactions

See Severs **CT344**, 568-614, for an edition of a version of *Le*

Livre de Mellibee et Prudence by Renaud de Louhans, an adaptation and abridgement of the *Liber consolationis et consilii;* the text is based on a 15th-century MS close to the one Chaucer used as his main source for *Mel*; see Severs **CT343**.

M221
Renaud de Louhans. *The Goodman of Paris (Le Ménagier de Paris): A Treatise on Moral and Domestic Economy by A Citizen of Paris (c. 1393)*, trans. Eileen Power (London 1928)
Power's translation is based on different MSS from Severs' edition of Louhans in **CT344**; see Power **B55**, 96-119 for a discussion of the work.

ALBERTUS MAGNUS (ca. 1200-1280)

Complete Works

M222
B. Alberti Magni ... opera omnia, ed. Auguste Borgnet. 38 vols. (Paris 1890-99)
Despite its title this edition is incomplete, but it includes the texts known to Chaucer.

De sensu et sensato

Edition

In **M222**, IX, 1-96.
See Pratt **CT208** for a discussion of the influence of this work on *SumT.*

De somno et vigilia

Edition

In **M222**, IX, 121-207
Pratt **CT372** demonstrates Chaucer's use of this work as a source for dream-lore in *NPT.*

AUGUSTINUS, AURELIUS [St. Augustine] (354-430)

Although Augustine is cited frequently in *ParsT* and occasionally
elsewhere, no text of his is listed here because Chaucer's certain use
has not been demonstrated for any single text of Augustine; most of
the citations were likely taken from another source, or from
florilegia. For a discussion of Augustine's influence on the Middle
Ages as a whole (and so on Chaucer), see Robertson **CrS66**; see
Kellogg **CT415** on the citations from Augustine in *ParsT*.

BERNARD SILVESTRIS (fl. 1145-1153)

Cosmographia

Edition

M223
Bernardus Silvestris. *Cosmographia,* ed. with intro. and notes
Peter Dronke. Textus minores 53 (Leiden 1978)
In *MLT* 197ff. Chaucer adapts a passage from the *Cosmographia*
on the fates written in the stars (Pt. I: *Megacosmos,* 1.3.33ff.);
some *CT* MSS have the Latin lines of the source written in the
margin. For another echo of the passage, see the note in
Robinson **M30** for *KnT* 2031-4. Dronke and Mann **M211**, 154-61
give a translation and discussion of the passage from Bernard
together with discussion of other ways in which the work may
have influenced Chaucer. Dronke's edition is based on Oxford,
Bodleian Library, MS. Laud misc. 515; it includes a lucid
summary of the work.

Translation

M224
The Cosmographia of Bernardus Silvestris, trans. with intro. and
notes Winthrop Wetherbee (New York and London 1973)
The passage cited by Chaucer in *MLT* 197ff. appears on p. 76. A
detailed introduction (pp. 1-62) and very full notes make important contributions to the study of the text.

THE BIBLE and THE LITURGY

For general studies see **B119-27**. For a select bibliography on the liturgy, see Pfaff **B128**.

The Bible

Edition

M225
Biblia sacra iuxta vulgatam versionem, ed. Robertus Weber et al. 2 vols. (Stuttgart 1969, 2nd rev. ed. 1975)
This edition is based on two modern critical editions: of the Old Testament by the Benedictines of St. Jerome's monastery in Rome and of the New Testament by J. Wordsworth and H.J. White (the Oxford edition). The text is printed without punctuation, and it includes a small selection of variants. Also included are the prologues of Jerome and many of the books now regarded as apocryphal. This edition is the basis for the standard modern concordance of the Vulgate: Bonifatius Fischer, *Novae concordantiae bibliorum sacrorum iuxta vulgatam versionem* (Stuttgart 1977).

Translation

M226
Bible, English (Douay-Rheims Version). *The Holy Bible, Translated from the Latin Vulgate* (Douay 1609, 1610; many reprints)
This translation is based on that of the New Testament by the English College at Rheims in 1582 and of the Old Testament by the English College at Douay which was included in the edition of 1609.

Studies of the Bible and the Liturgy

M227
Boyd, Beverly. *Chaucer and the Liturgy* (Philadelphia 1967)

Boyd examines Chaucer's liturgical allusions and gives background
on the liturgy in the Middle Ages. See also Rosenfeld **CT153**.
M228
Landrum, Grace W. 'Chaucer's Use of the Vulgate,' *PMLA* 39
(1924) 75-100
By analysing Chaucer's biblical references, Landrum attempts to
establish Chaucer's direct and comprehensive knowledge of the
Vulgate.
M229
Thompson, W. Meredith. 'Chaucer's Translation of the Bible' in
English and Medieval Studies Presented to J.R.R. Tolkien, ed. Norman
Davis and C.L. Wrenn (London 1962) 183-99
Thompson discusses the sources of Chaucer's biblical allusions and
quotations.
M230
Wenzel, Siegfried. 'Chaucer and the Language of Contemporary
Preaching,' *SP* 73 (1976) 138-61
Wenzel shows that Chaucer borrowed images and terms from
contemporary sermons.
M231
Wimsatt, James I. 'Chaucer and the Canticle of Canticles' in
Mitchell and Provost **CrS10**, 66-90.
Wimsatt reviews the exegetical and literary tradition of the Song of
Songs and suggests that Chaucer makes use of allusions to it for
comic effect in *MerchT* and *MillT;* he includes brief discussion of
allusions to the Canticle in *BD.* See also Kaske **CT131**.

BERSUIRE, PIERRE — see **M286-8**

BOETHIUS, ANICIUS MANLIUS SEVERINUS (ca. 480-524)

De consolatione philosophiae [*Consolatio philosophiae*]

The most influential of Chaucer's many Latin sources was the
Consolatio philosophiae of Boethius. Chaucer knew the work
intimately, because he translated it into Middle English with

considerable accuracy; where he felt his own version needed
explanation, he added material from Trivet's commentary. His
accomplishment is especially noteworthy because few philosophical
texts had been translated previously into Middle English; Chaucer
was creating new vocabulary as he worked and did the task so
successfully that most of his neologisms soon passed into English
usage. Consequently, his translation looks less original to modern
readers than it is.

The influence of the *Consolatio* is present throughout his work;
sometimes he incorporates passages he translates from the *Consolatio,* as in the song of Troilus, *Tr* III.1744-71; sometimes he adapts
its philosophical argument, as in the discourse of Troilus on free
will and predestination, *Tr* IV.960-1078; sometimes he uses the philosophical outlook of the *Consolatio* as part of a work's intellectual
setting, as in *KnT;* sometimes he incorporates ideas and phrases
from it into his work so completely that they seem integral to the
passage, not borrowings at all. Chaucer had, in brief, a translator's
knowledge of the *Consolatio,* and it remained central to his work
through his career as a poet.

Because a knowledge of the *Consolatio* and Chaucer's debts to it
are essential to the understanding of a major context of his poetry, a
relatively full selection of editions, translations, and studies of the
work is given here.

For items on Chaucer's translation of the *Consolatio* see **Bo1-3**
and their headnotes.

Editions

M232
Anicii Manlii Severini Boethii philosophiae consolatio, ed. Ludwig
Bieler. Corpus Christianorum, series Latina 94 (Turnhout 1957)
Bieler's is a standard critical edition.

M233
Boethius. *The Theological Tractates,* ed. and trans. H.F. Stewart
and E.K. Rand; *The Consolation of Philosophy with the English
translation of 'I.T.' (1609),* rev. H.F. Stewart. Loeb Classical
Library (London and Cambridge, Mass. 1918, many reprints)
This edition was reissued 1973 with a new translation of the
Consolation by S.J. Tester.

Concordance

M234

Cooper, Lane. *A Concordance of Boethius: The Five Theological Tractates and the Consolation of Philosophy* (Cambridge, Mass. 1928)
The concordance is based on the Loeb edition **M233**.

Translations

M235
Boethius. *The Consolation of Philosophy,* trans. with intro. and notes Richard Green. Library of Liberal Arts (Indianapolis 1962, repr. 1976)
Green's prose translation includes a summary of the argument, notes, index, and bibliography.
M236
Boethius. *The Consolation of Philosophy,* trans. with intro. V.E. Watts. Penguin Classics (Harmondsworth and Baltimore 1969)
Watts's translation follows the alternating verse and prose of the original; it includes glossary, notes, and full bibliography.
M237
Jean de Meun, trans. *Li Livres de confort de philosophie* in V.L. Dedeck-Héry, ed., 'Boethius' *De consolatione* by Jean de Meun,' *MS* 14 (1952) 165-275
In making his own translation, Chaucer probably used this French translation by Jean as well as the Latin original; see Lowes **Bo1**. This critical edition is based on a full study of the extant MSS as described in Dedeck-Héry, *Speculum* 15 (1940) 432-43.

Commentary

M238
Jourdain, Charles. 'Des commentaires inédits de Guillaume de Conches et de Nicholas Triveth sur *La Consolation de la philosophie* de Boèce,' *Notices et extraits des manuscrits de la Bibliothèque impériale et autres bibliothèques* 20 (1865) pt. II,

40-82; repr. in Jourdain, *Excursions historiques et philosophiques à travers le moyen âge* (Paris 1888, repr. Frankfurt 1966) 29-68 Jourdain provides a brief summary of the commentary by Nicholas Trivet, together with occasional quotations from the MSS; the commentary has not been edited. For Chaucer's use of this commentary in *Boece,* see Petersen **Bo2**.

Studies

For a study of Boethius' tendency to see opposed points of view and to find strategies for affirming both sides, and of a similar tendency in Chaucer, see Elbow **CrS40**, 19-48.

M239
Chadwick, Henry. *Boethius: The Consolations of Music, Logic, Theology, and Philosophy* (Oxford 1981)
Ch. V on 'Evil, Freedom, and Providence' provides a scholarly account of the *Consolatio* in its philosophical context. There is a full bibliography, pp. 261-84. For a readable, if somewhat outdated account of the historical context of Boethius, see Helen M. Barrett, *Boethius: Some Aspects of his Times and Work* (Cambridge 1940).
M240
Courcelle, Pierre, *'La Consolation de philosophie' dans la tradition littéraire: Antécédents et posterité de Boèce.* Études augustiniennes (Paris 1967)
Courcelle's important and detailed work is indispensable for the study of the influence of Boethius on the Middle Ages.
M241
Jefferson, Bernard L. *Chaucer and the 'Consolation of Philosophy' of Boethius* (Princeton 1917, repr. New York 1968)
Jefferson discusses in detail the influence of the *Consolatio* on Chaucer; he includes a list of passages in Chaucer's poetry showing Boethian influence and a list of passages from Boethius that influenced Chaucer.
M242
Patch, Howard Rollin. *The Tradition of Boethius: A Study of his Importance in Mediaeval Culture* (New York 1935)
Patch discusses the tradition and legend of Boethius, his

influence on medieval philosophy and theology, and translations and imitations of his work up to the 17th century.

'CATO'

Disticha Catonis [*Disticha de moribus ad filium*] (3rd c. A.D.?)

Edition

M243
Boas, Marcus, ed. with Henricus Johannes Botschuyver. *Disticha Catonis* (Amsterdam 1952)
The date of first compilation and the name of the original compiler of this collection of moral apothegms are not known. Proverbs in this collection were quoted near the end of the 2nd century, and by the end of the 4th century the early form of the compilation was enjoying an extensive vogue. It was associated with the name of Cato the Censor (234-149 B.C.), who wrote a similar work, the *Carmen de moribus,* but there is no evidence that Cato compiled this collection. It was expanded and translated frequently and, in its expanded, Christianized form, became a popular manual of instruction throughout the Middle Ages. Chaucer refers to it as 'Catoun' in *NPT* (2940) and *MerchT* (1377). This critical edition in Latin includes a full introduction, commentary, textual variants, and an *index verborum.*
Botschuyver completed the edition after the death of Boas.

Translation

M244
Dicta Catonis in *Minor Latin Poems,* ed. and trans. J. Wight Duff and Arnold M. Duff. Loeb Classical Library (Cambridge, Mass. and London 1934; rev. ed. 1935; repr. 1961, 1978) 583-639
The introduction gives a brief characterization of the work and its popularity in the Middle Ages. The text is based on the edition by E. Baehrens in *Poetae Latini minores,* 6 vols. (Leipzig 1879-83) III, 205-42. For another translation with parallel Latin also based on Baehrens' edition, see Wayland Johnson Chase, trans., *The*

Distichs of Cato, University of Wisconsin Studies in the Social
Sciences and History 7 (Madison 1922).

Study

M245
Hazelton, Richard. 'Chaucer and Cato,' *Speculum* 35 (1960)
357-80
Hazelton discusses the reputation of the *Disticha Catonis* in the
Middle Ages as an introductory treatise on ethics; he shows how
Chaucer uses it, often parodically, in *NPT, MillT, RvT, MerchT,*
and *MancT.*

CICERO, MARCUS TULLIUS (106-43 B.C.)

Much of Chaucer's knowledge of Cicero's works was probably
indirect: the *De amicitia* was quoted and summarized in the *Roman
de la rose;* the *De officiis* supplied many of the sententious sayings
in the *Liber consolationis et consilii* of Albertano da Brescia, the
ultimate source for *Mel;* other works provided brief quotations for
Boethius' *Consolatio philosophiae.* Chaucer cites Cicero in *FranklT*
722 as an authority on rhetoric, but probably did not know his *De
inventione* and *De oratore* directly; see Murphy **B170**. The *De re
publica* presents a special case: although it was not extant in its
entirety, the concluding section, the *Somnium Scipionis,* was known
and used by Chaucer because of its preservation in the commentary
of Macrobius; see **M271-2**.

De divinatione

Edition and Translation

M246
Cicero. De senectute, De amicitia, De divinatione, ed. and trans.
William Armistead Falconer. Loeb Classical Library (New York
and London 1923) 213-539
See Pratt **CT372** for a discussion of Chaucer's use of this work
in the discussions of dreams and prophesying in *NPT.*

De officiis

This work may have been known to Chaucer indirectly, through a 12th-century adaptation, *Moralium dogma philosophorum.*

Edition

M247
Holmberg, John, ed. *Das 'Moralium dogma philosophorum' des Guillaume de Conches: Lateinisch, altfranzösisch, und mittel-niederfränkisch.* 2 vols. (Uppsala 1929)
See Hazelton **CT414** for the argument that the *Moralium* was the ultimate source for parts of the section on the *remedia* for the seven sins in *ParsT.* This critical edition includes an introduction and the Latin text in vol. I, and an Old French and Middle Low Franconian translation in vol. II.

CLAUDIANUS, CLAUDIUS [Claudian] (355-ca. 404)

De raptu Proserpinae

Edition and Translation

M248
Claudian. *De raptu Proserpinae* in *Claudian,* ed. and trans. Maurice Platnauer. 2 vols. Loeb Classical Library (London and New York 1922) II, 292-377
Chaucer cites Claudian as an authority on the underworld in *HF* 449 and as an authority on the story of Proserpina in *MerchT* 2232; see Donovan **CT233**.

Study

M249
Pratt, Robert A. 'Chaucer's Claudian,' *Speculum* 22 (1947) 419-29
Pratt discusses the possible sources and extent of Chaucer's knowledge of Claudian, primarily the *De raptu Proserpinae,* with

some attention to *Laus Serenae*, which may have been a source for *LGWProl.* He points out that Chaucer could have read these works in a medieval school reader, the *Liber Catonianus*, and argues that studies of Chaucer's sources should include studies of the MSS in which the works were read.

COLONNE, GUIDO DELLE [Guido de Columnis] (fl. 1287)

Historia destructionis Troiae

Edition

M250
Guido de Columnis. *Historia destructionis Troiae*, ed. Nathaniel Edward Griffin. Mediaeval Academy of America Publications 26 (Cambridge, Mass. 1936; repr. New York 1969)
Guido's version of the story of Troy, although based largely on the romance version of Benoit de Sainte-More, was regarded in the Middle Ages as the authentic historical version, based on the eyewitness accounts of Dares of Troy and Dictys of Crete. It is a source for *Tr* and for the legend of Medea in *LGW* (1589ff.). See Benson **Tr16** and Hamilton **Tr17** for Guido's influence on *Tr.*

Translation

M251
Guido delle Colonne. *Historia destructionis Troiae*, trans. with intro. and notes Mary Elizabeth Meek (Bloomington, Ind. and London 1974)
Meek's translation is based on the Griffin edition **M250**; it includes a detailed index.

Study

M252
Benson, C. David. *The History of Troy in Middle English Literature: Guido delle Colonne's 'Historia destructionis Troiae' in Medieval England* (Woodbridge, Suffolk 1980)

Benson gives a careful analysis of Guido's text, its sources, and its distinctive character; he also uses the Middle English versions as a guide to the medieval English perception of the work. He traces the various lines of influence from Guido to Chaucer and from Chaucer to Lydgate.

DARES PHRYGIUS

Although Chaucer refers to Dares in *HF* 1467 as an important figure in upholding the fame of Troy, there is no clear evidence that he had firsthand knowledge of the *De excidio Troiae historia*, reputed to be an eyewitness account of the war from the Trojan viewpoint. His references to Dares in *Tr* I.146, and in V.1770-71, where he cites Dares more specifically as the recorder of the 'worthi dedes' of Troilus in battle, are likely to be based on the version of Dares by Joseph of Exeter, as Root **Tr20** has shown. Dares' version of the story of Troy is thus best viewed as an analogue, not a source, of *Tr;* see Frazer **Tr18** for a translation and discussion.

DICTYS CRETENSIS

See DARES PHRYGIUS above. The evidence for Chaucer's firsthand knowledge of the *Ephemerides belli Troiani libri*, reputed to be an eyewitness account of the war from the Greek viewpoint, is still more tenuous than the evidence for Chaucer's knowledge of Dares; although Chaucer makes reference to his work, he calls him 'Tytus' in *HF* 1467, and 'Dite' in *Tr* I.146. See Frazer **Tr18** for a translation and discussion.

FLORILEGIA and SCHOOL READERS

On the availability of classical texts in school readers and florilegia, see Harbert **M212** and Pratt **M140** and **M249**; see also Hammond **M1**, 89-90.

Study

M253
Pratt, Robert A. 'Chaucer and the Hand that Fed Him,' *Speculum* 41
(1966) 619-42
Pratt suggests that Chaucer may have used late 13th-century handbooks such as John of Wales's *Communiloquium* in *WBT, SumT,*
and *PardT;* he argues that Chaucer's knowledge of Seneca and
Valerius Maximus may also have derived from such a work.

GUILIELMUS PERALDUS (ca. 1200-ca. 1271)

Summa vitiorum [*Summa de vitiis*]

No modern edition of this text has been made; excerpts from it,
taken from the Basel 1497 edition, are printed in Dempster **CT413,**
741-4. Part of the section of *ParsT* on the seven sins (387-957)
derives ultimately from this work, but Chaucer's version is much
abbreviated and it also includes material not in Peraldus' *Summa;*
see Petersen **CT416.** See Wenzel **CT419** for the argument that
Chaucer knew Peraldus' *Summa* indirectly, through two treatises
derived from it, called *Quoniam* and *Primo.*

GUILLAUME DE CONCHES (1090-ca. 1160)

Moralium dogma philosophorum — *see* **M247.**

HIERONYMUS, SAINT [St. Jerome] (ca. 348-420)

The Vulgate translation of the Bible was attributed to St. Jerome;
see **M225-31.**

Epistola adversus Jovinianum

M254
S. Eusebii Hieronymi . . . adversus Jovinianum libri duo in *PL* 23
(1883): 221-352

The Wife of Bath cites this work (*WBProl* 674-5) as part of Jankyn's book of wicked wives, and it is an important source for *WBProl;* see Whiting **CT188**, who prints relevant excerpts from it. The part of the *Epistola* which had most influence on Chaucer is a lengthy passage which Jerome attributes to a treatise on marriage by the Greek philosopher Theophrastus (see below p. 94); the passage gives a series of antifeminist arguments (similar to Jerome's own) to support the view that a wise man should not take a wife. This passage is a source for several passages in *CT: MerchT* 1294-1310, where January disagrees with Theophrastus' view that a good servant is a better household manager than any wife; *MerchT* 1601-4, January's mental image of his wife; and *MancT* 148-53, on the folly of attempting to keep watch over any wife, bad or good. On Dorigen's complaint to Fortune in *FranklT* 1355-1456, see Morgan **CT270**; the passage is a condensed version of the six chapters in Jerome preceding the account of Theophrastus, which are echoed again in the speech of the God of Love in *LGWProl* 281-304, where the material is explicitly attributed to Jerome. The reference to Jovinian in *SumT* 1929-30 appears to derive from Jerome's description of the monk Jovinian, against whom the treatise was written. See the notes in Robinson **M30** and see Lounsbury **M138**, II, 292-7 for a summary account of the work and for other incidental borrowings from it.

HOLKOT, ROBERTUS [Robert Holkott] (ob. 1349)

Super libros sapientiae

Edition

M255
Robert Holkott. *Super libros sapientiae* (Hagenau 1494, repr. Frankfurt 1974)
Pratt **CT372** demonstrates Chaucer's use of this influential commentary on the biblical Book of Wisdom in *NPT;* see also Petersen **CT370**, 103-8. See Smalley **B154**, 133-202 for a discussion of Holkot and his works.

HORATIUS FLACCUS, QUINTUS [Horace] (65-08 B.C.)

The evidence for Chaucer's knowledge of Horace is extremely conjectural, and what passages he may have known may well have come from florilegia; see Lounsbury **M138**, II, 261-4 and Shannon **M214**, 359-60. See Kittredge **Tr21** for a passage from Horace which Chaucer may have found in John of Salisbury's *Policraticus.*

Studies

M256
Coffman, George R. 'Old Age from Horace to Chaucer: Some Literary Affinities and Adventures of an Idea,' *Speculum* 9 (1934) 249-77
Coffman compares Chaucer's discussions of old age with Horace's *Ars poetica* 169-74, and he provides a general account of the medieval literary tradition of describing old age.
M257
Seibert, Harriet. 'Chaucer and Horace,' *MLN* 31 (1916) 304-7
Of the eight passages usually viewed as borrowings from Horace, Seibert points out that at least seven could have been borrowed secondhand and that the eighth may have been proverbial; she doubts that Chaucer knew Horace's works at first hand.
M258
Wrenn, C.L. 'Chaucer's Knowledge of Horace,' *MLR* 18 (1923) 286-92
Wrenn attempts to make a case for Chaucer's firsthand knowlege of Horace's *Ars poetica,* and at least one of his *Odes,* on the basis of verbal parallels in Chaucer's works, particularly *Tr.*

INNOCENTIUS III [Pope Innocent III] (ca. 1160-1216)

De miseria condicionis humanae [*De contemptu mundi*]

Edition and Translation

M259
Lotario dei Segni (Pope Innocent III). *De miseria condicionis*

humane, ed. and trans. Robert E. Lewis. Chaucer Library
(Athens, Ga. 1978)
On Chaucer's lost translation of this work, see Lewis **M48**; for
the use of this work in *MLT,* see Lewis **CT151**. In this edition,
Lewis gives a critical text and translation; the introduction
discusses in detail Chaucer's use of the work.

JACOBUS DE VARAGINE [Voragine] (ca. 1230-1298)

Legenda aurea

Edition

M260
Jacobi a Voragine legenda aurea, ed. Th. Graesse. 2nd ed.
(Leipzig 1850)
On Chaucer's use of this work in *SecNT,* see Gerould **CT382**,
Kölbing **CT383**, and Reames **CT384**.

Translation

M261
The Golden Legend of Jacobus de Voragine, trans. Granger Ryan
and Helmut Ripperger. 2 vols. (London, New York, Toronto 1941;
repr. New York 1969)
This translation is based primarily on the edition of Graesse,
including the etymologies which preface most legends; some
passages involving points of theology are silently omitted. The
legend of St. Cecilia is printed on pp. 689-95.

JEROME, SAINT — see HIERONYMUS, SAINT.

JOHN OF SALISBURY [Ioannes Saresberiensis] (ca. 1115-1180)

Policraticus

Edition

M262
Ioannis Saresberiensis episcopi Carnotensis Policratici sive De nugis curialium et vestigiis philosophorum libri VIII, ed. Clemens C.I. Webb. 2 vols. (London 1909)
The denunciation of games of chance in *PardT* (591ff.) and the account of Stilbon (Chilon in *Policraticus*) *PardT* 603ff. are derived from this work; see the notes in Robinson **M30**. See Pratt **CT185** for the argument that Book VIII of the work is a source for some of Jankyn's stories of wicked wives, and Fleming **CT69** for the suggestion that the description of the Clerk parallels *Policraticus* 2.156-7. Kittredge **Tr21** suggests that the work may have been a source for Chaucer's fictive author 'Lollius.' See also Tupper **CT298** and see Lounsbury **M138**, II, 362-4 for other incidental borrowings.

Translations

M263
The Statesman's Book of John of Salisbury: Being the Fourth, Fifth, and Sixth Books, and Selections from the Seventh and Eighth Books of the 'Policraticus' ..., trans. and intro. John Dickinson (New York 1927; repr. 1955, 1963)
This translation includes only those sections of the work which deal directly with political theory.
M264
Frivolities of Courtiers and Footprints of Philosophers: Being a Translation of the First, Second, and Third Books and Selections from the Seventh and Eighth Books of the 'Policraticus' of John of Salisbury, trans. Joseph B. Pike (Minneapolis, Minn. and London 1938)
This translation includes all those sections of the work omitted in **M263**.

JOSEPH OF EXETER [Joseph Iscanus] (fl. 1180)

Iliad [*De bello Trojano*]

Edition

M265
Joseph Iscanus. *Frigii Daretis Yliados libri sex* in *Joseph Iscanus, Werke und Briefe,* ed. Ludwig Gompf. Mittellateinische Studien und Texte 4 (Leiden 1970) 77-211
Chaucer probably drew on Joseph's version of Dares' Trojan history for *Tr;* see Root **Tr20**.

Translation

M266
Joseph of Exeter. *The Iliad of Dares Phrygius,* trans. with intro. and notes Gildas Roberts (Cape Town 1970)
The introduction gives a brief survey of the medieval Troy legend and discusses Chaucer's use of Joseph's *Iliad;* Roberts includes a glossary of the principal persons in the text.

JUVENALIS, DECIMUS JUNIUS [Juvenal] (ca. 50-ca. 127)

'Satura X'

Edition and Translation

M267
Juvenal. 'Satura X' in *Juvenal and Persius,* ed. and trans. G.G. Ramsay. Loeb Classical Library (London and Cambridge, Mass. 1918; rev. ed. 1940, repr. 1950) 192-221
In *Tr* IV.197-201, Chaucer quotes from lines 2-4 of 'Satura X.'

LIVIUS, TITUS [Livy] (59 B.C.-A.D. 17)

Ab urbe condita

Edition and Translation

M268
Livy, ed. and trans. B.O. Foster, Frank Gardner Moore, Evan T. Sage, and Alfred C. Schlesinger. 14 vols. Loeb Classical Library (London, New York, and Cambridge, Mass. 1919-59) I, 196-209 [Lucrece, bk. 1, chs. 57-9]; II, 142-99 [Virginia, bk. 3, chs. 44-58] Livy is the original source of the story of Virginia, retold briefly by Jean de Meun in the *Roman de la rose* (see **M169**, lines 5589-5658 and **M171**, p. 114), where it is attributed to Livy; it is retold at greater length by Gower in *Confessio amantis* (7.5131-5306), and very briefly by Boccaccio in *De mulieribus claris* (ch. 56). All of these derivative versions of the tale were known to Chaucer, but his version in *PhysT* gives the full story as found in Livy and repeated in Gower. If *PhysT* antedates Gower's version as Tatlock argues in **M42**, 150-56, then Livy's original version can be taken as one of the sources of *PhysT*. See Shannon **CT284** for a Latin text of Livy with a discussion of its possible influence on Chaucer. Chaucer cites Livy (*LGW* 1680-1885), in addition to Ovid, as a source for the legend of Lucrece (*LGW* 1680-1885), but there is no clear evidence that Chaucer made use of Livy's version of the story of Lucrece; see Shannon **M214**.

LUCANUS, MARCUS ANNAEUS [Lucan] (39-65)

Pharsalia

Edition

M269
Lucan. *Pharsalia,* ed. C.E. Haskins, intro. W.E. Heitland (London 1887, repr. Hildesheim and New York 1971) Chaucer claims the *Pharsalia* is the principal source of the

tragedy of Julius Caesar in *MkT* (*CT* 2671-2726), and he refers elsewhere to Lucan as an authority on Caesar (*MLT* 401), but without any indication that he has detailed knowledge of the text; see Shannon **M214**, 333-9 for a discussion of Chaucer's problematical knowledge of the text, and Robinson **M30**, 750, n. 2671 for the possibility that Chaucer's story of Caesar derives in part from a French version by Jehan de Tuim.

Translation

M270
Lucan. *Pharsalia: Dramatic Episodes of the Civil Wars,* trans. Robert Graves (Harmondsworth and Baltimore 1956)
The translation includes a detailed introduction.

MACROBIUS, AMBROSIUS AURELIUS THEODOSIUS (fl. 375)

Commentary on the 'Somnium Scipionis'

Edition

M271
Ambrosii Theodosii Macrobii commentarii in Somnium Scipionis, vol. II of *Saturnalia ... In Somnium Scipionis commentarios,* ed. Jacobus Willis. 2 vols. Bibliotheca scriptorum Graecorum et Romanorum Teubneriana (Leipzig 1963, 2nd ed. 1970)
Macrobius' commentary on the *Somnium Scipionis,* which formed part of Cicero's *De re publica,* is the source for Chaucer's version of the dream of Scipio in *PF* 29-98; in *BD* 284-8, Chaucer describes Macrobius as the author of the *Somnium* itself, following a similar allusion in the *Roman de la rose.* Macrobius was known for his elaborate classification of types of dreams to which Chaucer may be alluding in *HF* 7-11. This edition includes a selection of variant readings, an index of topics, an index of authors mentioned by Macrobius, and, in vol. I, a bibliography.

Translation

M272

Macrobius. *Commentary on the Dream of Scipio,* trans. with
intro. and notes William Harris Stahl. [Columbia University]
Records of Civilization, Sources and Studies 48 (New York and
London 1952)
The introduction summarizes and analyses the work, and dis-
cusses its significance in the Middle Ages.

MAP, WALTER (ca. 1137-1209)

Dissuasio Valerii ad Ruffinum philosophum ne uxorem ducat

Edition

M273

Map, Walter. 'Dissuasio Valerii ad Ruffinum philosophum ne
uxorem ducat (A Dissuasion of Valerius to Ruffinus the
Philosopher, that he should not take a Wife),' dist. 4, chs. 3-5, in
De nugis curialium, ed. M.R. James. Anecdota Oxoniensia,
Mediaeval and Modern Series 14 (Oxford 1914), pp. 143-59. A
translation, *Walter Map's 'De Nugis Curialium',* by M.R. James,
ed. E. Sidney Hartland with notes by Sir John Edward Lloyd, was
published separately, Cymmrodorion Record Series 9 (1923) pp.
160-72. James' text and translation have recently been reissued
as *De nugis curialium Courtiers' Trifles,* ed. and trans. M.R. James,
revised by C.N.L. Brooke and Sir R.A.B. Mynors, Oxford
Medieval Texts (Oxford 1983), pp. 289-315
The Wife of Bath refers to 'Valerie' in describing Jankyn's book
of wicked wives (*WBProl* 671), and most of the examples of
wicked wives in lines 715ff. are mentioned in this work. The
Dissuasio circulated as an anonymous treatise (sometimes called
the *Epistola Valerii*), either separately or together with the
Adversus Jovinianum of Jerome (see **M254**). See Whiting **CT188**
and **CT192** for the relevant excerpts, and Pratt **CT186** for an
account of the work in the tradition of Jankyn's Oxford.

Translation

M274
Master Walter Map's Book, De nugis curialium (Courtiers' Trifles),
trans. Frederick Tupper and Marbury Blanden Ogle (London
1924) 183-98
This translation is based on the James edition **M273**.

MARTIANUS CAPELLA (fl. 410-439)

De nuptiis Philologiae et Mercurii

Edition

M275
Martianus Capella, ed. Adolfus Dick (Leipzig 1925). Rev. ed.
Adolfus Dick, addenda and corrections Jean Préaux. Bibliotheca
scriptorum Graecorum et Romanorum Teubneriana (Stuttgart
1978)
Chaucer refers to the wedding of Philology and Mercury in
MerchT 1732-5; in *HF* 985, he cites 'Marcian' together with the
Anticlaudianus of Alan of Lille as authorities on the heavens. See
Dronke and Mann **M211**, 161-3 for an analysis of the reference
in *HF.* This edition of *De nuptiis* includes critical apparatus in
Latin plus an index.

Translation

M276
Martianus Capella. *The Marriage of Philology and Mercury,* vol.
II of *Martianus Capella and the Seven Liberal Arts,* trans. William
Harris Stahl and Richard Johnson with E.L. Burge. 2 vols.
[Columbia University] Records of Civilization, Sources and
Studies 84 (New York 1977)
This translation into English prose is based on the first edition of
Dick **M275**; it includes full explanatory notes and an index. Vol. I
provides a discussion of the background of the work, 'Latin
Traditions in the Mathematical Sciences' by Stahl (pp. 1-79), and

an interpretive analysis, 'The Allegory and the Trivium' by
Johnson with Burge (pp. 81-243).

MĀSHĀ' ALLĀH [Messahala] (ca. 740-ca. 815)

See Skeat **Astr2** and Gunther **Astr3** for Chaucer's use of his *Compositio et operatio astrolabii* together with a collotype facsimile of
the work; see Kennedy **Eq2** for the horoscope by Messahala in *Eq.*

MATHEOLUS (ob. ca. 1320)

Lamentationes

Edition and Translation

M277
*Les Lamentations de Matheolus et le Livre de Leesce de Jehan le
Fèvre, de Ressons (poèmes français du XIV siècle),* ed. A.G. van
Hamel. Bibliothèque de l'Ecole des hautes études, Sciences
philologiques et historiques, fasc. 95-6, (Paris 1892-1905)
See Moore **CT184** and Thundy **CrS18**, 24-58, for the argument
that the *Lamentationes* (late 13th century) is the source for much
of the polemical matter of *WBProl.* This edition includes the
original *Lamentationes* in Latin, a popular French translation (ca.
1371-2) attributed in several MSS to Le Fèvre, and a rebuttal of
Matheolus by Le Fèvre, entitled variously *Livre de Leesce* or
Rebours de Matheolus (Le Resolu en mariage), defending
marriage and celebrating the merits of women.

NICHOLAS OF LYNN (fl. 1386)

Kalendarium

Edition

M278
The Kalendarium of Nicholas of Lynne, ed. Sigmund Eisner,

trans. Gary Mac Eoin and Sigmund Eisner. Chaucer Library (Athens, Ga.

1980)
Eisner provides an introduction explaining the medieval use of the *Kalendarium* and its influence on Chaucer; for a full statement on Chaucer's use of it in *CT*, see Eisner **CT9**.

ORIGEN (185/6-254/5)

In *LGW* F428 and G418 Chaucer refers to a translation he is said by Alceste to have made of 'Origenes upon the Maudelayne'; for the meaning of this reference, see the headnote to Lost Works (p. 16) and also McCall **M49**.

OVIDIUS NASO, PUBLIUS [Ovid] (43 B.C.-A.D. 17)

Among classical Latin authors, Ovid is by far the best known to Chaucer; see Shannon **M214** and Harbert **M212**. See Skeat **M31**, VI, 387-8 and Dillon **M69**, 162-71 for lists of parallel passages in Chaucer and Ovid. Although parallels can be found with all of the major works of Ovid, there is no clear evidence that Chaucer knew the *Amores, Ars amatoria,* and *Remedia amoris* at first hand, because so much of this material had by Chaucer's time become part of a long and complex medieval literary tradition of Ovidian quotation, adaptation, and commentary; see Fyler **M282** for the argument that Chaucer shares certain habits of mind with these works whether or not he knew them at first hand. Even for the works that Chaucer is certain to have known directly, the full extent of his indebtedness to Ovid cannot be detailed here. Only the most important borrowings are listed below. See Hoffman **CT10** for a detailed study of Chaucer's use of Ovid in *CT*.

Fasti

Edition and Translation

M279
Ovid's Fasti, ed. and trans. James George Frazer. Loeb Classical

Library (Cambridge, Mass. and London 1931; repr. 1967)
The *Fasti* (2.685-848) is the main source for the story of Lucrece
in *LGW* 1680-1873.

Heroides

Edition and Translation

M280
Ovid. *The Heroides* in *Heroides and Amores,* ed. and trans. Grant
Showerman. Loeb Classical Library (Cambridge, Mass. and
London 1914; 2nd ed. G.P. Goold 1977)
The *Heroides* is a main source for four of the stories in *LGW:*
Hypsipyle and Medea, *LGW* 1368-1679 (*Heroides* 6 and 12);
Ariadne, *LGW* 2185-2217 (*Heroides* 10); Phyllis, *LGW* 2404-2554
(*Heroides* 2); and Hypermnestra, *LGW* 2562-2722 (*Heroides* 14).
Dido's letter, *LGW* 1355-65, shows a few similarities to *Heroides*
7. The *Heroides* is also the basic source for the catalogue of
abandoned women in *HF* 388-426. See Dean **SP5** for the
argument that Chaucer's 'Complaint' is a genre derived from the
Heroides. See Meech **LGW7** for the argument that Chaucer used
an Italian translation of the *Heroides* ascribed to Filippo Ceffi in
addition to Ovid's text.

Metamorphoses

Edition and Translation

M281
Ovid. *Metamorphoses,* ed and trans. Frank Justus Miller. 2 vols.
Loeb Classical Library (Cambridge, Mass. and London 1916; 3rd
ed. G.P. Goold 1977)
The *Metamorphoses* is a main source for the description of the
house of Rumour in *HF* 1918-85 (*Met.* 12.39-63), and for the story
of Ceyx and Alcyone in *BD* 62-220 (*Met.* 11.410-728). Four of the
stories in *LGW* also derive from *Metamorphoses:* Pyramus and
Thisbe, *LGW* 706-915 (*Met.* 4.155-66); Hypsipyle and Medea,
LGW 1368-1679 (*Met.* 7); Ariadne, *LGW* 1894-1921 (*Met.* 8.6-

182); and Philomela, *LGW* 2244-2382 (*Met.* 6.424-600). The main source for *MancT* is Ovid's tale of Apollo and Coronis (*Met.* 2.531-632); see Work **CT403**.

Studies

M282
Fyler, John M. *Chaucer and Ovid* (New Haven and London 1979)
Concentrating on the *Ars amatoria,* the *Remedia amoris,* and the *Amores,* Fyler assesses Ovid's influence on Chaucer's skeptical cast of mind and ambiguous stance as fallible narrator; his discussion of Chaucer focusses on *HF, BD, PF, LGW, Tr,* and *NPT.*

OVID: MEDIEVAL ALLEGORIZATIONS

The text of Ovid was subject to allegorical interpretation, moralization, and expansion by a variety of authors in the Middle Ages. Chaucer knew texts that allegorized Ovid's work; relevant items are included here because Chaucer's poetic treatment of Ovidian material often reflects this tradition.

General Studies

M283
Born, Lester K. 'Ovid and Allegory,' *Speculum* 9 (1934) 362-79
Born discusses the influence of medieval commentaries on the understanding of Ovid in the Middle Ages.

M284
Twycross, Meg. *The Medieval Anadyomene: A Study in Chaucer's Mythography.* Medium Ævum Monographs n.s. 1 (Oxford 1972, repr. 1977)
In the course of her discussion of the origins of the citole of Chaucer's Venus in *KnT* and the comb in *HF,* Twycross provides a useful introduction to medieval mythography and allegorical commentary on Ovid, particularly to the *Ovidius moralizatus* of Pierre Bersuire.

M285

Wilkins, Ernest H. 'Descriptions of Pagan Divinities from Petrarch to Chaucer,' *Speculum* 32 (1957) 511-22

Wilkins attempts to trace the line of descent from Petrarch through Bersuire to the image of Venus in *HF* and *KnT;* he argues that Chaucer used a condensed version of Bersuire, the *Libellus de imaginibus deorum.*

Texts

BERSUIRE, PIERRE [Petrus Berchorius] (ca. 1290-1362)

Reductorium morale

Book 15, generally called the *Ovidius moralizatus,* was probably the only part of this work that Chaucer knew. The first chapter of Book 15 was known as 'De formis figurisque deorum.' For possible use of other sections of this work, see Steadman **CT373**.

M286

Petrus Berchorius. *Reductorium morale, Liber XV, cap. I: De formis figurisque deorum,* ed. J. Engels. Werkmateriaal, Instituut voor Laat Latijn der Rijksuniversiteit (Utrecht 1960)

This edition is based on the first redaction of the work (ca. 1335-40) as originally published in 1509 and attributed to Thomas Walleys.

M287

Petrus Berchorius. *Reductorium morale, Liber XV, cap. ii-xv: 'Ovidius moralizatus,'* ed. J. Engels. Werkmateriaal 2, Instituut voor Laat Latijn der Rijksuniversiteit (Utrecht 1962)

This work is a continuation of **M286**.

M288

Petrus Berchorius. *Reductorium morale, Liber XV: Ovidius moralizatus, cap. i: De formis figurisque deorum,* ed. J. Engels. Werkmateriaal 3, Instituut voor Laat Latijn der Rijksuniversiteit (Utrecht 1966)

This edition of the first chapter of the *Ovidius moralizatus* is based on the second redaction (ca. 1359) of that text.

Ovide moralisé

Edition

M289
'Ovide moralisé,' poème du commencement du quatorzième siècle,
ed. C. de Boer. 5 vols. Verhandelingen der Koninklijke
Akademie van Wetenschappen te Amsterdam, Afdeeling
Letterkunde n.s. 15 [bks. 1-3], 21 [bks. 4-6], 30, No. 3 [bks. 7-11],
37 [bks. 10-13], 43 [bks. 14-15] (Amsterdam 1915-38)
This work may have had both direct and indirect influence on
Chaucer, since the second redaction of Bersuire is based in part
on it. See Meech **LGW8** and Work **CT403** for its influence on the
tale of Ariadne (in *LGW* and *HF*) and on *MancT.*

Study

M290
Lowes, John Livingston. 'Chaucer and the *Ovide moralisé,*'
PMLA 33 (1918) 302-25
Lowes demonstrates Chaucer's use of this work in the story of
Ariadne in *LGW* and *HF,* and in the story of Philomela in *LGW.*
See also Meech **LGW8.**

PAMPHILUS DE AMORE (ca. 1200)

Edition

M291
Becker, Franz G., ed. *Pamphilus: Prolegomena zum Pamphilus (de
amore) und kritische Textausgabe.* Beihefte zum 'Mittellateinischen
Jahrbuch' 9 (Ratingen, Kastellaun, Düsseldorf 1972)
In *FranklT* 1110 and *Mel* 1556, Chaucer refers to Pamphilus as an
example of a model lover, and one line from the Latin work is cited
on the margin of the Ellesmere MS. Becker provides very full textual
apparatus on the many MSS and early editions of *Pamphilus.* See
Garbáty **Tr23** for the argument that this work is a source for *Tr.*

Translation and Study

M292

Garbáty, Thomas Jay. '*Pamphilus: De amore:* An Introduction and Translation,' *ChauR* 2 (1967-8) 108-34
The introduction discusses the popularity and influence of the work. The translation is based on the edition by Jacobus Ulrich, *Pamphilus: Comoedia elegiaca medioevalis — ex codice Turicensi* (Zürich 1893)

PERSIUS FLACCUS, AULUS (34-62)

Persi saturae

Edition and Translation

In **M267**, 310-401; Prologue, 310-11
Chaucer quotes the second line of the Prologue to the *Satires* of Persius at *FranklT* 721. Skeat **CT272** argues that Chaucer also used line 14 of the same prologue at *SqT* 207.

PETRUS RIGA [Peter Riga] (ca. 1140-1209)

Aurora

Edition

M293

Aurora: Petri Rigae biblia versificata. A Verse Commentary on the Bible, ed. Paul E. Beichner, CSC. 2 vols. Publications in Mediaeval Studies, University of Notre Dame 19 (Notre Dame, Ind. 1965)
In *BD* 1160-69, Chaucer refers to 'Aurora' as his source for Tubal as the inventor of music and Pictagoras as the inventor of painting. The introduction to this edition includes a discussion of the popularity and influence of the work.

Study

M294

Young, Karl. 'Chaucer and Peter Riga,' *Speculum* 12 (1937)
299-303
Young shows that Chaucer's allusion to the *Aurora* as his source
for Tubal as the inventor of music can be authenticated from MSS
of the work available in Chaucer's time.

RAYMUNDUS DE PENNAFORTE [Raymond of Peñaforte, Saint]
(ca. 1175-1270)

'De poenitentiis et remissionibus'

Edition

M295

Summa Sancti Raymundi de Peniafort Barcinonensis de
poenitentia, et matrimonio (Rome 1603; repr. Farnborough,
Hants. 1967)
The *Summa* has three books entitled *De poenitentia;* the fourth
book is separately referred to as *De matrimonio.* See Petersen
CT416 for Chaucer's use in *ParsT* of 'De poenitentiis et
remissionibus,' the last chapter (34) of bk. 3 of the *Summa,* pp.
437-502.

SACROBOSCO, JOHANNES DE [John de Sacrobosco] (ca. 1190-
ca. 1255)

De sphaera

Edition and Translation

M296

Johannes de Sacrobosco. *De sphaera* in *'The Sphere' of*

Sacrobosco and its Commentators, ed., trans., and intro. Lynn
Thorndike (Chicago 1949) 76-142
See Harvey **Astr4** for Chaucer's use of this work in *Astr.*
Thorndike's study includes editions of three of the important
commentaries on the work and a discussion (pp. 1-76) of the
significance of the work in the history of science.

Study

M297
Veazie, Walter B. 'Chaucer's Text-Book of Astronomy; Johannes
de Sacrobosco,' *University of Colorado Studies,* Series B: Studies
in the Humanities 1 (1939-41) 169-82
Veazie provides a summary of *De sphaera* and discusses its
influence in the Middle Ages.

SENECA, LUCIUS ANNAEUS (ca. 4 B.C.-A.D. 65)

There is no clear evidence that Chaucer knew the works of Seneca
at first hand. Passages he knew may well have come from florilegia
or from quotation in other works such as the *Roman de la rose;*
consequently, no texts or translations of Seneca's works are cited
here. See Hart **CT207** for a possible borrowing from Seneca's *De
ira.*

Study

M298
Ayres, Harry Morgan. 'Chaucer and Seneca,' *Romanic Review* 10
(1919) 1-15
Ayres discusses Chaucer's use of passages from Seneca's *Epistles,*
especially in *Tr;* for the argument that Chaucer did not know the
Epistles at first hand, see Pratt **M253**.

STATIUS, PUBLIUS PAPINIUS (ca. 45-96)

Thebaid

Edition and Translation

M299
Statius. *Thebaidos* in *Statius,* ed. and trans. J.H. Mozley. 2 vols.
Loeb Classical Library (London and New York 1928) I, 340-571
and II, 2-505
Chaucer knew the *Thebaid* directly as well as through
Boccaccio's adaptation in *Teseida.* It is an important source for
KnT and a source for *Tr,* which includes Latin verse summaries
in many of the MSS.

Studies

M300
Clogan, Paul M. 'Chaucer and the *Thebaid* Scholia,' *SP* 61 (1964)
599-615
Clogan discusses the glosses and commentaries found in
medieval MSS of the *Thebaid* and assesses their influence on
Chaucer's works, especially *HF, Anel, Tr,* and *KnT.*

M301
Magoun, Francis P., Jr. 'Chaucer's Summary of Statius' *Thebaid*
II-XII,' *Traditio* 11 (1955) 409-20
Magoun prints the Latin verse summaries of the *Thebaid* that
appear in fourteen of the sixteen MSS of *Tr* at V.1485-1510; he
gives English translations and offers detailed comparisons with
Chaucer's narrative.

M302
Wise, Boyd Ashby. *The Influence of Statius upon Chaucer*
(Baltimore 1911)
Wise examines Chaucer's use of Statius' *Thebaid,* discussing
both his direct borrowings and his use of adaptations of the
Thebaid in Boccaccio's *Teseida.*

THEOPHRASTUS ['Theofraste'] (ca. 370-288/5 B.C.)

In his treatise *Adversus Jovinianum*, Jerome quotes at length from a work he calls 'the splendid book of Theophrastus, *On Marriage*' *(aureolus Theophrasti liber de nuptiis)* as evidence for the high regard that pagan philosophers had for the virtue of virginity. In the Middle Ages, on the authority of Jerome, *De nuptiis* (sometimes called *Liber aureolus de nuptiis* from a misunderstanding of the passage by Jerome, see **M273**, p. 311n.) was widely believed to be a Latin translation of a treatise on marriage by Theophrastus, the Greek philosopher who studied with Aristotle and succeeded him as head of the Peripatetic School in Athens (P. Delhaye, 'Le Dossier anti-matrimonial de l'*Adversus Iovinianum* et son influence sur quelques écrits latins du XIIe siècle,' *MS* 13 [1951] 65-86). Apart from the passages given by Jerome, however, there is no other evidence for the existence of either the Latin translation or a Greek original, and no treatise on marriage was listed in the four catalogues of the works of Theophrastus given by Diogenes Laertius (first half of the 3rd century A.D.). 'Theofraste' is one of the titles Jankyn gives for his book of wicked wives in *WBProl* 671 and 'Theofraste' is cited as an antifeminist authority in *MerchT* 1294-5 and 1310. For Chaucer's knowledge of Jerome's account of *De nuptiis,* see **M254**; the relevant passages are printed in **CT188**, 211-12.

VALERIUS MAXIMUS (fl. A.D. 31)

Factorum et dictorum memorabilium

Edition

M303
Valerius Maximus. *Factorum et dictorum memorabilium libri novem cum Iulii Paridis et Ianuarii Nepotiani epitomis,* ed. Carolus Kempf (Leipzig 1888, repr. Stuttgart 1966)
See Shannon **M214** 335ff. for the argument that Chaucer's story of Caesar in *MkT* was based on Valerius, as the Monk himself

claims (2120); the Wife of Bath also cites Valerius as the source of her exemplum of Tullius Hostilius. For parallels with *NPT*, see Hulbert **CT367**. See Pratt **M253** for the argument that Chaucer's knowledge of Valerius was derived from florilegia.

Translation

M304
Valerius Maximus. *Romae antiquae descriptio. A view of the religion, laws, customs, manners, and dispositions of the ancient Romans, and others:... now carefully rendred into English, ...* [by Samuel Speed] (London 1678)
This, the only complete English translation, is not widely available, but there are modern translations in French and Italian: *Valère Maxime: Actions et paroles mémorables* by Pierre Constant, 2 vols. (Paris 1935), and *Detti e fatti memorabili di Valerio Massimo* by Rino Faranda (Turin 1971).

VERGILIUS MARO, PUBLIUS [Virgil] (70-19 B.C.)

Aeneid

Edition and Translation

M305
Virgil. *The Aeneid* in *Virgil,* ed. and trans. H. Rushton Fairclough, 2 vols. Loeb Classical Library (London 1916-18, rev. ed. 1924-34; repr. 1960, 1967)
The *Aeneid* is the ultimate source for the story of Aeneas and Dido in *HF* 143-465 as well as for the story of Dido in *LGW*.

Studies

See Harbert **M212** and Shannon **M214**.

M306
Hall, Louis Brewer. 'Chaucer and the Dido-and-Aeneas Story,' *MS* 25 (1963) 148-59

Comparing Chaucer's two versions of the story in *HF* and *LGW* with each other and with five medieval adaptations of Virgil, Hall argues that Chaucer's versions of the story should not only be set against the classical source but also be seen in the context of medieval adaptations.

VINCENT DE BEAUVAIS [Vincent of Beauvais, Vincentius Bellovacensis] (ca. 1190-ca. 1264)

Speculum maius

Edition

M307
Vincentius Bellovacensis. *Speculum quadruplex, sive speculum maius: Naturale, doctrinale, morale, historiale.* 4 vols. (Douai 1624, photographic repr. Graz 1964-5)
See Aiken **CT101** for the argument that this encyclopedia was the source for details of Arcite's illness in *KnT*, **CT202** for the argument that it was a source for the demonology in *FrT*, **CT350** for its use as a source for *MkT*, **CT364** for its use as a source for Pertelote's knowledge of medicine in *NPT*, and Brown **CT365** for the *Speculum historiale* as the ultimate source for the phrase 'mulier est hominis confusio' (*NPT* 3164); Aiken **CT389** for its use as a source for alchemical information in *CYT* and **LGW2** for its use as a source for the story of Cleopatra.

De eruditione filiorum nobilium

Edition

M308
Vincent of Beauvais. *De eruditione filiorum nobilium,* ed. Arpad Steiner (Cambridge, Mass. 1938)
See Young **CT286** and Robinson **M30**, 727, note to lines 41ff. for a discussion of this work as a source for *PhysT* 35-120.

VINSAUF, GEOFFREY DE [Geoffrey of Vinsauf] (fl. 1210)

Poetria nova

Edition

M309
Geoffroi de Vinsauf. *Poetria nova* in Faral **B166**, 197-262
The nature and extent of the influence of the *Poetria nova* on
Chaucer is a matter of dispute; see Manly **B167** and Murphy
B170. Chaucer does, however, translate and refer to passages
from the work in *Tr* I.1065ff. and *NPT* 3347-51 and 3358-9. For
the argument that the reference to Geoffrey's lament for Richard
I in *NPT* 3347-51 is good evidence for Chaucer's knowledge of
the work, see Young **CT374**.

Translation

M310
'*Poetria nova*' *of Geoffrey of Vinsauf,* trans. Margaret F. Nims
(Toronto 1967)
The translation includes an introductory analysis of the work
together with textual and explanatory notes.

WIREKER, NIGELLUS [Nigel de Longchamps] (ca. 1130-early
12th c.)

Nigel's name in Latin is Nigellus de Longo Campo, in French Nigel
de Longchamps. Raymo points out, **M311**, Intro. n. 1 (pp. 123-4),
that the surname Wireker given Nigel 'in manuals and histories of
medieval literature derives solely from J. Bale,' a 16th-century
antiquarian. Although spurious, the name Wireker is kept here
because of its continuing use in bibliographical references to Nigel.

Speculum stultorum

Edition

M311
Nigel de Longchamps. *Speculum stultorum,* ed. with intro. and notes John H. Mozley and Robert R. Raymo (Berkeley and Los Angeles 1960)
See Mann **CT369** for Chaucer's use of this work in *NPT,* and see Dronke and Mann **M211** for a general discussion of its influence on Chaucer.

Translations

M312
The Book of Daun Burnel the Ass: Nigellus Wireker's 'Speculum stultorum,' trans. Graydon W. Regenos (Austin, Tex. 1959)
The translation is in verse.
M313
Nigel Longchamp. *A Mirror for Fools, or The Book of Burnel the Ass,* trans. J.H. Mozley (Oxford 1961)
This abridged translation is in prose.

II
Chaucer's Works

The first section of Part II contains general critical studies and includes books and articles that concern several of Chaucer's works. The rest of the sections in Part II are devoted to the individual works of Chaucer, presented here in the order in which they are printed in the standard modern edition, Robinson **M30**; each section is divided further, usually into three parts, one on editions (and textual studies where relevant), one on sources and analogues, and one on critical studies.

GENERAL CRITICAL STUDIES

Collections of Essays

Many of the articles in the collections described here are listed
separately, under the appropriate headings, elsewhere in this bibliography. See Brewer **B8** for a collection of essays on Chaucer's
intellectual background.

CrS1
Bethurum, Dorothy, ed. *Critical Approaches to Medieval Literature:
Selected Papers from the English Institute 1958-59* (New York and
London 1960, 4th repr. 1967)
Bethurum prints essays selected from four sessions of the confer-
ence: patristic exegesis in the criticism of medieval literature
(E. Talbot Donaldson, R.E. Kaske, Charles Donahue); folklore,
myth, and ritual (Francis Lee Utley); classical fable and English
poetry in the 14th century (Richard Hamilton Green); and Chaucer
and Dante (Howard Schless).

CrS2
Bloomfield, Morton W. *Essays and Explorations: Studies in Ideas,
Language, and Literature* (Cambridge, Mass. 1970)
This volume reprints eighteen essays and reviews, four of them on
Chaucer and others on closely related topics.

CrS3
Brewer, Derek, ed. *Chaucer: The Critical Heritage.* 2 vols. Critical
Heritage Series, gen. ed. B.C. Southam (London 1978)
Brewer edits selected excerpts from Chaucer criticism; the work is
valuable as a supplement to Spurgeon **CrS16**. Vol. I includes 103
excerpts from 1385-1837; II includes 52 excerpts from 1837-1933.
Each volume includes a lengthy essay tracing the history of
criticism of Chaucer and a list of the principal editions of Chaucer's
works during the period.

CrS4
_____ *Chaucer and Chaucerians: Critical Studies in Middle English
Literature* (London and University, Ala. 1966)
Brewer prints nine essays written for the volume, covering
Chaucer's major works as well as selected ancillary subjects:

Chaucer's relation to literary tradition, the Scottish Chaucerians, the English Chaucerians, images of Chaucer 1386-1901. Each essay takes as its point of departure Chaucer's language and rhetoric.
CrS5
Burrow, J.A., ed. *Geoffrey Chaucer: A Critical Anthology.* Penguin Critical Anthologies, gen. ed. Christopher Ricks (Harmondsworth and Baltimore 1970)
This collection includes representative brief excerpts arranged in three sections: criticism contemporary with Chaucer, criticism from Hoccleve to the end of the 19th century, and 20th-century criticism. A selected bibliography of other works of criticism is included.
CrS6
Cawley, A.C., ed. *Chaucer's Mind and Art* (Edinburgh and London 1969)
This collection includes four new and six reprinted essays, together with selected bibliographies, topically arranged.
CrS7
Donaldson, E.T. *Speaking of Chaucer* (New York 1970)
This influential collection of twelve reprinted essays contains some of the best of Donaldson's deft and witty criticism; eight essays are on specifically Chaucerian topics.
CrS8
Economou, George D., ed. *Geoffrey Chaucer: A Collection of Original Articles* (New York 1975)
Economou prints eight essays on important general themes and topics in Chaucer, each written for this volume and directed at an audience of students and teachers of Chaucer.
CrS9
Esch, Arno, ed. *Chaucer und seine Zeit: Symposion für Walter F. Schirmer.* Buchreihe der *Anglia, Zeitschrift für englische Philologie* 14 (Tübingen 1968)
This collection of twenty-one essays written for this volume includes nine essays on Chaucer, some in English, some in German.
CrS10
Mitchell, Jerome and William Provost, eds. *Chaucer the Love Poet* (Athens, Ga. 1973)
This volume is a printed record of a conference held at the University of Georgia in 1971 under the auspices of the South Atlantic Graduate English cooperative agreement; it includes four essays

and the round-table discussion which followed their presentation.
CrS11
Newstead, Helaine, ed. and intro. *Chaucer and his Contemporaries: Essays on Medieval Literature and Thought.* Literature and Ideas Series, gen. ed. Irving Howe (Greenwich, Conn. 1968)
This collection includes seventeen essays, most reprinted or excerpted from longer works, arranged in three sections: excerpts from contemporary descriptions of the Black Death (Boccaccio) and the Peasants' Revolt (Froissart); essays on topics related to Chaucer, such as science, technology, and courtly love; and essays on Chaucer and his works.
CrS12
Robbins, Rossell Hope, ed. *Chaucer at Albany* (New York 1975)
This collection of ten essays is based on the Chaucer Conference at SUNY Albany in 1973.
CrS13
Rowland, Beryl, ed. *Companion to Chaucer Studies* (New York, Toronto, London 1968; rev. ed. New York and Oxford 1979)
The revised edition includes twenty-two essays reviewing scholarship up to 1978 on the major works of Chaucer and on important topics in Chaucer criticism.
CrS14
_____ *Chaucer and Middle English Studies in Honour of Rossell Hope Robbins* (London 1974)
This collection includes thirty-six essays written for this volume, fourteen of them on Chaucer.
CrS15
Schoeck, Richard J. and Jerome Taylor, eds. *Chaucer Criticism.* 2 vols. (Notre Dame, Ind. 1960-61)
This collection includes thirty-three essays, mostly reprinted or excerpted from longer works. Vol. I includes essays on *CT,* vol. II essays on *Tr* and the minor poems.
CrS16
Spurgeon, Caroline F.E. *Five Hundred Years of Chaucer Criticism and Allusion, 1357-1900.* 7 pts. Chaucer Society 2nd ser. 48-50, 52-6 (London 1914-25, for 1908-17); repr. in 3 vols. (Cambridge 1925, New York 1960)
Spurgeon's work is the most comprehensive collection of English editions and allusions to Chaucer up to 1800; between 1800 and

1867 she includes only the most important or interesting allusions; from 1867 to 1900 she limits herself to the chief editions and a few noteworthy allusions. An appendix gives some attention to Latin, French, and German allusions. For corrections of errata and an annotated update through 1952 see William L. Alderson, 'A Check-List of Supplements to Spurgeon's Chaucer Allusions,' *PQ* 32 (1953) 418-27. See Brewer **CrS3** for additional references and for a continuation of the collection through 1933. For a discussion of the history of Chaucer's literary reputation, see Lounsbury **M138**, III, 1-279.

CrS17
Sullivan, Sheila, ed. *Critics on Chaucer.* Readings in Literary Criticism 6 (London 1970)
Sullivan prints twenty-two brief excerpts from criticism, from Dryden to the present.

CrS18
Vasta, Edward and Zacharias P. Thundy, eds. *Chaucerian Problems and Perspectives: Essays Presented to Paul E. Beichner, CSC* (Notre Dame, Ind. 1979)
The collection includes sixteen essays written for this volume.

CrS19
Wagenknecht, Edward, ed. *Chaucer: Modern Essays in Criticism* (New York 1959, many reprints)
Wagenknecht reprints twenty-six essays and excerpts from longer works.

Critical Studies

The studies listed here are those that treat more than two of Chaucer's works; studies which deal with one or two works only are listed under those works. Studies of groups of tales within the *Canterbury Tales* are listed in the *CT* section. For general studies of Chaucer's sources and literary background see **M134-313** and **B158-72**, in addition to the items listed here. For general studies of text, MSS, and canon, see **M32-42**. For general studies in language and versification see **M60-105**.

CrS20
Baum, Paull F. *Chaucer: A Critical Appreciation* (Durham, N.C. 1958; repr. 1961)

Baum criticizes the complexity and obscurity of some modern critical approaches to Chaucer and argues for a return to an appreciation of the poet as storyteller and humorist.

CrS21
Bethurum, Dorothy. 'Chaucer's Point of View as Narrator in the Love Poems,' *PMLA* 74 (1959) 511-20; repr. in abridged form in Schoeck and Taylor **CrS15**, II, 211-31
Bethurum sets Chaucer's love poems in the tradition of the dream-vision and analyses Chaucer's contributions to the tradition.

CrS22
Bloomfield, Morton W. 'Chaucer's Sense of History,' *JEGP* 51 (1952) 301-13; repr. in Bloomfield **CrS2**, 13-26
Bloomfield sees evidence in *LGW, Tr,* and *CT* of an increasing preoccupation with accurate chronology and cultural diversity.

CrS23
_____ 'Authenticating Realism and the Realism of Chaucer,' *Thought* 39 (1964) 335-58; repr. in Bloomfield **CrS2**, 174-98
Bloomfield defines and analyses a variety of strategies Chaucer uses to give an air of realism to his fictions, such as the dream and the pilgrimage as framing devices, the use of a narrator *persona*, and the use of familiar circumstantial details.

CrS24
_____ 'The Gloomy Chaucer' in *Veins of Humor*, ed. Harry Levin. Harvard English Studies 3 (Cambridge, Mass. 1972) 57-68
Bloomfield discusses Chaucer's use of an imaginary 'querulous objector' as one means of conveying the multiplicity of perspectives characteristic of Chaucer's humour.

CrS25
Boitani, Piero. 'Chaucer's Temples of Venus,' *Studi inglesi* 2 (1975) 9-31
Boitani gives a thorough analysis of the descriptions of Venus' temple in *HF, PF,* and *KnT.*

CrS26
Brewer, D.S. 'The Ideal of Feminine Beauty in Medieval Literature, especially "Harley Lyrics," Chaucer, and Some Elizabethans,' *MLR* 50 (1955) 257-69
Brewer discusses the literary tradition of feminine beauty and Chaucer's use of it in *BD, Tr, KnT,* and *MillT.*

CrS27
_____ 'Class Distinction in Chaucer,' *Speculum* 43 (1968) 290-305

Brewer analyses three different but overlapping systems of class distinction in Chaucer's works: the 'ladder of degree,' the binary system of 'gentils' and 'churls,' and the three-fold classification according to function of knights, clergy, and plowmen.
CrS28
_____ 'Towards a Chaucerian Poetic.' Sir Israel Gollancz Memorial Lecture, *Proceedings of the British Academy* 60 (1974) 219-52; also issued separately
Brewer suggests that Chaucer's poetic art is based on innovative use and re-creation of traditional tales.
CrS29
Bronson, Bertrand H. *In Search of Chaucer.* Alexander Lectures for 1958-59, University of Toronto (Toronto 1960; repr. 1963, 1967)
Bronson surveys fashions in Chaucer criticism and advocates literal reading and increased historical investigation; his own criticism focusses on Chaucer's use of dreams and books and his depiction of everyday life.
CrS30
Burlin, Robert B. *Chaucerian Fiction* (Princeton 1977)
Burlin offers a complex analysis of Chaucer's relations to his audience (poetic fictions), to the creative imagination (philosophic fictions), and to the motives of his tellers of tales (psychological fictions).
CrS31
Burrow, J.A. *Ricardian Poetry: Chaucer, Gower, Langland, and the 'Gawain' Poet* (London 1971)
Burrow argues that Chaucer and his great contemporaries constitute a school of poetry; he examines the characteristics shared by these poets and discusses their distinctive emphases.
CrS32
Clemen, Wolfgang. *Der junge Chaucer: Grundlagen und Entwicklung seiner Dichtung.* Kölner Anglistische Arbeiten 33 (Bochum-Langendreer 1938); rev. ed. *Chaucers frühe Dichtung* (Göttingen 1963) publ. simultaneously in English as *Chaucer's Early Poetry,* trans. C.A.M. Sym (London 1963, repr. London and New York 1980)
Clemen gives a close analysis of *BD, HF, PF,* and some of the short poems; the work is an excellent introduction to these poems.
CrS33
Coghill, Nevill. *The Poet Chaucer* (London, New York, Toronto 1949; many reprints)

Coghill offers a good introduction and traces Chaucer's poetic career.

CrS34

Crosby, Ruth. 'Chaucer and the Custom of Oral Delivery,' *Speculum* 13 (1938) 413-32

Crosby discusses Chaucer's references to oral delivery as evidence for the view that his poetry was meant to be read aloud.

CrS35

Curry, Walter Clyde. *Chaucer and the Mediaeval Sciences* (New York and Oxford 1926, repr. 1942; rev. ed. New York and London 1960)

Curry's work was a pioneering study, but more recent works should be consulted on specific details.

CrS36

David, Alfred. *The Strumpet Muse: Art and Morals in Chaucer's Poetry* (Bloomington, Ind. and London 1976)

David traces the changes in Chaucer's conception of poetry and its relation to moral values.

CrS37

Dempster, Germaine. *Dramatic Irony in Chaucer* (Stanford and London 1932, repr. New York 1959)

Dempster discusses dramatic irony in *Tr,* in the fabliaux in *CT,* in *WBT, FranklT, NPT, PardT,* and in the frame of *CT.*

CrS38

Donaldson, E. Talbot. 'The Masculine Narrator and Four Women of Style' in Donaldson **CrS7**, 46-64

Donaldson shows how Chaucer's seemingly simple style masks complex descriptions of characters like Emily, Criseyde, May, and the Prioress.

CrS39

_____ 'Chaucer's Three "P's": Pandarus, Pardoner, and Poet,' *Michigan Quarterly Review* 14 (1975) 282-301

Donaldson analyses the resemblances among Pandarus, the Pardoner, and Chaucer himself as creative artists.

CrS40

Elbow, Peter. *Oppositions in Chaucer* (Middletown, Conn. 1975)

In this stimulating study Elbow describes a pattern of thinking common to Boethius and Chaucer, the tendency to see opposed points of view and to devise strategies for maintaining both sides of a question without rejecting either.

CrS41

Fifield, Merle. 'Chaucer the Theatre-goer,' *Papers on Language and Literature* 3, Supplement (1967) 63-70

Drawing on a study of contemporary dramatic records Fifield argues that in *FranklT, MerchT,* and *SqT* Chaucer shows his awareness of contemporary theatre. See also Harder **CT130.**

CrS42

French, Robert Dudley. *A Chaucer Handbook* (New York 1927, 2nd ed. 1947)

This beginner's companion, which includes introductions to Chaucer's life, time, and works, contains translations of some of the sources and analogues to *CT.*

CrS43

Gray, Douglas. 'Chaucer and "Pite",' in *J.R.R. Tolkien, Scholar and Storyteller: Essays in Memoriam,* ed. Mary Salu and Robert T. Farrell (Ithaca and London 1979) 173-203

Gray explores the concept of *pite* in human love in a variety of contexts and argues that emphasis on pathos is a dominant characteristic of Chaucer's narrative art.

CrS44

Hieatt, Constance B. *The Realism of Dream Visions: The Poetic Exploitation of the Dream-Experience in Chaucer and his Contemporaries.* De proprietatibus litterarum, series practica 2 (The Hague 1967)

Hieatt discusses the ways in which *BD, HF, PF,* and *LGW* resemble real dreams; she relates medieval dream theories to modern psychological dream theories, Freudian and post-Freudian.

CrS45

Hussey, Maurice, A.C. Spearing, and James Winny. *An Introduction to Chaucer* (Cambridge 1965)

This handbook for students contains chapters on 'Chaucer's England,' 'The Church,' 'Chaucer's Science' as well as discussions of Chaucer's life and language; an appendix discusses difficult Chaucerian words like *pite.*

CrS46

Jordan, Robert M. *Chaucer and the Shape of Creation* (Cambridge, Mass. 1967)

Analysing the coordinated inconsistencies in Gothic architecture, Jordan develops an aesthetic theory that he applies to *CT* and *Tr.*

CrS47

_____ 'Chaucerian Narrative' in Rowland **CrS13**, 95-116
Jordan surveys selected scholarship on poetic theory, rhetoric, and
stylistics with reference to narrative structure in Chaucer's works.

CrS48

Kane, George. *The Autobiographical Fallacy in Chaucer and
Langland Studies.* Chambers Memorial Lecture 1965 (London 1965)
Kane shows that apparently autobiographical statements in the
works of Chaucer and Langland cannot be taken at face value.

CrS49

Kean, P.M. *Chaucer and the Making of English Poetry.* 2 vols.
(London and Boston 1972)
Kean discusses Chaucer as an heir to and a creator of English
poetic tradition; she divides her discussion into studies of the
traditions of love-vision and debate and of the tradition of
narrative.

CrS50

Kittredge, George Lyman. *Chaucer and his Poetry* (Cambridge,
Mass. 1915; many reprints; with intro. by B.J. Whiting, 1976)
Kittredge's classic study is dated in some respects, but is still
valuable, especially for its discussions of the Marriage Group and of
the dramatic aspects of *CT.*

CrS51

Lawlor, John. *Chaucer* (London 1968)
Lawlor focusses on Chaucer as a narrative poet and on the tension
he establishes between experience and authority.

CrS52

Lowes, J. Livingston. *Geoffrey Chaucer and the Development of his
Genius* (Cambridge, Mass. 1934); repr. as *Geoffrey Chaucer:
Lectures Delivered in 1932 on the William J. Cooper Foundation in
Swarthmore College* (Oxford 1944); repr. as *Geoffrey Chaucer*
(Bloomington, Ind. 1958; many reprints)
Lowes provides a clear and informative analysis of Chaucer's
poetry in its historical context.

CrS53

McCall, John P. 'Chaucer's May 3,' *MLN* 76 (1961) 201-5
McCall suggests that the May 3 date in *KnT, NPT,* and *Tr* is
associated with irrational love or lust, since Ovid assigned May 3 to
Flora and her celebration.

CrS54

_____ *Chaucer among the Gods: The Poetics of Classical Myth*
(University Park, Pa. and London 1979)
McCall suggests that an important part of Chaucer's poetic art is
his creative use of classical mythology.

CrS55

Mehl, Dieter. 'Chaucer's Audience,' *Leeds Studies in English* 10
(1978) 58-73
Mehl argues that Chaucer creates a fictional audience in each of his
works and that its function is to direct and provoke the reader's
response to the work.

CrS56

Miskimin, Alice S. *The Renaissance Chaucer* (New Haven and
London 1975)
Miskimin discusses the changing perceptions of Chaucer and his
work in the Renaissance, focussing primarily on the figure of
Chaucer the poet and his enigmatic and ironic attitudes towards his
art; she includes an extended account of early editions of Chaucer
and a full discussion of the story of Troilus as told by Boccaccio,
Chaucer, Henryson, Shakespeare, and Dryden.

CrS57

Muscatine, Charles. *Chaucer and the French Tradition: A Study in
Style and Meaning* (Berkeley and Los Angeles 1957, repr. 1964)
This important and influential study concerns Chaucer's style in
relation to Old and Middle French poetic traditions and presents a
valuable account of Chaucerian 'realism' in terms of poetic style.

CrS58

_____ *Poetry and Crisis in the Age of Chaucer.* University of Notre
Dame Ward-Phillips Lectures in English Language and Literature 4
(Notre Dame, Ind. and London 1972)
Muscatine begins with a characterization of the spirit of the age,
and in ch. IV discusses Chaucer's use of pathos as an alternative to
irony.

CrS59

Nims, Margaret F. 'Translatio: "Difficult Statement" in Medieval
Poetic Theory,' *UTQ* 43 (1973-4) 215-30
Nims discusses the capacity for words and objects to have multiple
meanings in medieval poetic usage, using examples from Chaucer,
as well as from Geoffrey of Vinsauf and Alan of Lille.

CrS60
Norton-Smith, John. *Geoffrey Chaucer.* Medieval Authors (London and Boston 1974)
This is a general study of Chaucer's work; it pays particular attention to Chaucer's general intellectual debt to the Latin classics.

CrS61
Patch, Howard Rollin. *On Rereading Chaucer* (Cambridge, Mass. 1939; repr. 1948)
Patch focusses on Chaucer's humour.

CrS62
Payne, Robert O. *The Key of Remembrance: A Study of Chaucer's Poetics* (New Haven and London 1963; repr. Westport, Conn. 1973)
Payne's book gives an account of Chaucer's poetics in the context of rhetorical tradition. See also Payne **B159**.

CrS63
_____ 'Chaucer's Realization of Himself as *rhetor*' in *Medieval Eloquence: Studies in the Theory and Practice of Medieval Rhetoric,* ed. James J. Murphy (Berkeley, Los Angeles, London 1978) 270-87
Payne suggests that Chaucer makes characters out of his narrators as a way of forcing his audience to evaluate his rhetoric consciously.

CrS64
Robbins, Rossell Hope. 'Geoffroi Chaucier, poète français, Father of English Poetry,' *ChauR* 13 (1978-9) 93-115
Robbins suggests that Chaucer's now-lost early poetry was written in French.

CrS65
Robertson, D.W., Jr. 'The Doctrine of Charity in Medieval Literary Gardens: A Topical Approach through Symbolism and Allegory,' *Speculum* 26 (1951) 24-49; repr. in Robertson **CrS67**, 21-50
Robertson examines a number of medieval gardens from *Beowulf* through *MerchT* and argues that the ideal of charity is the higher meaning of medieval poetic allegory.

CrS66
_____ *A Preface to Chaucer: Studies in Medieval Perspectives* (Princeton 1962)
In this important and controversial book, Robertson discusses medieval views on aesthetics and the morality of art and argues that Chaucer's poetry and, indeed, all medieval poetry was intended to

be interpreted allegorically by the exegetical methods applied to the Bible. Critical response to Robertson's theory has been mixed, and the debate continues; numerous books and articles have appeared, which either apply Robertson's method to specific works, or argue against it. For reviews see especially the following: Francis L. Utley, 'Robertsonianism Redivivus,' *Romance Philology* 19 (1965) 250-60, repr. as 'Chaucer and Patristic Exegesis' in Cawley **CrS6**, 69-85; and R.E. Kaske, 'Chaucer and Medieval Allegory,' *ELH* 30 (1963) 175-92. See also Robert O. Payne,'The Historical Criticism We Need,' and Martin Stevens, 'Chaucer and Modernism: An Essay in Criticism' in Robbins **CrS12**, 179-91 and 193-216. For a symposium on 'Patristic Exegesis in the Criticism of Medieval Literature' see Bethurum **CrS1**.

CrS67
_____ *Essays in Medieval Culture* (Princeton, N.J. 1980)
This volume includes twenty-four essays, most of them reprints, on a variety of medieval subjects; four focus on Chaucerian subjects and five others deal with questions of literary theory closely related to Chaucerian studies.

CrS68
Root, Robert Kilburn. *The Poetry of Chaucer: A Guide to its Study and Appreciation* (Boston and New York 1906, rev. ed. 1922; many reprints)
Although many of its references are now out of date, Root's book is still valuable as an introduction to the study of Chaucer.

CrS69
Rowland, Beryl. 'Chaucer's Imagery' in Rowland **CrS13**, 117-42
Rowland surveys the history of the study of Chaucer's imagery and the contributions to that study made by related work in irony, rhetoric, and lexicography; a selective bibliography is included.

CrS70
Spearing, A.C. *Medieval Dream-Poetry* (Cambridge 1976) 48-110
Spearing examines *BD, HF, PF,* and *LGWProl* in the context of medieval dream-poetry in general, and late medieval English dream-poetry in particular.

CrS71
Speirs, John. *Chaucer the Maker* (London 1951; rev. ed. 1960, repr. 1962)
Speirs presents a critical reading of Chaucer from the perspectives of Freudian analysis and new criticism.

CrS72
Windeatt, Barry. 'Gesture in Chaucer,' *Medievalia et humanistica* 9
(1979) 143-61
Windeatt discusses the significance of the physical gestures
Chaucer often adds to his version of a story.

CrS73
Wood, Chauncey. *Chaucer and the Country of the Stars: Poetic Uses
of Astrological Imagery* (Princeton 1970)
Wood takes a Robertsonian approach to Chaucer's astrological
imagery. See Robertson **CrS66**.

THE CANTERBURY TALES

Editions and Textual Studies

See Robinson **M30**, 1-265, 649-773, 883-98. See also Skeat **M31**, IV, vii-xxiv (introduction), 1-644 (text); V, ix-xxvi (introduction to notes), 1-476 (notes). Robinson's edition follows the order of the tales found in the Ellesmere MS, Skeat's follows the Chaucer Society rearrangement (see Furnivall **CT6**). For studies on the order of the tales see **CT4-7**. For a facsimile of the Ellesmere MS see **M22**. Editions of separate tales are listed tale by tale.

CT1
Manly, John M. and Edith Rickert, eds. *The Text of the 'Canterbury Tales,' Studied on the Basis of All Known Manuscripts. Prepared with the Aid of Mabel Dean, Helen McIntosh, and Others; with a Chapter on Illuminations by Margaret Rickert.* 8 vols. (Chicago 1940)
This monumental work is indispensable for study of the text of *CT.*
CT2
Pratt, R.A., ed. *The Tales of Canterbury, Complete* (Boston 1974)
This is an illustrated student's edition; difficult words are glossed in the margin, explanatory notes appear at the bottom of the page, and there is a brief but useful introduction. The text is based on Robinson **M30**, with several changes designed to bring the edition closer to Manly's 'latest common original of all extant mss.' (see Manly and Rickert **CT1**). Pratt accepts headless nine-syllable lines, avoids fillers to complete metrically imperfect lines, and appends a list of readings which differ from Robinson's; the order of the tales follows the Bradshaw order, based on the arguments in Pratt **CT7**.
CT3
Tyrwhitt, Thomas, ed. *The Canterbury Tales of Chaucer: To Which are Added an Essay on his Language and Versification, and an Introductory Discourse, together with Notes and a Glossary.* 5 vols. (London 1775-8; 2nd ed. Oxford 1798, repr. 1822; see comment for later reprints)
Although his text has no critical value, Tyrwhitt did most of the pioneer work on the sources of the individual tales of *CT,* eliminated many spurious poems from the Chaucer canon, and produced a set of notes that are still, in many ways, the basis for all following

commentary on *CT*. He was also the first to perceive and describe the principles underlying Chaucer's vowel-pronunciation and prosody. Tyrwhitt's apparatus is reprinted in vols. 1-3 of Nichol's Library Edition of the British Poets (*The Canterbury Tales... to Which are Added an Essay... with Notes and a Glossary by Thomas Tyrwhitt, with Memoir and Critical Dissertation by George Gilfillan* [Edinburgh 1841, repr. 1850 and 1860]); the text of that edition is a modernized version by Charles Cowden Clarke. This Tyrwhitt-Clarke-Gilfillan combination was also reprinted, under the same title, in Edinburgh (1868) and in London (1875). Tyrwhitt's introduction has been reprinted recently under the title *An Introductory Discourse to the 'Canterbury Tales'* (Philadelphia 1977)

Order

See Tupper **CT311** and Keiser **CT316** for the argument that FragVII was designed to follow FragII.

CT4
Benson, Larry D. 'The Order of *The Canterbury Tales*,' *Studies in the Age of Chaucer* 3 (1981) 77-120
After a careful review of the evidence from the MSS and of the scholarship on the question, Benson concludes that what 'Chaucer actually did was to leave us the Type *a*-Ellesmere order, imperfect and blemished though it be' (p. 117).
CT5
Donaldson, E.T. 'The Ordering of the *Canterbury Tales*' in *Medieval Literature and Folklore Studies: Essays in Honor of Francis Lee Utley*, ed. Jerome Mandel and Bruce A. Rosenberg (New Brunswick, N.J. 1970) 193-204
Donaldson supports the Ellesmere order of *CT* as the best way of accounting for all the MS evidence.
CT6
Furnivall, F.J. 'Arrangement of the Tales and their Component Parts' in Furnivall, *A Temporary Preface to the Six-Text Edition of Chaucer's Canterbury Tales*, pt. I: *Attempting to Show the True Order of the Tales, and the Days and Stages of the Pilgrimage, etc. etc.*
Chaucer Society 2nd ser. 3 (London 1868) 9-44
This study presents the first notice in print of the 'Bradshaw shift.'

Furnivall discusses the order of the tales and the sequence of events on the pilgrimage, explaining and elaborating upon the suggestion made to him by Henry Bradshaw, that locating Ellesmere FragVII (Chaucer Society B^2) between Fragments II (B^1) and III (D) would eliminate certain inconsistencies in the Ellesmere order of the tales. In the edition published by the Chaucer Society, there was a further shift in which Ellesmere FragVI (Chaucer Society C) was located between VII (B^2) and III (D).

CT7
Pratt, Robert A. 'The Order of the *Canterbury Tales,*' *PMLA* 66 (1951) 1141-67
Pratt argues convincingly against the order of the *CT* proposed by the Chaucer Society and presents a persuasive case for the Bradshaw order: A B^1 B^2 D E-F C G H I. The article includes a summary of criticism on the order of *CT.*

Sources and Analogues

This section includes general source studies; source studies of individual tales are listed under the tale. For texts and translations of analogues to Chaucer's fabliaux, see Benson and Andersson **M156**. For texts of analogues to *CT* in Boccaccio's *Decameron* see **M195** and **M198**. For background material on the medieval English pilgrimage see Hall **B93**. Some studies which discuss the sources of two or more tales are listed in the section on Chaucer's sources and influences above: see Fyler **M282** for the influence of Ovid, Hazelton **M245** for Chaucer's use and parody of Cato in *CT,* Lowes **M154** for his use of the *Miroir de mariage,* and Pratt **M253** for borrowings from handbooks like John of Wales' *Communiloquium.* See McPeek **B146** for the influence of Goliardic poetry on *CT.*

CT8
Bryan, W.F. and G. Dempster, eds. *Sources and Analogues of Chaucer's 'Canterbury Tales'* (Chicago 1941, repr. New York 1958)
This collaborative study presents detailed discussions of the sources and analogues of each tale, accompanied by texts in the original languages. Each chapter is prepared by a specialist in the field. Specific references to each chapter appear below in the sections on

individual tales. For the analogues to the frame narrative of *CT* see Pratt and Young **CT11**.

CT9

Eisner, Sigmund. 'Chaucer's Use of Nicholas of Lynn's Calendar,' *E&S* n.s. 29 (1976) 1-22

Eisner suggests that Chaucer drew on Nicholas' *Kalendarium* for ways of describing times and dates throughout *CT*; see Nicholas of Lynn **M278** for an edition.

CT10

Hoffman, Richard L. *Ovid and 'The Canterbury Tales'* (Philadelphia 1966)

Hoffman argues that Shannon **M214** was wrong in thinking that the influence of Ovid on Chaucer ended with *LGW*, and presents evidence of Ovidian influence in fifteen of the *CT*.

CT11

Pratt, Robert Armstrong and Karl Young. 'The Literary Framework of the *Canterbury Tales*' in Bryan and Dempster **CT8**, 1-81

Pratt and Young provide a thorough account of precedents for Chaucer's use of a frame-narrative, printing the Proemio and Intermezzi from Sercambi's *Novelle* in Italian, with English marginal glosses.

Critical Studies of the *Canterbury Tales* as a Whole

In addition to the studies listed below, see those listed under **CrS** above; many have valuable and extensive discussions of *CT*, for example Kittredge **CrS50** and Muscatine **CrS57**.

CT12

Baldwin, Ralph. *The Unity of 'The Canterbury Tales'*. Anglistica 5 (Copenhagen 1955); repr. in part in Schoeck and Taylor **CrS15**, I, 14-51

Baldwin explores the theological background of the opening of *GenProl, ParsT,* and *Retr,* arguing that the metaphor of the heavenly pilgrimage is sustained throughout *CT*.

CT13

Bennett, J.A.W. *Chaucer at Oxford and at Cambridge* (Toronto and Oxford 1974)

Quoting extensively from contemporary sources, Bennett sketches the Oxford and Cambridge of Chaucer's time, describing their connections with Chaucer's life and poetry, especially *MillT* and *RvT.*

CT14
Brewer, D.S. 'The Fabliaux' in Rowland **CrS13**, 296-325
Brewer presents a review of scholarship with bibliography for *MillT, RvT, FrT, SumT, MerchT,* and *ShipT.*

CT15
Bronson, Bertrand H. 'Chaucer's Art in Relation to his Audience' in *Five Studies in Literature* [no ed.]. University of California Publications in English 8, no. 1 (Berkeley 1940) 1-53
This study is a careful and illuminating examination of the ways in which Chaucer designed his poetry for oral delivery and a listening audience.

CT16
Coghill, Nevill. 'Chaucer's Narrative Art in *The Canterbury Tales*' in Brewer **CrS4**, 114-39
Coghill suggests that Chaucer devised his own rules for story-telling, and he discusses some of his methods.

CT17
Craik, T.W. *The Comic Tales of Chaucer* (London 1964)
Craik presents an appreciation of the comic art of *MillT, RvT, CkT, FrT, SumT, MerchT, ShipT, Thop, NPT,* and *CYT;* the study is aimed at the general reader.

CT18
Dempster, Germaine. 'Manly's Conception of the Early History of the *Canterbury Tales*,' *PMLA* 61 (1946) 379-415
Dempster summarizes conclusions drawn from Manly and Rickert **CT1** about the condition of *CT* MSS at Chaucer's death and in the 15th century.

CT19
Donaldson, E. Talbot. 'Chaucer the Pilgrim,' *PMLA* 69 (1954) 928-36; repr. in Donaldson **CrS7**, 1-12; in Schoeck and Taylor **CrS15**, I, 1-13; and in abridged form in Owen **CT32**, 18-24
In this influential study, Donaldson suggests that Chaucer the pilgrim narrator is neither the poet nor the man Chaucer, but a *persona* who is ironically presented as obtuse, although he claims to be an accurate reporter. See Major **CT27** for an opposing view.

CT20
Heist, William W. 'Folklore Study and Chaucer's Fabliau-like Tales,' *Papers of the Michigan Academy of Science, Arts, and Letters* 36 (1950) 251-8
In a general study of the influence of modern folklore studies on Chaucerian scholarship, Heist points out that a recorded medieval analogue is not necessarily a source for the tale it resembles, because a source in oral tradition is a likely possibility.

CT21
Howard, Donald R. *The Idea of the 'Canterbury Tales'* (Berkeley, Los Angeles, London 1976)
Defining a 'literary idea' broadly as the complex of ideas and feelings in the author's mind as well as the style and shape of the resulting work, Howard draws on a wide variety of medieval sources and analogues as well as modern scholarship to discover ways in which *CT* may be seen as 'unfinished but complete.' After an introductory chapter defining 'idea,' Howard discusses a series of interrelated topics: *CT* as a book about the world; style in *CT;* memory and form; a theory of the structure of the tales, which are divided into four groups; and the Pardoner and the Parson.

CT22
Huppé, Bernard F. *A Reading of the 'Canterbury Tales'* (New York 1964)
Following the methodology of Robertson **CrS66**, Huppé reads *CT* as a Christian allegory.

CT23
Lawrence, William Witherle. *Chaucer and the 'Canterbury Tales'* (New York 1950)
Lawrence offers a useful account of problems in *CT;* the chapter on MS tradition and the order of the tales is particularly helpful.

CT24
Leyerle, John. 'Thematic Interlace in *The Canterbury Tales,*' *E&S* n.s. 29 (1976) 107-21
Leyerle describes the interlacing of significant themes, such as food and drink, gold, sex, and death, as a means of creating coherence in *CT.*

CT25
Lumiansky, Robert M. *Of Sondry Folk: The Dramatic Principle in the 'Canterbury Tales'* (Austin, Tex. 1955)

Lumiansky examines the tales and links as related elements in a dramatic structure; he discusses the relations between the tales and their tellers, focussing attention on the Knight, the Wife of Bath, the Pardoner, and the Prioress, and on the quarrels between the Miller and Reeve and between the Friar and Summoner.

CT26

Macdonald, Donald. 'Proverbs, *sententiae,* and *exempla* in Chaucer's Comic Tales: The Function of Comic Misapplication,' *Speculum* 41 (1966) 453-65

Macdonald discusses Chaucer's skill in using the tradition of arguing by proverb, sententia, and exemplum for comic purposes in tales like *MillT.*

CT27

Major, John M. 'The Personality of Chaucer the Pilgrim,' *PMLA* 75 (1960) 160-62

Major disagrees with the views presented by Donaldson **CT19**.

CT28

Manly, John Matthews. *Some New Light on Chaucer: Lectures Delivered at the Lowell Institute* (New York 1926, repr. 1951; repr. Gloucester, Mass. 1959) 70-252

Manly suggests that several of the pilgrims represent real persons and he documents the lives of those he suggests as Chaucer's models.

CT29

Miller, Robert P. 'Allegory in *The Canterbury Tales*' in Rowland **CrS13**, 326-51

Miller surveys selected studies of allegory and provides a bibliography.

CT30

Muscatine, Charles. 'The *Canterbury Tales:* Style of the Man and Style of the Work' in Brewer **CrS4**, 88-113

Muscatine argues that Chaucer uses a mixed style which is not confined by ideas of literary decorum and which juggles perspective and tone, even within an individual work.

CT31

Newstead, Helaine. 'Chaucer's *Canterbury Tales*' in *Recent Middle English Scholarship and Criticism: Survey and Desiderata,* ed. J. Burke Severs (Pittsburgh 1971) 97-107

Newstead offers a good starting-point for students unfamiliar with recent trends in *CT* criticism; she discusses recent editions and summarizes the work of the most influential modern critics.
CT32
Owen, Charles A., Jr., ed. *Discussions of the 'Canterbury Tales'* (Boston 1966)
Owen gives short excerpts from important modern critical studies.
CT33
_____ *Pilgrimage and Storytelling in the 'Canterbury Tales': The Dialectic of 'ernest' and 'game'* (Norman, Okla. 1977)
Owen summarizes and expands his earlier work (Rowland **CrS13**, 221-42) on the order of *CT* and Chaucer's final plan. He argues that a return journey was intended, and that Chaucer revised his earlier, 'earnest' plan to accommodate 'game' and comic elements.
CT34
Piper, Edwin Ford. 'The Miniatures of the Ellesmere Chaucer,' *PQ* 3 (1924) 241-56, 8 pp. of pls.
Piper describes the miniatures (reproduced in black and white) and suggests that they reflect the artist's close study of *GenProl*, the links, and the tales.
CT35
Ramsey, Vance. 'Modes of Irony in *The Canterbury Tales*' in Rowland **CrS13**, 352-79
Ramsey surveys scholarship on irony and provides a selective bibliography.
CT36
Richardson, Janette. *Blameth Nat Me: A Study of Imagery in Chaucer's Fabliaux* (The Hague and Paris 1970)
Richardson shows how Chaucer interweaves imagery with other narrative elements in the fabliaux, and she describes image clusters in some of the tales.
CT37
Ruggiers, Paul G. *The Art of the 'Canterbury Tales'* (Madison, Milwaukee, London 1965; repr. 1967)
Ruggiers gives a critical analysis of *CT,* tale by tale.
CT38
Severs, J. Burke. 'Chaucer's Clerks' in Rowland **CrS14**, 140-52
Severs provides historical background on 14th-century clerks.

CT39

───── 'The Tales of Romance' in Rowland **CrS13**, 271-95
Severs surveys current criticism and provides a selected
bibliography for *KnT, MLT, WBT, ClT, SqT, FranklT,* and *Thop.*

CT40

Szittya, Penn R. 'The Antifraternal Tradition in Middle English
Literature,' *Speculum* 52 (1977) 287-313
Szittya discusses some literary precedents for Chaucer's descrip-
tions of friars.

CT41

Wallis, N. Hardy. *Canterbury Colloquies: A New Arrangement of the
Prologue and End-Links of the 'Canterbury Tales' to Show their
Dramatic Significance* (London 1957)
Wallis prints *GenProl* (rearranged) and the text of the endlinks as a
drama, assigning lines to speakers and specifying time and place.

CT42

Whittock, Trevor. *A Reading of the 'Canterbury Tales'* (Cambridge
1968)
Whittock argues that the multiplicity of points of view represented
in *CT* is an essential part of the design of the work.

CT43

Williams, Arnold. 'Chaucer and the Friars,' *Speculum* 28 (1953)
499-513
Williams argues that since a hostile attitude to friars was common
in the period, Chaucer's characterization of friars may reflect
contemporary attitudes, not a personal view.

CT44

Zacher, Christian K. *Curiosity and Pilgrimage: The Literature of
Discovery in Fourteenth-Century England* (Baltimore and London
1976)
Zacher sets Chaucer's description of the Canterbury pilgrimage in
the context of medieval 'literature of discovery,' a term he uses to
include pilgrimage narratives as well as works of 'curiosity,' such as
Richard of Bury's *Philobiblon.* He argues that throughout *CT* there
is a conflict between the bond of pilgrim brotherhood as a force of
order and the disorderly forces of 'curiosity.'

Fragment I
(*GenProl, KnT, MillT, RvT, CkT*)

CRITICAL STUDIES

The studies listed in this section deal with relations among two or more tales in FragI. Studies of relationships between *GenProl* and other parts of *CT* are listed under *GenProl*, the next section. See Stanley **CT147** for the relationship between *CkT* and *RvT*.

CT45
Dean, Christopher. 'Imagery in the *Knight's Tale* and the *Miller's Tale*,' *MS* 31 (1969) 149-63
Dean gives a perceptive and detailed examination of the contrasting images used in the two poems.

CT46
Olson, Paul A. 'The *Reeve's Tale:* Chaucer's *Measure for Measure*,' *SP* 59 (1962) 1-17
Olson analyses the working out of justice in the Reeve's 'quityng' of the Miller.

CT47
Owen, Charles A., Jr. 'Chaucer's *Canterbury Tales:* Aesthetic Design in Stories of the First Day,' *ES* 35 (1954) 49-56
Owen shows that the Miller contrasts Nicholas and Absolon with Palamon and Arcite, as Chaucer contrasts the Reeve and Miller with both pairs.

CT48
Stokoe, William C., Jr. 'Structure and Intention in the First Fragment of the *Canterbury Tales*,' *UTQ* 21 (1951-2) 120-27
Stokoe argues that *MillT* is a conscious re-telling of *KnT* from the Miller's point of view, and he discusses some of the parallels.

GENERAL PROLOGUE

Editions

Robinson **M30**, 17-25 (text); 650-69, 889-90 (notes). Skeat **M31**, IV, 1-25
(text); V, 1-59 (notes).

CT49

Hodgson, Phyllis, ed. *The General Prologue to the Canterbury Tales* (London 1969)
Hodgson's edition is based on the Ellesmere text; it includes an introduction and several appendices.

CT50

Schmidt, A.V.C., ed. *The General Prologue to the Canterbury Tales and the Canon's Yeoman's Prologue and Tale* (London 1974)
This student's edition has an introduction, commentary, and notes.

Sources and Analogues

See Pratt and Young in Bryan and Dempster **CT8**, 3-6 for the tradition of the literary portrait.

CT51

Cunningham, J.V. 'The Literary Form of the Prologue to the *Canterbury Tales*,' *MP* 49 (1952) 172-81; repr. as 'Convention as Structure: The Prologue to the *Canterbury Tales*' in Cunningham, *Tradition and Poetic Structure: Essays in Literary History and Criticism* (Denver 1951) 59-75
Cunningham suggests that Chaucer took the idea of an introductory set of portraits from the opening of the *Roman de la rose*.

CT52

Lumiansky, R.M. 'Benoit's Portraits and Chaucer's General Prologue,' *JEGP* 55 (1956) 431-8
Lumiansky examines Chaucer's indebtedness to literary portraiture in Benoit de Sainte-More, and discusses techniques common to both authors.

CT53

Mann, Jill. *Chaucer and Medieval Estates Satire: The Literature of Social Classes and the 'General Prologue to the Canterbury Tales'* (Cambridge 1973)
In this important study, Mann traces literary antecedents for the portraits of *GenProl*, emphasizing their moral ambiguity.

CT54

Tuve, Rosemond. *Seasons and Months: Studies in a Tradition of Middle English Poetry* (Paris 1933; repr. Cambridge and Totowa, N.J. 1974, Folcroft, Pa. 1974) 46-70, 170-91

Tuve discusses literary precedents for the description of the seasons in Chaucer and shows that *GenProl* draws on a rich and ancient tradition of the seasons, typified by the *Secreta secretorum*. Effective use is made of illustrated treatises on the calendar and Books of Hours. A full bibliography and an appendix of illustrative quotations are included.

Critical Studies of the *General Prologue* as a Whole

See Wood **CrS73**, 161-71 and Owen **CT66** for a discussion of the date.

CT55
Bowden, Muriel. *A Commentary on the 'General Prologue to the Canterbury Tales'* (New York 1948, 2nd ed. 1967; repr. London 1973)
Bowden provides a valuable guide to *GenProl*, combining original research with references to many studies on individual pilgrims; she includes a bibliography.

CT56
Brooks, Harold F. *Chaucer's Pilgrims: The Artistic Order of the Portraits in the Prologue* (London 1962)
This short general study stresses the contrasts in Chaucer's presentation of the pilgrims.

CT57
Brown, Carleton. 'The Squire and the Number of the Canterbury Pilgrims,' *MLN* 49 (1934) 216-22
Brown suggests that Chaucer inserted a description of the Squire after the rest of *GenProl* had been written, increasing the number of pilgrims to thirty, but forgetting to alter line 24, which gives the number as twenty-nine; for a review of work on this discrepancy see Eckhardt **CT59**.

CT58
Dent, A.A. 'Chaucer and the Horse,' *Proceedings of the Leeds Philosophical and Literary Society* (Literary and Historical Section) 9 (1959) 1-12, 4 pp. of pls.
Dent examines the language Chaucer uses to describe horses, and comments on the Ellesmere miniatures.

CT59
Eckhardt, Caroline D. 'The Number of Chaucer's Pilgrims: A Review and Reappraisal,' *Yearbook of English Studies* 5 (1975) 1-18

Eckhardt provides an account of previous work on the problem of the number of pilgrims; she argues that the numbers have symbolic value and that the confusions are an intentionally ironic reflection on Chaucer the pilgrim.

CT60
Hoffman, Arthur W. 'Chaucer's Prologue to Pilgrimage: The Two Voices,' *ELH* 21 (1954) 1-16
Hoffman explores the implications of the relations between some of the pilgrims (Knight and Squire, Parson and Plowman, Summoner and Pardoner); he shows that each pilgrim is described in terms of whom or what he loves.

CT61
Kirby, Thomas A. 'The *General Prologue*' in Rowland **CrS13**, 243-70
Kirby surveys criticism and critical issues involving *GenProl* through 1978 and includes a selected bibliography.

CT62
Lenaghan, R.T. 'Chaucer's *General Prologue* as History and as Literature,' *Comparative Studies in Society and History* 12 (1970) 73-82
Lenaghan examines the pilgrims' place in the economy of 14th-century England.

CT63
Morgan, Gerald. 'The Design of the *General Prologue to the Canterbury Tales*,' *ES* 59 (1978) 481-98
Morgan uses contemporary discussions of social rank and class to suggest how the portraits of *GenProl* are organized.

CT64
Nevo, Ruth. 'Chaucer: Motive and Mask in the *General Prologue*,' *MLR* 58 (1963) 1-9
Nevo shows that money is mentioned in all the portraits of the *GenProl* and that each pilgrim is assessed according to his attitude towards money; she argues that the pilgrims are arranged according to an economic scheme, beginning with the rich upper classes and ending with the parasites.

CT65
Norman, Philip. 'The Tabard Inn, Southwark, The Queen's Head, William Rutter, and St. Margaret's Church,' *Surrey Archaeological Society Collections* 13 (1897) 28-38

Norman prints acts and documents relating to the Tabard Inn as it was in the 16th century, including a deed which lists the inn's rooms and furniture as they may have been in Chaucer's day.

CT66
Owen, Charles A., Jr. 'The Twenty-Nine Pilgrims and the Three Priests,' *MLN* 76 (1961) 392-7
Owen suggests that *GenProl* was composed during two separate periods: 1387-8 and 1396.

CT67
Steadman, John M. 'Chaucer's Thirty Pilgrims and *activa vita*,' *Neophilologus* 45 (1961) 224-30
Steadman points out that the number 30 is associated with the active life, especially with marriage, and that many of the pilgrims' and the poet's concerns are with the active life.

CT68
Woolf, Rosemary. 'Chaucer as Satirist in the *General Prologue to the Canterbury Tales*,' *Critical Quarterly* 1 (1959) 150-57
Woolf offers a brief and lucid discussion of satirical techniques in *GenProl.*

Critical Studies of Individual Portraits

See Manly **CT28** and Bowden **CT55** for suggested real-life originals and social backgrounds for some of the portraits; see Mann **CT53** for discussions of the literary tradition of each portrait. See Robertson **B57** for comments on the way recent work on social and economic history casts light on the portraits. Many of the studies listed under the individual tales discuss the portraits as well. The studies below are organized under the name of the pilgrim discussed and are in alphabetical order. Portraits without significant separate studies are not listed below.

Clerk

See Severs **CT38**.

CT69
Fleming, John. 'Chaucer's Clerk and John of Salisbury,' *ELN* 2 (1964) 5-6

Fleming shows that the description of the Clerk in *GenProl* 308
closely parallels John of Salisbury, *Policraticus* 2.156-7; Chaucer
quotes from this work in *PardT* 591-2 and 603ff.

Cook

CT70
Hieatt, Constance B. ' "To boille the chiknes with the
marybones": Hodge's Kitchen Revisited' in Vasta and Thundy
CrS18, 149-63
Hieatt offers a brief discussion of medieval cookery as
background for the portrait of the Cook.

Franklin

See Manly **CT28**, 157-68.

CT71
Gerould, Gordon Hall. 'The Social Status of Chaucer's Franklin,'
PMLA 41 (1926) 262-79; repr. in rev. form as 'The Social Status
of the Franklin' in Gerould, *Chaucerian Essays* (Princeton, N.J.
1952; repr. 1968) 33-54
Gerould cites historical evidence that refutes the notion that a
franklin could not have been a gentleman.

CT72
Pearcy, Roy J. 'Chaucer's Franklin and the Literary Vavasour,'
ChauR 8 (1973-4) 33-59
Pearcy provides information on the *vavasour* in medieval society
and literature.

Friar

See Szittya **CT40** and Williams **CT43**

CT73
Spargo, John Webster. 'Chaucer's Love-Days,' *Speculum* 15
(1940) 36-56
Spargo traces the historical background of love-days, days set
aside for the amicable settlement of legal disputes, and concludes

that the Friar's interference in love-days was illegal.
CT74
Williams, Arnold. 'The "Limitour" of Chaucer's Time and his "Limitacioun",' *SP* 57 (1960) 463-78
Williams provides background information on the office of *limitour*.

Guildsmen — see Tradesmen

Host

See Manly **CT28**, 77-83.

CT75
Malone, Kemp. 'Harry Bailly and Godelief,' *ES* 31 (1950) 209-15
Malone directs attention away from the search for real-life models for Harry Bailly and towards Chaucer's artistry in creating the comic figure of the Host as the controlling figure of the storytelling contest.
CT76
Page, Barbara. 'Concerning the Host,' *ChauR* 4 (1970-71) 1-13
Page gives a convenient summary of critical opinions on the Host; she argues that he is a timekeeper, as well as a comic character whose remarks contribute to the marriage debate.
CT77
Richardson, Cynthia C. 'The Function of the Host in *The Canterbury Tales*,' *TSLL* 12 (1970-71) 325-44
Richardson suggests that to Chaucer Harry Bailly represents the shallow and uncritical contemporary audience; she shows that Harry's demand for *sentence* and *solas* is in accord with medieval aesthetics, and demonstrates that he is consistently associated with the passing of time.

Knight

See Kaske **CT359**.

CT78
Cook, Albert Stanburrough. 'The Historical Background of

Chaucer's Knight,' *Transactions of the Connecticut Academy of Arts and Sciences* 20 (1916) 161-240; repr. separately (New York 1966)
Cook gives detailed discussion of the historical personages and events which, he argues, provide the context for the Knight and his military exploits.

Man of Law — see Sergeant-of-the-Law

Merchant

See Manly **CT28**, 181-200.

CT79
Rickert, Edith. 'Extracts from a Fourteenth-Century Account Book,' *MP* 24 (1926-7) 111-19, 249-56, 1 pl.
Rickert quotes from records of mercantile life to illustrate the background of the Merchant.

Monk

See Kaske **CT359**.

CT80
Beichner, Paul E., CSC. 'Daun Piers, Monk and Business Administrator,' *Speculum* 34 (1959) 611-19; repr. in Schoeck and Taylor **CrS15**, I, 52-62
Beichner defines *outrider* as an administrator and uses contemporary sources to explain the duties involved; he suggests that the Monk is criticised, not for assuming wordly duties, but for allowing worldly duties to take precedence over the monastic life.
CT81
Grennen, Joseph E. 'Chaucerian Portraiture: Medicine and the Monk,' *NM* 69 (1968) 569-74
Grennen discusses echoes of contemporary medical lore in the Monk's portrait.
CT82
Reiss, Edmund. 'The Symbolic Surface of the *Canterbury Tales:*

The Monk's Portrait,' [Pt. I] *ChauR* 2 (1967-8) 254-72; [Pt. II]
ChauR 3 (1968-9) 12-28
Reiss argues that the Monk's portrait is symbolic of his inner
moral state; he devotes special attention to animal imagery and
to the evidence of deceptive appearances in the portrait.

Pardoner

See also **CT299-302**. See Curry **CrS35**, 54-70 for an account of
the Pardoner's physiognomy; Curry classifies the Pardoner as a
congenital eunuch.

CT83
Bloomfield, Morton W. 'The Pardons of Pamplona and the
Pardoner of Rounceval: *Piers Plowman* B XVII 252 (C XX 218),'
PQ 35 (1956) 60-68
Bloomfield gives a clear account of the connections between
Pamplona, headquarters of the order of Nuestra Señora de
Roncesvalles, and the Hospital of St. Mary of Rounceval, the
daughter house in London.
CT84
Hamilton, Marie P. 'The Credentials of Chaucer's Pardoner,'
JEGP 40 (1941) 48-72
Hamilton suggests that the Pardoner is an authorized *quaestor*,
an Augustinian canon regular, and an agent for the Hospital of
St. Mary of Rounceval.
CT85
Kellogg, Alfred L. and Louis A. Haselmayer. 'Chaucer's Satire of
the Pardoner,' *PMLA* 66 (1951) 251-77
Kellogg and Haselmayer provide historical data on pardoners
and abuses of their office.
CT86
Miller, Robert P. 'Chaucer's Pardoner, the Scriptural Eunuch,
and the *Pardoner's Tale*,' *Speculum* 30 (1955) 180-99; repr. in
Schoeck and Taylor **CrS15**, I, 221-44 and in Faulkner **CT306**,
43-69
Quoting from biblical commentaries, Miller argues that the
Pardoner is a type of the spiritual eunuch *in malo,* who willfully

rebels against God, and that he is contrasted with the Parson, a spiritual eunuch *in bono*, who practises chastity out of obedience.

CT87

Moore, Samuel. 'Chaucer's Pardoner of Rouncival,' *MP* 25 (1927-8) 59-66

Moore prints contemporary documents which reveal the abuses practised by hospitals like St. Mary Rounceval and the existence of fraudulent alms collections for hospitals.

CT88

Schaut, Quentin L. 'Chaucer's Pardoner and Indulgences,' *Greyfriar* [The Greyfriar Lectures] 4 (1961) 25-39

Schaut quotes from contemporary sources to demonstrate that Chaucer's treatment of the Pardoner was not an exaggerated portrait.

Physician

CT89

Ussery, Huling E. *Chaucer's Physician: Medicine and Literature in Fourteenth-Century England.* Tulane Studies in English 19 (New Orleans 1971)

Drawing on research on 14th-century physicians, Ussery argues that the Physician is a highly qualified practitioner as well as a cleric and that this status is reflected in his tale.

Plowman

CT90

Stillwell, Gardiner. 'Chaucer's Plowman and the Contemporary English Peasant,' *ELH* 6 (1939) 285-90

Stillwell argues that Chaucer's portrait of the Plowman is an ideal figure designed to symbolize the medieval idea of an ordered society at a time when real plowmen were revolting against that order.

Prioress

See Manly **CT28**, 202-20.

CT91

Madeleva, Sister M., CSC. 'Chaucer's Nuns' in Madeleva, *Chaucer's Nuns and Other Essays* (New York 1925) 3-42
Madeleva supplies information on medieval nuns as background for Chaucer's portrait of the Prioress.

CT92

Moorman, Charles. 'The Prioress as Pearly Queen,' *ChauR* 13 (1978-9) 25-33
Moorman suggests that the Prioress is more Cockney than aristocrat.

Sergeant-of-the-Law

See Manly **CT28**, 131-57

CT93

McKenna, Isobel. 'The Making of a Fourteenth-Century Sergeant of the Lawe,' *Revue de l'Université d'Ottawa* 45 (1975) 244-62
McKenna gives background information on sergeants-of-the-law in the age of Chaucer.

Shipman

See Manly **CT28**, 169-81.

CT94

Galway, Margaret. 'Chaucer's Shipman in Real Life,' *MLR* 34 (1939) 497-514
Galway argues that the Shipman was probably Basque and may have been modelled after John Piers, a Basque who settled in Dartmouth.

CT95

Karkeek, P.Q. 'Chaucer's Schipman and his Barge "The Maudelayne" with Notes on Chaucer's Horses' in Chaucer Society 2nd ser. 19, *Essays on Chaucer, his Words and Works,* Pt. V, item 15 (London n.d. for 1884) 453-500
Karkeek provides information on shipping in Chaucer's time, and proof of the existence of a Dartmouth ship called 'The Maudelayne.'

Summoner

See Manly **CT28**, 102-22

CT96
Haselmayer, Louis A., Jr. 'The Apparitor and Chaucer's Summoner,' *Speculum* 12 (1937) 43-57
Haselmayer provides information on the office of summoner.
CT97
Kaske, R.E. 'The Summoner's Garleek, Onyons and eek Lekes,' *MLN* 74 (1959) 481-4
Kaske examines exegetical interpretations of biblical parallels and concludes that the line implies the Summoner is spiritually as well as physically deformed.

Tradesmen

CT98
McCutchan, J. Wilson. ' "A solempne and a greet fraternité",' *PMLA* 74 (1959) 313-17
McCutchan gives background information on the craft guilds, especially the Company of the Drapers, to which Chaucer's Tradesmen might have belonged.

Wife of Bath

See **CT193-5** and Manly **CT28**, 225-34.

THE KNIGHT'S TALE

Editions

Robinson **M30**, 25-47 (text); 669-83, 890 (notes). Skeat **M31**, IV, 26-88 (text); V, 60-94 (notes).

CT99
Bennett, J.A.W., ed. *The Knight's Tale* (London 1954, rev. ed. 1958)

In this student's edition Bennett prints the text of the Ellesmere MS
and includes an introduction, notes, glossary, and a brief summary
of the *Teseida.*
CT100
Spearing, A.C., ed. *The Knight's Tale* (Cambridge 1966)
This is a student's edition with Robinson's text, a long introduction,
notes, and a glossary.

Sources and Analogues

The main source of *KnT* is Boccaccio's *Teseida;* see **M195** for a text
and **M204** for a translation; see Wright **M197**, 45-58 for an
extended comparison of *Teseida* and *KnT.* For a discussion of the
influence of Boethius, see Lumiansky **CT25** and Jefferson **M241**;
for Chaucer's descriptions of pagan deities, see McCall **CrS54**.

CT101
Aiken, Pauline. 'Arcite's Illness and Vincent of Beauvais,' *PMLA* 51
(1936) 361-9
Aiken suggests that Vincent of Beauvais was Chaucer's main
source for the details of Arcite's illness.
CT102
Boitani, Piero. *Chaucer and Boccaccio.* Medium Ævum
Monographs n.s. 8 (Oxford and Cambridge 1977)
Boitani provides a close comparison of *KnT* and the *Teseida.*
CT103
Lowes, John Livingston. 'The Loveres Maladye of Hereos,' *MP* 11
(1913-14) 491-546
Lowes chronicles the history of *amor hereos* from Galen to Robert
Burton, and examines the transmutations of its meaning as a lover's
malady.
CT104
Pratt, Robert A. 'The *Knight's Tale*' in Bryan and Dempster **CT8**,
82-105
Pratt gives an English summary of the *Teseida* as well as an
account of Chaucer's use of the poem, and briefer discussions of the
influence of the *Thebaid* of Statius and the anonymous *Roman de
Thèbes.* He also lists the minor sources: Ovid, Boethius, Vincent of

Beauvais, the *Roman de la rose,* and English romances.
CT105
_____ 'Conjectures Regarding Chaucer's Manuscript of the
Teseida,' SP 42 (1945) 745-63
Through the examination of Chaucer's use of the *Teseida,* Pratt
concludes that Chaucer's copy of Boccaccio's poem must have been
fairly corrupt and lacked the author's commentary.
CT106
_____ 'Chaucer's Use of the *Teseida,' PMLA* 62 (1947) 598-621
Pratt gives a detailed account of the relationship between the
Teseida and *KnT.*
CT107
Wilson, H.S. 'The *Knight's Tale* and the *Teseida* Again,' *UTQ* 18
(1948-9) 131-46
Wilson summarizes the *Teseida* and interprets *KnT* as 'an
exemplum of the power of love which overrules all fellowship.'

Critical Studies

See Curry **CrS35,** 119-65 for an analysis of the astrological framework of *KnT,* and for the argument that the conflict between the
two knights represents the strife between the forces of Saturn and
Mars. See Dean **CT45** for the imagery of the poem. See Elbow
CrS40, 73-94 for a discussion of the conflict between freedom and
necessity in *KnT.* See Leyerle **Tr45,** 118-21 for the argument that
bonds are the 'poetic nucleus' of *KnT.* See McCall **CrS53** for the
significance of the date May 3. See Muscatine **CrS57,** 175-90
(printed in an earlier form in *PMLA* 65 [1950] 911-29; repr. in
Wagenknecht **CrS19,** 60-82), for the influential view that the poem
is a symmetrical 'poetic pageant' which reveals the conflict between
the ordered character of the noble life and the forces of chaos.

CT108
Brooks, Douglas and Alistair Fowler. 'The Meaning of Chaucer's
Knight's Tale,' MAE 39 (1970) 123-46
Brooks and Fowler suggest that the mythological episodes and the
descriptions of Lygurge and Emetreus may be fitted into an overall
interpretation of the poem as a vision of the Four Ages of Man.

CT109

Cowgill, Bruce Kent. 'The *Knight's Tale* and the Hundred Years'
War,' *PQ* 54 (1975) 670-79
Cowgill argues that the tournament described in Part IV is of a type
obsolete in Chaucer's day, and that it is intended to emphasize the
Knight's archaic chivalry and the decadence of the Hundred Years'
War. See Robertson **CT121** and Kahrl **CT259** for an opposing view.

CT110

French, W.H. 'The Lovers in the *Knight's Tale*,' *JEGP* 48 (1949)
320-28
French discusses Chaucer's use of the tradition of the knightly
lover.

CT111

Frost, William. 'An Interpretation of Chaucer's *Knight's Tale*,' *RES*
25 (1949) 289-304; repr. in Schoeck and Taylor **CrS15**, I, 98-116
Frost suggests that *KnT* has three main areas of interest: the rivalry
of lovers, the ethical conflict between love and friendship, and 'the
method by which a just providence fully stabilizes a disintegrating
human situation.'

CT112

Haller, Robert S. 'The *Knight's Tale* and the Epic Tradition,' *ChauR*
1 (1966-7) 67-84
Haller discusses the poem in terms of the classical epic tradition,
and argues that love takes the place of the usual political centre of
the classical epic.

CT113

Halverson, John. 'Aspects of Order in the *Knight's Tale*,' *SP* 57
(1960) 606-21
Halverson explores three aspects of order, which he sees as the
poem's central theme: the order of nature, the order of society, and
the divine order of the cosmos.

CT114

Hieatt, A. Kent. *Chaucer, Spenser, Milton: Mythopoeic Continuities
and Transformations* (Montreal and London 1975) 29-58
Hieatt compares *KnT* with *PF*.

CT115

Lumiansky, Robert M. 'Chaucer's Philosophical Knight,' *Tulane
Studies in English* 3 (1952) 47-68; repr. in rev. form as 'The Knight'

in Lumiansky **CT25**, 29-48

Lumiansky suggests that in *KnT* Chaucer set a chivalric romance within a Boethian framework, and that this combination suits the character of the Knight.

CT116

Mather, Frank J., Jr. 'On the Date of the *Knight's Tale*' in *An English Miscellany presented to Dr. Furnivall in Honour of his Seventy-Fifth Birthday* [no ed.] (Oxford 1901) 300-13

Mather suggests that *KnT* was written after *Tr*, in 1381-2; the date of completion of *Tr* is now thought to be 1385.

CT117

Meier, T.K. 'Chaucer's Knight as "Persona": Narration as Control,' *English Miscellany* 20 (1969) 11-21

Meier suggests that the poem's structure and meaning express the pessimism and stoicism of the Knight's world-view.

CT118

Mitchell, Edward R. 'The Two Mayings in Chaucer's *Knight's Tale*,' *MLN* 71 (1956) 560-64

Mitchell discusses the medieval May Day celebrations and argues that the Mayings in *KnT* derive both from English observance and from French literary tradition.

CT119

Pratt, Robert A. ' " Joye after wo" in the *Knight's Tale*,' *JEGP* 57 (1958) 416-23

Pratt argues that the plot of the poem illustrates the theme of 'joye after wo.'

CT120

Reidy, John. 'The Education of Chaucer's Duke Theseus' in *The Epic in Medieval Society: Aesthetic and Moral Values,* ed. Harald Scholler (Tübingen 1977) 391-408

Reidy argues that Theseus is presented as a successful military commander of Chaucer's period, one whose vision of life has broadened by the end of the poem.

CT121

Robertson, Stuart. 'Elements of Realism in the *Knight's Tale*,' *JEGP* 14 (1915) 226-55

Robertson argues that the accounts of single combat and the tournament in *KnT* reflect practices in Chaucer's time. See

Cowgill **CT109** for an opposing view.
CT122
Salter, Elizabeth. *Chaucer: The Knight's Tale and the Clerk's Tale* (London 1962; repr. 1965, 1967, 1969) 9-37
Salter provides a perceptive discussion of theme and language in the poem; she suggests that Chaucer raises questions about the relation between divine providence and human happiness.
CT123
Schmidt, A.V.C. 'The Tragedy of Arcite: A Reconsideration of the *Knight's Tale,*' *Essays in Criticism* 19 (1969) 107-17
Schmidt argues that Arcite is the hero of the story.
CT124
Underwood, Dale. 'The First of *The Canterbury Tales,*' *ELH* 26 (1959) 455-69
Underwood discusses the poem in terms of three realms of order: the disorderly order of Fortune, the orderly disorder of the human, and the true order of God.
CT125
Webb, Henry J. 'A Reinterpretation of Chaucer's Theseus,' *RES* 23 (1947) 289-96
Webb argues that Chaucer's Theseus is more cruel and savage than Boccaccio's Teseo.
CT126
Westlund, Joseph. 'The *Knight's Tale* as an Impetus for Pilgrimage,' *PQ* 43 (1964) 526-37
Westlund argues that *KnT* presents 'the continual subversion of noble efforts to bring order out of disorder.'
CT127
Whittock, Trevor. 'Chaucer's *Knight's Tale,*' *Theoria* 13 (1958) 27-38
Whittock examines the diction of the poem.

THE MILLER'S PROLOGUE AND TALE

Editions

Robinson **M30**, 47-55 (text); 683-6, 890-91 (notes). Skeat **M31**, IV, 89-111 (text); V, 95-111 (notes).

CT128
Hieatt, Constance B., ed. *The Miller's Tale* (New York 1970)
This is a student's edition with introduction, notes, bibliography, a
note on language, a translation of the tale's closest analogue, and a
glossary.
CT129
Winny, James, ed. *The Miller's Prologue and Tale* (London 1971;
repr. 1974, 1975)
This is a student's edition, with introduction, notes, and glossary.

Sources and Analogues

See Benson and Andersson **M156** for translations of analogues.

CT130
Harder, Kelsie B. 'Chaucer's Use of the Mystery Plays in the
Miller's Tale,' *MLQ* 17 (1956) 193-8
Harder gives examples of Chaucer's parody of mystery plays.
CT131
Kaske, R.E. 'The *Canticum canticorum* in the *Miller's Tale*,' *SP* 59
(1962) 479-500
Kaske lists possible borrowings from the Song of Songs and shows,
with reference to exegetical tradition, how they intensify the
comedy of the tale while subtly emphasizing an underlying moral
theme. See also Wimsatt **M231**.
CT132
Thompson, Stith. 'The *Miller's Tale*' in Bryan and Dempster **CT8**,
106-23
Thompson discusses the three principal folklore motifs, giving texts
of four of the closest analogues and a list of other analogues.

Critical Studies

See Dean **CT45**, Owen **CT47**, and Stokoe **CT48** for discussions of
the relationship of *MillT* to *KnT*. See Bennett **CT13** for the contemporary background. See Brewer **CrS26** for the description of
Alisoun. See Leyerle **Tr45**, 122-3 for the argument that holes are the
'poetic nucleus' of *MillT*. See Olson **CT46** for the Reeve's 'quityng'
of the Miller.

CT133

Beichner, Paul E., CSC. 'Characterization in *The Miller's Tale*' in Schoeck and Taylor **CrS15**, I, 117-29

Beichner shows that Absolon is characterized as a weak, effeminate city-dweller, contrasted with Alisoun the forthright country girl; he discusses the term *hende,* applied to Nicholas, as a many-sided pun.

CT134

Bloomfield, Morton W. 'The Miller's Tale — An UnBoethian Interpretation' in *Medieval Literature and Folklore Studies: Essays in Honor of Francis Lee Utley,* ed. Jerome Mandel and Bruce A. Rosenberg (New Brunswick, N.J. 1970) 205-12

Bloomfield argues that the universe of *MillT* is irrational and unjust.

CT135

Bolton, W.F. 'The *Miller's Tale:* An Interpretation,' *MS* 24 (1962) 83-94, 1 pl.

Bolton views the tale as a combination of opposites: 'courtly and common, sacred and profane, realistic and fatalistic.'

CT136

Donaldson, E.T. 'Idiom of Popular Poetry in the *Miller's Tale*' in *English Institute Essays 1950,* ed. Alan S. Downer (New York 1951) 116-40; repr. in *Explication as Criticism: Selected Papers from the English Institute 1941-52,* ed. W.K. Wimsatt, Jr. (New York and London 1963) 27-51, and in Donaldson **CrS7**, 13-29

Donaldson explores the use of words in and out of their conventional contexts in *MillT.*

CT137

O'Connor, John J. 'The Astrological Background of the *Miller's Tale,*' *Speculum* 31 (1956) 120-25

O'Connor suggests that Nicholas convinces John to believe his astrological forecast of a flood by pointing out that Noah himself foresaw the Flood by means of astrology.

THE REEVE'S PROLOGUE AND TALE

Editions

Robinson **M30**, 55-60 (text); 686-8, 891 (notes). Skeat **M31**, IV, 112-25 (text); V, 112-27 (notes).

Sources and Analogues

See Benson and Andersson **M156** for translations of analogues.

CT138
Hart, Walter Morris. 'The *Reeve's Tale:* A Comparative Study of
Chaucer's Narrative Art,' *PMLA* 23 (1908) 1-44; repr. in part in
Brewer **CrS3**, II, 268-80
Hart gives a detailed comparison of the tale with its closest fabliau
analogue.

CT139
_____ 'The *Reeve's Tale*' in Bryan and Dempster **CT8**, 124-47
Hart discusses the principal analogue, *Le Meunier et les .II. clers,* and
prints two versions of this tale.

CT140
Hellman, Robert and Richard O'Gorman, trans. 'The Miller and the
Two Clerics' in *Fabliaux: Ribald Tales from the Old French* (New
York 1965) 51-8
Hellman and O'Gorman give a translation of the principal Old
French analogue, printed in Hart **CT139**.

Critical Studies

See Bennett **CT13** for the contemporary background, and
Muscatine **CrS57**, 197-204 for an influential study. See Olson **CT46**
for the Reeve's 'quityng' of the Miller.

CT141
Copland, M. 'The *Reeve's Tale:* Harlotrie or Sermonyng?' *MAE* 31
(1962) 14-32
Copland examines the quarrel between the Reeve and the Miller,
revealing the correspondences and contrasts between the two
antagonists.

CT142
Jones, George Fenwick. 'Chaucer and the Medieval Miller,' *MLQ* 16
(1955) 3-15
Jones discusses the use of the tradition of satire on millers in *RvT*
and gives information on the social position of medieval millers.

CT143

Lancashire, Ian. 'Sexual Innuendo in the *Reeve's Tale*,' *ChauR* 6 (1971-2) 159-70

Lancashire discusses puns and sexual allusions associated with the themes of horsemanship and milling.

CT144

Tolkien, J.R.R. 'Chaucer as a Philologist: The *Reeve's Tale*,' *Transactions of the Philological Society* (1934) 1-70

Tolkien examines Chaucer's remarkable use of Northern dialect for dramatic realism, as evidence of the poet's private interest in philology and as the basis of a humour dependent on linguistic prejudices.

THE COOK'S PROLOGUE AND TALE

Editions

Robinson **M30**, 60-61 (text); 688-9 (notes). Skeat **M31**, IV, 126-9 (text); V, 128-31 (notes).

Sources and Analogues

CT145

Lyon, Earl DeWitt. 'The *Cook's Tale*' in Bryan and Dempster **CT8**, 148-54

Lyon discusses types of possible analogues to the tale, especially stories of the London underworld.

Critical Studies

CT146

Braddy, Haldeen. 'Chaucerian Minutiae,' *MLN* 58 (1943) 18-20 [pt. I]; repr. in Braddy, *Geoffrey Chaucer: Literary and Historical Studies* (Port Washington, N.Y. 1971) 96-101 [pt. I]

Braddy quotes a 1396 indenture of apprenticeship and shows that Perkyn violates three of its most important stipulations.

CT147

Stanley, E.G. ' "Of this cokes tale maked Chaucer na moore",'

Poetica: An International Journal of Linguistic-Literary Studies 5
(Tokyo 1976) 36-59
Stanley discusses the Cook's comments on *RvT* in relation to his
own fragmentary tale, especially with reference to the idea of
'herbergage.'

Fragment II
(*MLT*)

See Tupper **CT311** for the argument that FragVII was designed to
follow FragII.

THE MAN OF LAW'S INTRODUCTION, PROLOGUE, AND TALE

Editions

Robinson **M30**, 62-75 (text); 689-97, 891 (notes). Skeat **M31**, IV,
130-64 (text); V, 132-64 (notes).

CT148
Coghill, Nevill and Christopher Tolkien, eds. *The Man of Law's
Tale* (London 1969)
This is a student's edition with introduction, notes, and glossary.

Sources and Analogues

CT149
Block, Edward A. 'Originality, Controlling Purpose, and Craftsman-
ship in Chaucer's *Man of Law's Tale,*' *PMLA* 68 (1953) 572-616
Block compares *MLT* with its source in Trivet and finds in many of
Chaucer's changes evidence of a conscious artistic purpose.
CT150
Isaacs, Neil D. 'Constance in Fourteenth-Century England,' *NM* 59
(1958) 260-77
Isaacs gives a comparison, with facing-page summaries, of the
three Middle English versions of the Constance story (Chaucer's,
Gower's, and *Emare*).
CT151
Lewis, Robert Enzer. 'Chaucer's Artistic Use of Pope Innocent III's

De miseria humane conditionis in the Man of Law's Prologue and Tale,' PMLA 81 (1966) 485-92

Lewis suggests that two of the passages in MLT taken from De miseria (421-7, 1132-8) are added in order to emphasize the principle of 'wo after gladnesse,' an important theme in Chaucer's version of the tale. For a text and translation of De miseria see **M259**.

CT152

Paull, Michael R. 'The Influence of the Saint's Legend Genre in the Man of Law's Tale,' ChauR 5 (1970-71) 179-94

Paull suggests that MLT deliberately exploits the saint's legend genre, and he reads the events of the tale as types of the Passion of Christ.

CT153

Rosenfeld, Mary-Virginia. 'Chaucer and the Liturgy,' MLN 55 (1940) 357-60 [pt. 2]

Rosenfeld shows that Constance's prayer (II, 456-62) is a translation of certain antiphons for the feast of the Exaltation of the Cross. See also Boyd **M227** for Chaucer's use of the liturgy.

CT154

Schlauch, Margaret. Chaucer's Constance and Accused Queens (New York 1927, repr. 1973)

Schlauch explores the literary background of MLT, discussing the forms of folk-literature in which the story appears, with some examples.

CT155

_____ 'The Man of Law's Tale' in Bryan and Dempster **CT8**, 155-206

Schlauch discusses Trivet's version of the story, its closest analogues, and their possible sources in Byzantine legend; she prints Trivet's Life of Constance and Gower's Tale of Constance. For the full text of Gower's Confessio amantis, in which the Tale of Constance appears, see **M145**. For another edition of Trivet, with an English translation, see **M190**.

Critical Studies

See David **CrS36** and Wood **CrS73** for the argument that MLT is a comment on its teller; see Curry **CrS35**, 164-94 for astrology in MLT.

CT156
Beichner, Paul E., CSC. 'Chaucer's Man of Law and *disparitas cultus,*' *Speculum* 23 (1948) 70-75
Beichner shows that the discussion of the 'diversitee' between Christian and Moslem laws (*MLT* 220-21) is accurate in its legal details; he suggests that the emphasis by the Man of Law on the legal aspect of the marriage is appropriate.

CT157
Bloomfield, Morton W. 'Il *Racconto dell'uomo di legge:* La tragedia di una vittima e la commedia cristiana,' *Strumenti critici* 3 (1969) 195-207; trans. and repr. as 'The *Man of Law's Tale:* A Tragedy of Victimization and a Christian Comedy,' *PMLA* 87 (1972) 384-90
Bloomfield suggests that *MLT* hovers between comedy and tragedy and that it is designed to distance the reader from the story in a way that parallels the *contemptus mundi* perspective advocated in the poem.

CT158
Clasby, Eugene. 'Chaucer's Constance: Womanly Virtue and the Heroic Life,' *ChauR* 13 (1978-9) 221-33
On the basis of a close reading of the tale in light of Boethius' *Consolatio philosophiae,* Clasby argues that *MLT* describes a woman's gradual spiritual growth until she is finally able to adopt a Boethian view of life.

CT159
Clogan, Paul M. 'The Narrative Style of *The Man of Law's Tale,*' *Medievalia et humanistica* 8 (1977) 217-33
Clogan places the tale in the tradition of 'hagiographical romance,' a tradition that is based on a series of exemplary episodes.

CT160
Hamilton, Marie P. 'The Dramatic Suitability of *The Man of Law's Tale*' in *Studies in Language and Literature in Honour of Margaret Schlauch,* ed. Mieczysław Brahmer et al. (Warsaw 1966, New York 1971) 153-63
Hamilton suggests that the attention to legal details, in the debate over Constance's proposed marriage with the Sultan and her trial, is appropriate in a tale told by the Man of Law.

CT161
Loomis, Dorothy Bethurum. 'Constance and the Stars' in Vasta and Thundy **CrS18,** 207-20
Loomis sets the tale in the context of medieval astrology and argues

that Chaucer is stressing both the power of the stars to influence events and the power of God to prevent or remedy harmful influences of the stars.

CT162
Smith, Roland M. 'Chaucer's *Man of Law's Tale* and Constance of Castile,' *JEGP* 47 (1948) 343-51
Smith finds parallels between events in the lives of Chaucer's Custance and Constance of Castile, the second wife of John of Gaunt, arguing that Chaucer altered his source in Trivet to make the parallels less striking and so to avoid giving offence; the argument implies a date for *MLT* before 1390.

CT163
Stevens, Martin. 'Malkyn in the Man of Law's Headlink,' *Leeds Studies in English* n.s. 1 (1967) 1-5
Stevens argues, against Skeat (**M31**, V, 135), that the Man of Law's allusion to 'Malkynes maydenhede' was not proverbial but an allusion to Malyne in *RvT;* he suggests that the presence of the allusion invalidates the theory that *MLT* was originally the first of the tales.

CT164
Weissman, Hope Phyllis. 'Late Gothic Pathos in *The Man of Law's Tale,*' *Journal of Medieval and Renaissance Studies* 9 (1979) 133-53
Weissman maintains that the tale is designed to reveal the tendency to public displays of sentimentalism in Chaucer's time.

The 'Marriage Group'

CRITICAL STUDIES

See Kittredge **CrS50**, 185-210 for the initial formulation of the argument that the prologues and tales of the Wife of Bath, Clerk, Merchant, and Franklin constitute a debate about marriage. See Helmholz **B68** and Kelly **B47** for information on marriage in theory and practice in Chaucer's time. See Utley **M21** for listings of many Marriage Group analogues.

CT165
Brown, Carleton. 'The Evolution of the Canterbury "Marriage Group",' *PMLA* 48 (1933) 1041-59

Brown points out that study of *CT* MSS provides various clues to the development of the Marriage Group block.

CT166

Dempster, Germaine. 'A Period in the Development of the *Canterbury Tales* Marriage Group and of Blocks B² and C,' *PMLA* 68 (1953) 1142-59

Dempster argues that the Marriage Group should be expanded to include *Mel,* the *Mel-Mk* link, and *NPT.*

CT167

Hinckley, Henry Barrett. 'The Debate on Marriage in the *Canterbury Tales,*' *PMLA* 32 (1917) 292-305

In this reply to Kittredge **CrS50** (pp. 185-210), Hinckley argues that the Marriage Group is not a well-organized or highly finished 'act' within *CT,* that the tales involved are not primarily stories about marriage, and that *SecNT* provides a better conclusion than *FranklT;* see also Howard **CT169**.

CT168

Hodge, James L. 'The Marriage Group: Precarious Equilibrium,' *ES* 46 (1965) 289-300

Hodge argues that Chaucer deliberately neglected to conclude the Marriage Group.

CT169

Howard, Donald R. 'The Conclusion of the Marriage Group: Chaucer and the Human Condition,' *MP* 57 (1959-60) 223-32

Howard suggests that in the final arrangement of *CT, SecNT* might have followed *FranklT,* crowning the Marriage Group with a description of virginal marriage, the highest kind of marriage, according to some patristic authorities.

CT170

Kaske, R.E. 'Chaucer's Marriage Group' in Mitchell and Provost **CrS10**, 45-65

Kaske argues that the Marriage Group is organized around two central themes, the questions of the distribution of authority and of the importance of sex in marriage. He suggests that man's authority decreases and woman's increases as the importance of sex increases in the scale of values implied in each of the tales in the Group.

CT171

Lawrence, William Witherle. 'The Marriage Group in the *Canterbury Tales,*' *MP* 11 (1913-14) 247-58

Questioning the view of Kittredge **CrS50** (pp. 185-210), that the Marriage Group is set off from the rest of *CT,* Lawrence discusses the relationship of *Mel* and *NPT* to *WBProl* and *WBT* and the rest of the Marriage Group; he suggests that Group B^2 (FragVII), which includes *Mel* and *NPT,* may have originally been planned to precede Group D (FragIII), which included *WBT.*

CT172
Lyons, Clifford P. 'The Marriage Debate in the *Canterbury Tales,*' *ELH* 2 (1935) 252-62
Lyons attacks the theory of Kittredge **CrS50** (pp. 185-210), arguing that although the problem of sovereignty in marriage is a theme in the tales, they do not constitute a consciously articulated debate on marriage.

CT173
Mogan, Joseph J., Jr. 'Chaucer and the *bona matrimonii,*' *ChauR* 4 (1970) 123-41
Focussing on *MillT, MLT, WBProl, MerchT,* and *ParsT,* Mogan discusses Chaucer's adaptations of various medieval interpretations of Augustine's doctrine of the three 'goods' of marriage: offspring, faithfulness, and sacrament.

Fragment III
(*WBT, FrT, SumT*)

CRITICAL STUDIES

CT174
Beichner, Paul E., CSC. 'Baiting the Summoner,' *MLQ* 22 (1961) 367-76
Beichner argues that the Friar's purpose in telling his tale is to provoke the Summoner.

CT175
Cawley, A.C. 'Chaucer's Summoner, the Friar's Summoner, and the *Friar's Tale,*' *Proceedings of the Leeds Philosophical and Literary Society* (Literary and Historical Section) 8, pt. 3 (1957) 173-80
Cawley discusses parallels between the summoner in *FrT* and Chaucer's Summoner and between the curses in *FrT* and the curses in a formal excommunication.

CT176
Merrill, Thomas F. 'Wrath and Rhetoric in *The Summoner's Tale*,'
TSLL 4 (1962-3) 341-50
Merrill suggests that the digression on anger in Friar John's sermon
is intended by the Summoner as an attack on the wrathful Friar
Huberd, and that anger is a major issue in the encounter between
the Summoner and the Friar. See also Tupper **CT179**.
CT177
Richardson, Janette. 'Friar and Summoner: The Art of Balance,'
ChauR 9 (1974-5) 227-36
Richardson discusses parallels between the Friar's and Summoner's
tales and prologues.
CT178
Szittya, Penn R. 'The Green Yeoman as Loathly Lady: The Friar's
Parody of the *Wife of Bath's Tale*,' *PMLA* 90 (1975) 386-94
Szittya discusses close verbal and structural parallels between *WBT*
and *FrT*, and suggests that these tales, together with *SumT*, form a
triad similar in structure to that formed by *KnT*, *MillT*, and *RvT*.
CT179
Tupper, Frederick. 'The Quarrels of the Canterbury Pilgrims,'
JEGP 14 (1915) 256-70
Tupper interprets the quarrel between the Friar and the Summoner
as typifying the deadly sin of wrath. See also Merrill **CT176**.
CT180
Zietlow, Paul N. 'In Defence of the Summoner,' *ChauR* 1 (1966-7)
4-19
Zietlow suggests that the Summoner comes off better than the Friar
in their exchange because he exposes the Friar as stupid, unobser-
vant, and unable to control his tongue, like Friar John in the tale.

THE WIFE OF BATH'S PROLOGUE AND TALE

Editions

Robinson **M30**, 76-88 (text); 697-704, 891-2 (notes). Skeat **M31**, IV,
320-56 (text); V, 291-321 (notes).

CT181
Winny, James, ed. *The Wife of Bath's Prologue and Tale*
(Cambridge 1965)
This is a student's edition, with introduction, notes, and glossary.

Sources and Analogues

Prologue

See Lowes **M154**, 305-21 for Chaucer's use of Deschamps'
Miroir de mariage and Utley **M21** for a guide to medieval
antifeminist literature.

CT182
Boren, James L. 'Alysoun of Bath and the Vulgate "Perfect
Wife",' *NM* 76 (1975) 247-56
Boren argues that the allusion to 'the Parables of Solomon' in
Jankyn's collection refers to the Vulgate *Encomium mulieris fortis*
(Prov. 31:10-31), and that Chaucer shaped his portrait of the
Wife as an antithesis to this biblical account of the perfect wife.
CT183
Matthews, William. 'The Wife of Bath and All her Sect,' *Viator* 5
(1974) 413-43
Matthews provides a thorough analysis of the Wife's antecedents
in classical and medieval Latin poetry and in fabliaux.
CT184
Moore, Arthur K. 'Chaucer and Matheolus,' *Notes and Queries*
190 (1946) 245-8
Moore demonstrates that the *Lamentations* of Matheolus contains
three-fourths of the polemical matter of *WBProl;* he cites parallel
passages from both the original *Lamentations* and the popular
French version by Le Fèvre (1371-2). For a similar argument and
a text of the *Lamentations,* see **M277**.
CT185
Pratt, Robert. 'A Note on Chaucer and the *Policraticus* of John of
Salisbury,' *MLN* 65 (1950) 243-6
Pratt suggests that Book VIII of the *Policraticus* is the source of
some of Jankyn's stories of wicked wives; the stories recorded
there are the closest known parallels to *WBT* 765-71, and appear

in precisely the same order. For a text and translation of the *Policraticus* see **M262-3**.

CT186

_____ 'Jankyn's Book of Wikked Wyves: Medieval Antimatrimonial Propaganda in the Universities,' *Annuale mediaevale* 3 (1962) 5-27

Pratt discusses three of Jankyn's main sources: Jerome, *Epistola adversus Jovinianum;* Theophrastus, *De nuptiis;* and Walter Map, *Dissuasio Valerii ad Ruffinum,* as well as some medieval commentaries on them. For a text of *Adversus Jovinianum* and the work attributed to Theophrastus see **M254** and p. 94. For a text and translation of *Dissuasio Valerii* see **M273**.

CT187

Steele, R. 'Chaucer and the "Almagest",' *Library* ser. 3, 10 (1919) 243-7

Noting that Tyrwhitt, Lounsbury, and Skeat could not find the passages in Ptolemy's *Almagest* quoted in the *Prologue,* Steel draws on an article by Ewald Flügel (*Anglia* 18 [1896] 133-40) to point out that the translation of the *Almagest* by Gerard of Cremona contains a number of gnomic sentences attributed to Ptolemy; among them are the Wife's quotations. For a study of the *Almagest* see Pedersen **B233**. The translation by Gerard of Cremona has not been edited.

CT188

Whiting, Bartlett J. 'The *Wife of Bath's Prologue*' in Bryan and Dempster **CT8**, 207-22

Whiting gives illustrative passages from four medieval antifeminist works used in *WBProl:* Jerome's *Epistola adversus Jovinianum,* Deschamps' *Miroir de mariage,* Walter Map's *Dissuasio Valerii ad Ruffinum,* and Jean de Meun's part of the *Roman de la rose.*

Tale

For the use of Ovid in the digression on Midas, see Hoffman **CT10**, 145-9.

CT189

Eisner, Sigmund. *A Tale of Wonder: A Source Study of 'The Wife of Bath's Tale'* (Wexford, Ire. 1957)

Eisner examines Irish analogues.

CT190

Lowes, John Livingston. 'Chaucer and Dante's *Convivio*,' *MP* 13 (1915-16) 19-33

Lowes compares Dante's discussion of *gentilezza* with Chaucer's discussion of *gentilesse* in *WBT* 1109-76, and concludes that Dante's entire argument is summarized in Chaucer's lines. Lowes also notes allusions to the *Convivio* elsewhere in Chaucer's works. For a text and translation of the *Convivio* see **M208-9**.

CT191

Silverstein, Theodore. 'Wife of Bath and the Rhetoric of Enchantment; or, How to Make a Hero See in the Dark,' *MP* 58 (1960-61) 153-73

Silverstein compares the tale to its analogues, showing how it is constructed to suit the Wife.

CT192

Whiting, Bartlett J. 'The *Wife of Bath's Tale*' in Bryan and Dempster **CT8**, 223-68

Whiting describes *WBT* as 'an *exemplum* which clinches, by an appeal to authority, an argument which in the prologue was largely derived from experience' (p. 223); he prints three medieval sources which combine the two main motifs: the transformation of a loathly lady and the search for the correct answer to a life-or-death question.

Critical Studies

Prologue

The critical studies that deal with the *Prologue* usually also discuss the portrait of the Wife in *GenProl*. See Robertson **CrS66**, 317-51 for the Wife as exegete. See Curry **CrS35**, 91-118 for an account of the Wife based on her horoscope.

CT193

Kernan, Anne. 'The Archwife and the Eunuch,' *ELH* 41 (1974) 1-25

Kernan compares the Wife of Bath and the Pardoner; she examines patristic views of sex within marriage and relates them

to the Wife's discussion.
CT194
Margulies, Cecile Stoller. 'The Marriages and the Wealth of the Wife of Bath,' *MS* 24 (1962) 210-16
Margulies explains how the Wife accumulated wealth through her first three marriages and how she retained control of her property even after she married Jankyn.
CT195
Pratt, Robert A. 'The Development of the Wife of Bath' in *Studies in Medieval Literature in Honor of Professor Albert Croll Baugh*, ed. MacEdward Leach (Philadelphia and London 1961) 45-79
In this influential study, Pratt examines the portrait of the Wife in *GenProl* as well as her *Tale* and *Prologue* in order to show how Chaucer developed her complex character and story.

Tale

CT196
Carruthers, Mary. 'The Wife of Bath and the Painting of Lions,' *PMLA* 94 (1979) 209-22
Arguing that the economic context of Alisoun's experience as a clothier makes her opinions on marital power comprehensible, Carruthers discusses the tale as a parodic rejection of the ideal pictures of genteel marriages painted by the aristocratic writers of medieval manuals of deportment.
CT197
Coffman, George R. 'Chaucer and Courtly Love Once More — The *Wife of Bath's Tale*,' *Speculum* 20 (1945) 43-50
Coffman discusses the incongruity between the tale's courtly setting and the hag's lecture on *gentilesse*.
CT198
Roppolo, Joseph P. 'The Converted Knight in Chaucer's *Wife of Bath's Tale*,' *CE* 12 (1950-51) 263-9
Roppolo shows how the folk-motif of the converted knight is modified to suit the Wife's outlook; he also gives a useful review of scholarship on the *Tale* (as distinct from the *Prologue*).
CT199
Schlauch, Margaret. 'The Marital Dilemma in the *Wife of Bath's*

Tale,' PMLA 61 (1946) 416-30
Schlauch discusses the patristic and late medieval tradition
behind the choice offered to the knight, showing how it unifies
Tale and *Prologue.*
CT200
Slade, Tony. 'Irony in the *Wife of Bath's Tale,' MLR* 64 (1969)
241-7
Slade suggests that the tale sometimes illuminates and sometimes
mocks the Wife's own views.

THE FRIAR'S PROLOGUE AND TALE

Editions

Robinson **M30**, 89-93 (text); 704-6, 892 (notes). Skeat **M31**, IV, 357-
69 (text); V, 322-9 (notes).

CT201
Havely, N.R., ed. *The Friar's, Summoner's and Pardoner's Tales from
'The Canterbury Tales'* (London 1975)
This student's edition has an introduction, glosses at the foot of the
page, and notes.

Sources and Analogues

See Birney **CT206** for Chaucer's adaptations of the folktale.

CT202
Aiken, Pauline. 'Vincent of Beauvais and the Green Yeoman's
Lecture on Demonology,' *SP* 35 (1938) 1-9
Aiken suggests that Chaucer is indebted to Vincent of Beauvais for
his information on demonology. For an edition of the *Speculum
maius* see **M307**.
CT203
Mroczkowski, Przemysław. 'The *Friar's Tale* and its Pulpit Back-
ground' in *English Studies Today: Second Series,* ed. G.A. Bonnard
(Berne 1961) 107-20
Mroczkowski examines the sermon influence on *FrT* and interprets

the tale as an exemplum of greed.

CT204

Nicholson, Peter. 'The Analogues of Chaucer's *Friar's Tale*,' *ELN* 17 (1979) 93-8

Nicholson revises and refines the discussion of analogues in Taylor **CT205**.

CT205

Taylor, Archer. 'The *Friar's Tale*' in Bryan and Dempster **CT8**, 269-74

Taylor prints three exempla as analogues to the tale and discusses variations in medieval and later versions of the story.

Critical Studies

See Beichner **CT174** for the Friar's baiting of the Summoner. See Szittya **CT178** for the relation of *FrT* to *WBT*. See Cawley **CT175** for the connection between the Summoner and the summoner in *FrT*. See Merrill **CT176** and Tupper **CT179** for the theme of wrath. See Richardson **CT36**, 73-85 (repr. in Cawley **CrS6**, 155-65) for the imagery of the hunter and prey.

CT206

Birney, Earle. ' "After his ymage" — The Central Ironies of the *Friar's Tale*,' *MS* 21 (1959) 17-35

Birney gives a close analysis of the various ironies of the tale, and of Chaucer's modifications of the folktale on which it is based.

THE SUMMONER'S PROLOGUE AND TALE

Editions

Robinson **M30**, 93-100 (text); 706-8, 892 (notes). Skeat **M31**, IV, 370-88 (text); V, 330-441 (notes). See Havely **CT201** for a student's edition.

Sources and Analogues

CT207

Hart, Walter Morris. 'The *Summoner's Tale*' in Bryan and

Dempster **CT8**, 275-87
Hart prints the most important analogue to *SumT, Li Dis de le vescie à prestre* of Jacques de Baisieux, and the passages from Seneca's *De ira* in which the exempla on anger appear.
CT208
Pratt, Robert A. 'Albertus Magnus and the Problem of Sound and Odor in the *Summoner's Tale*,' *PQ* 57 (1978) 267-8
Pratt proposes the *Liber de sensu et sensato* of Albertus Magnus as the source for the idea that sound and odour both proceed in a circular and wave-like manner. For a text of the *Liber* see **M222**.

Critical Studies

See Merrill **CT176** and Tupper **CT179** for the theme of anger. See Zietlow **CT180** for the relation between the Summoner and his tale. See Szittya **CT178** for background on antimendicant satire.

CT209
Adams, John F. 'The Structure of Irony in *The Summoner's Tale*,' *Essays in Criticism* 12 (1962) 126-32
Adams discusses the sophistry of Friar John.
CT210
Fleming, John V. 'The Antifraternalism of the *Summoner's Tale*,' *JEGP* 65 (1966) 688-700
Fleming relates *SumT* to other examples of antimendicant literature.
CT211
Levitan, Alan. 'The Parody of Pentecost in Chaucer's *Summoner's Tale*,' *UTQ* 40 (1970-71) 236-46
Levitan shows that the 'departynge' of the fart by means of a cart-wheel is a parody of Pentecost iconography.

Fragment IV
(*ClT, MerchT*)

See **CT165-73**, especially Kaske **CT170**, for parallels between the two tales.

THE CLERK'S PROLOGUE AND TALE

Editions

Robinson **M30**, 101-14 (text); 708-12, 892 (notes). Skeat **M31**, IV, 389-425 (text); V, 342-52 (notes).

CT212
Sisam, Kenneth, ed. *Chaucer: The Clerkes Tale of Oxenford* (Oxford 1923; repr. 1925, 1930)
This is a student's edition with introduction, notes, and glossary.
CT213
Winny, James, ed. *The Clerk's Prologue and Tale* (Cambridge 1966)
This student's edition has an introduction, notes, and glossary.

Sources and Analogues

CT214
Bettridge, William Edwin and Francis Lee Utley. 'New Light on the Origin of the Griselda Story,' *TSLL* 13 (1971-2) 153-208
The authors print and discuss several versions of a folktale analogue closer to *ClT* than any previously suggested.
CT215
Cate, Wirt Armistead. 'The Problem of the Origin of the Griselda Story,' *SP* 29 (1932) 389-405
Cate corrects some of the errors in Griffith **CT217**.
CT216
Craig, Barbara H., ed. *L'Estoire de Griseldis.* University of Kansas Publications, Humanistic Series 31 (Lawrence 1954)
Craig's edition of this analogue, a dramatized French version of Petrarch's tale, has an extensive introduction and bilbliography.
CT217
Griffith, Dudley David. *The Origin of the Griselda Story.* University of Washington Publications in Language and Literature 8, no. 1 (Seattle 1931) 1-120
Griffith suggests that *ClT* ultimately derives from the Cupid-Psyche group of fables; see also Bettridge and Utley **CT214** and Cate **CT215**.

CT218
Kellogg, Alfred L. 'The Evolution of the *Clerk's Tale:* A Study in Connotation' in Kellogg, *Chaucer, Langland, Arthur: Essays in Middle English Literature* (New Brunswick, N.J. 1972) 276-329
Kellogg analyses the pattern of scriptural allusion added to Boccaccio's story by Petrarch and further amplified by Chaucer.
CT219
Severs, J. Burke. 'The *Clerk's Tale*' in Bryan and Dempster **CT8**, 288-332
Severs notes that Chaucer used both Petrarch's Latin and the Old French versions of the Griselda story; Chaucer's version is a paraphrase with significant alterations. Severs prints the text of Petrarch's letter containing the story (*Epistolae seniles* 17, 3) and the Old French *Le Livre Griseldis.* For a translation of Petrarch's letter see French **CrS42**, 291-311.
CT220
_____ *The Literary Relationships of Chaucer's 'Clerkes Tale'* (New Haven 1942)
Severs expands on his discussion in **CT219**, explaining how he determined the two chief sources of the tale and established the texts of both.
CT221
Utley, Francis Lee. 'Five Genres in the *Clerk's Tale,*' *ChauR* 6 (1971-2) 198-228
Utley analyses *ClT* as a story about marriage, a folktale, an exemplum of patience, a realistic narrative, and an allegory of the Blessed Virgin.

Critical Studies

See Muscatine **CrS57**, 190-97 for a defence of *ClT* as a religious tale symbolizing the necessity for absolute obedience to God; see Salter **CT122**, 37-65 for the contradiction between the harsh religious lesson of the tale and the Clerk's own humane outlook.

CT222
Cunningham, J.V. 'Ideal Fiction: The *Clerk's Tale,*' *Shenandoah: The Washington and Lee University Review* 19 (1968) 38-41

Cunningham defends *ClT* as idealized fiction, a story which the audience does not expect to be realistic.

CT223

Grennen, Joseph E. 'Science and Sensibility in Chaucer's Clerk,' *ChauR* 6 (1971-2) 81-93

Grennen suggests that for the Clerk *ClT* is merely an exercise in logic; the Clerk posits the perfectly patient woman and the result is Griselda.

CT224

Hawkins, Harriett. 'The Victim's Side: Chaucer's *Clerk's Tale* and Webster's *Duchess of Malfi*,' *Signs* 1 (1975) 339-61; repr. in Hawkins, *Poetic Freedom and Poetic Truth* (Oxford 1976) 26-54

Hawkins gives a detailed and sensitive examination of the poetic injustice of Griselda's ordeal.

CT225

McCall, John P. 'The *Clerk's Tale* and the Theme of Obedience,' *MLQ* 27 (1966) 260-69

McCall suggests that Griselda's behaviour reflects both the obedience owed by a religious to his superior and the ideal Christian's complete submission of his will to God's.

CT226

McNamara, John. 'Chaucer's Use of the Epistle of St. James in the *Clerk's Tale*,' *ChauR* (1972-3) 184-93

McNamara argues that the theme of *ClT* is patience as described in the Letter of James, especially 1:2-4.

CT227

Morse, J. Mitchell. 'The Philosophy of the Clerk of Oxenford,' *MLQ* 19 (1958) 3-20

Morse suggests that the philosophical background of the poem is the realist-nominalist controversy, and that the Clerk is a nominalist attempting to raise questions about freedom and authority in his audience.

CT228

Sledd, James. 'The *Clerk's Tale:* The Monsters and the Critics,' *MP* 51 (1953-4) 73-82; repr. in Schoeck and Taylor **CrS15**, I, 160-74 and in Wagenknecht **CrS19**, 226-39

Sledd reviews criticism on the tale and argues that Chaucer's narrative skill makes it effective both as a story and as an exemplum of patience.

CT229
Steinmetz, David C. 'Late Medieval Nominalism and the *Clerk's Tale*,' *ChauR* 12 (1977-8) 38-54
Steinmetz suggests that the Clerk's story allegorizes the nominalist doctrine of justification.

THE MERCHANT'S PROLOGUE AND TALE

Editions

Robinson **M30**, 115-27 (text); 713-16, 893-4 (notes). Skeat **M31**, IV, 426-60 (text); V, 353-69 (notes).

CT230
Hussey, Maurice, ed. *The Merchant's Prologue and Tale* (Cambridge 1966)
This student's edition has an introduction, notes, and glossary.

Sources and Analogues

See Dempster **CT8**, 46-58 and Lowes **M154** for the use of Deschamps' *Miroir de mariage;* for the text see **M153**. See Hoffman **CT10** for Chaucer's use of Ovid. See Economou **CT241** for a borrowing from the *Roman de la rose.*

CT231
Bassan, Maurice. 'Chaucer's "cursed monk," Constantinus Africanus,' *MS* 24 (1962) 127-40
Bassan gives background on Constantinus, the author of *De coitu,* who is mentioned in the tale (line 1810).
CT232
Dempster, Germaine. 'The *Merchant's Tale*' in Bryan and Dempster **CT8**, 333-56
Dempster prints passages from the probable main source, Deschamps' *Miroir de mariage,* as well as selections from Boccaccio's *Ameto,* and folktales, as parallels to three elements in *MerchT:* the discussion of marriage, the relationship between an old husband and a young wife, and the pear-tree episode.

CT233
Donovan, Mortimer J. 'The Image of Pluto and Proserpine in the *Merchant's Tale*,' *PQ* 36 (1957) 49-60
Donovan shows that Chaucer borrowed from Claudian's *De raptu Proserpinae* as well as from the *Miroir de mariage* for the story of Pluto and Proserpina. For a text and translation of *De raptu* see **M248**.

CT234
McGalliard, John C. 'Chaucer's *Merchant's Tale* and Deschamps' *Miroir de mariage*, *PQ* 25 (1946) 193-220
McGalliard gives a detailed comparison of Chaucer's tale and its source in Deschamps.

CT235
Wentersdorf, Karl P. 'Chaucer's *Merchant's Tale* and its Irish Analogues,' *SP* 63 (1966) 604-29
Attacking the theory that the lost second source of *MerchT* was a French fabliau, Wentersdorf discusses Irish analogues which seem closer to *MerchT* than the continental ones usually cited.

Critical Studies

See Jordan **CrS46**, 132-51 for an analysis of the non-dramatic design of the tale.

CT236
Bloomfield, Morton W. *'The Merchant's Tale:* A Tragicomedy of the Neglect of Counsel — The Limits of Art' in *Medieval and Renaissance Studies: Proceedings of the Southeastern Institute of Medieval and Renaissance Studies, Summer 1975,* ed. Siegfried Wenzel. Medieval and Renaissance Series 7 (Chapel Hill 1978) 37-50
Bloomfield suggests that the tale is about limits and the tragi-comic implications of their transgression.

CT237
Brown, Emerson, Jr. 'Biblical Women in the *Merchant's Tale:* Feminism, Antifeminism, and Beyond,' *Viator* 5 (1974) 387-412
Brown shows how the Merchant alters the traditional descriptions of certain biblical women to suit his view of woman as deceitful.

CT238
_____ *'Hortus inconclusus:* The Significance of Priapus and

Pyramus and Thisbe in the *Merchant's Tale*,' *ChauR* (1970-71) 31-40
Brown shows that the passing references to Priapus, Pyramus, and
Thisbe fit into the overall design of the tale.

CT239
Burnley, J.D. 'The Morality of *The Merchant's Tale*,' *Yearbook of
English Studies* 6 (1976) 16-25
Burnley traces the pattern of biblical and liturgical allusions in the
poem.

CT240
Burrow, J.A. 'Irony in the *Merchant's Tale*,' *Anglia* 75 (1957) 199-208
Burrow shows that *MerchT* owes as much to allegory as to fabliau,
and suggests that the key to the story is 'fantasye.' He sees January's
delusions as common to all mankind, and the irony of the tale as
gentle.

CT241
Economou, George D. 'Januarie's Sin against Nature: The
Merchant's Tale and the *Roman de la rose*,' *Comparative Literature*
17 (1965) 251-7
Economou shows how the mirror image borrowed from the *Roman*
functions in *MerchT*.

CT242
McGalliard, John C. 'Chaucerian Comedy: *The Merchant's Tale*,
Jonson, and Molière,' *PQ* 25 (1946) 343-70
McGalliard suggests that the plot of *MerchT* derives ultimately
from the characterization, and that in this respect Chaucer
anticipates Jonson and Molière; he sees *MerchT* as a comedy both
of manners and of character.

CT243
Olson, Paul A. 'Chaucer's Merchant and January's "hevene in erthe
heere",' *ELH* 28 (1961) 203-14
Olson notes that, according to medieval teaching, the desire to
possess any physical object is avarice; therefore, the Merchant
and January are both avaricious, one for money and the other for
May.

CT244
_____ 'The Merchant's Lombard Knight,' *TSLL* 3 (1961-2) 259-63
Olson discusses the rivalry between English and Lombard
merchants and the bad reputation of the Lombards in England.

CT245
Otten, Charlotte F. 'Proserpine: *Liberatrix suae gentis*,' *ChauR* 5

(1970-71) 277-87

Otten shows how the references to Proserpine and to the biblical women discussed in lines 1362-74 assist the comic development of the tale.

CT246

Schlauch, Margaret. 'Chaucer's *Merchant's Tale* and Courtly Love,' *ELH* 4 (1937) 201-12

Schlauch sees a continuing change in Chaucer's attitude towards courtly love, from admiring acceptance in the early poems to bitter satire in *MerchT*.

CT247

Sedgewick, G.G. 'The Structure of *The Merchant's Tale*,' *UTQ* 17 (1947-8) 337-45

Sedgewick notes the irony directed at January by the narrator and at the narrator by Chaucer the poet.

CT248

Tatlock, J.S.P. 'Chaucer's *Merchant's Tale*,' *MP* 33 (1935-6) 367-81

Tatlock emphasizes the tale's cynical bitterness.

CT249

Wentersdorf, Karl P. 'Theme and Structure in *The Merchant's Tale*: The Function of the Pluto Incident,' *PMLA* 80 (1965) 522-7

Wentersdorf shows that the Pluto incident reinforces the tale's double moral: that youth and age should not marry, and that husband and wife bear equal responsibility in marriage.

CT250

White, Gertrude M. ' "Hoolynesse or dotage": The Merchant's January,' *PQ* 44 (1965) 397-404

White suggests that January's character and delusions are the centre of interest, and that he is to be both pitied and condemned.

Fragment V
(*SqT, FranklT*)

CRITICAL STUDIES

CT251

Berger, Harry, Jr. 'The F-Fragment of the *Canterbury Tales*,' *ChauR* 1 (1966-7) 88-102, 135-56

Berger discusses the relation between the Squire and the Franklin

and their tales; he sees *FranklT* as a mature and controlled version
of the type of romantic narrative represented by *SqT.*
CT252
Duncan, Charles F., Jr. ' "Straw for your gentilesse": The Gentle
Franklin's Interruption of the Squire,' *ChauR* 5 (1970-71) 161-4
Duncan discusses the dramatic quality of the Franklin's
interruption, and suggests that the Franklin is, apart from the
Knight, the only pilgrim high-ranking enough to interrupt the
Squire without rudeness.

THE SQUIRE'S INTRODUCTION AND TALE

Editions

Robinson **M30**, 128-35 (text); 717-21, 894 (notes). Skeat **M31**, IV,
461-79 (text); V, 370-87 (notes).

CT253
Bethurum, Dorothy, ed. *Chaucer: The Squire's Tale* (Oxford 1965)
This student's edition has an introduction, notes, glossary, and a
brief account of Chaucer's life and language.

Sources and Analogues

CT254
Jones, H.S.V. 'The *Squire's Tale*' in Bryan and Dempster **CT8**,
357-76
Noting that no direct source of *SqT* is known, Jones gives, as
analogues to certain features of the poem, sections from the letter of
Prester John (in Latin and German), excerpts from the French
romance of *Cléomadès*, and Hindu and Arabic analogues to the
episode of Canacee and the falcon.
CT255
Stillwell, Gardiner, 'Chaucer in Tartary,' *RES* 24 (1948) 177-88
Stillwell examines characteristically Chaucerian adaptations of the
romantic material of *SqT.*
CT256
Whiting, B.J. 'Gawain: His Reputation, his Courtesy, and his
Appearance in Chaucer's *Squire's Tale,*' *MS* 9 (1947) 189-234

In Part V (pp. 231-4), Whiting argues that Chaucer probably read *Sir Gawain and the Green Knight* and drew on it for the opening of *SqT* and the reference to Gawain.

Critical Studies

CT257
Braddy, Haldeen. 'The Genre of Chaucer's *Squire's Tale*,' *JEGP* 41 (1942) 279-90; repr. in Braddy, *Geoffrey Chaucer: Literary and Historical Studies* (Port Washington, N.Y. 1971) 85-95
Braddy suggests that Canacee's love-story was intended as the frame for a narrative like the *Thousand and One Nights.*
CT258
Göller, Karl Heinz. 'Chaucers *Squire's Tale:* "The knotte of the tale" ' in Esch **CrS9**, 163-88
Concentrating on the falcon episode, Göller shows how Chaucer mixes passages of good poetry with inept rhetoric that makes the Squire look silly. This article is in German.
CT259
Kahrl, Stanley J. 'Chaucer's *Squire's Tale* and the Decline of Chivalry,' *ChauR* 7 (1972-3) 194-209
Analysing tone and rhetoric, Kahrl suggests that *SqT* presents the 'impulse towards exoticism and disorder' characteristic of late medieval chivalry, in contrast to the celebration of order that characterizes the presentation of chivalry in *KnT*. See Cowgill **CT109** and Robertson **CT121**.
CT260
McCall, John P. 'The Squire in Wonderland,' *ChauR* 1 (1966-7) 103-9
McCall suggests that *SqT* is designed as an example of rhetorical ineptitude and that it follows a pattern of elaborate inconsequence, incongruity, and downright bathos.
CT261
Neville, Marie. 'The Function of the *Squire's Tale* in the Canterbury Scheme,' *JEGP* 50 (1951) 167-79
Neville discusses the social context of *SqT* and the tale's place in the plan of *CT*.
CT262
Pearsall, D.A. 'The Squire as Story-Teller,' *UTQ* 34 (1964-5) 82-92

Pearsall examines the Squire's language, especially his modest disclaimers of rhetorical ability, and shows that he is neither modest nor a good storyteller.

THE FRANKLIN'S PROLOGUE AND TALE

Editions

Robinson **M30**, 135-44 (text); 721-6, 894 (notes). Skeat **M31**, IV, 482-508 (text); V, 387-99 (notes).

CT263
Hodgson, Phyllis, ed. *Chaucer: The Franklin's Tale* (London 1960)
This student's edition has an introduction, notes, glossary, and several appendices, including one on astronomy, astrology, and magic.
CT264
Spearing, A.C., ed. *The Franklin's Prologue and Tale* (London 1966)
This student's edition has an introduction, notes, and glossary.

Sources and Analogues

CT265
Dempster, Germaine and J.S.P. Tatlock. 'The *Franklin's Tale*' in Bryan and Dempster **CT8**, 377-97
Dempster and Tatlock print the main source, Questione IV of Boccaccio's *Il filocolo,* as well as illustrative excerpts from selected Breton lays and short extracts from Geoffrey of Monmouth's *Historia regum Britanniae* and Jerome's *Epistola adversus Jovinianum.* For a full text of the *Filocolo* see **M195**.
CT266
Donovan, Mortimer J. 'The *Anticlaudian* and Three Passages in the *Franklin's Tale*,' JEGP 56 (1957) 52-9
Donovan gives analogues to lines 723-5, 829-34, and 1614.
CT267
_____ 'Chaucer and the *Franklin's Tale*' in Donovan, *The Breton Lay: A Guide to Varieties* (Notre Dame, Ind. and London 1969) 173-89

Donovan discusses Chaucer's use of the traditions of the Breton lay in *FranklT* and suggests that for Chaucer the essence of the genre was the idealism associated with *courtoisie* in some of the lays.
CT268
Loomis, Laura Hibbard. 'Chaucer and the Breton Lays of the Auchinleck MS,' *SP* 38 (1941) 14-33
Loomis discusses some lays that Chaucer could have known and suggests that the description of a Breton lay in *CT* V.709-13 is a summary of the introduction on Breton lays found in the Auchinleck MS (Edinburgh, National Library, Advocates MS. 19.2.1). See also Loomis **CT330**.
CT269
Lowes, John Livingston. 'The *Franklin's Tale,* the *Teseide,* and the *Filocolo,*' *MP* 15 (1917-18) 689-728
Lowes examines the relations among the texts and offers some general observations on Chaucer's characteristic handling of his sources.
CT270
Morgan, Gerald. 'A Defence of Dorigen's Complaint,' *MÆ* 46 (1977) 77-97
Morgan gives close analysis of the artistic adaptation of the exempla taken from Jerome's *Epistola adversus Jovinianum.* For a text of the *Epistola* see **M254**.
CT271
Reisner, Thomas A. and Mary Ellen Reisner. 'A British Analogue for the Rock-Motif in the *Franklin's Tale,*' *SP* 76 (1979) 1-12
The authors propose as an analogue one of the best-known miracles of St. Balred, who, out of pity for sailors, moved a dangerous rock out of the Firth of Forth.
CT272
Skeat, Walter W. 'Chaucer's Two Allusions to Persius,' *Notes and Queries* ser. 10, 12 (1909) 6
Skeat points out parallels to the *Satires* of Persius in the *Franklin's Prologue.*

Critical Studies

See Beidler **CT281** for a comparison with *PhysT,* and Berger **CT251** for *FranklT* as a mature version of *SqT.* See Lumiansky

CT25, 349-56 for the tension between marriage and courtly love in the tale and the contradictory character of the teller. For discussion of *FranklT* as part of the 'Marriage Group' see CT165-73. See Wood CrS73, 245-58 for an astrological explanation of the magic in *FranklT.*

CT273
Baker, Donald C. 'A Crux in Chaucer's *Franklin's Tale:* Dorigen's Complaint,' *JEGP* 60 (1961) 56-64
Baker suggests that the apparently confused ordering of exempla in Dorigen's complaint is intended to reveal her state of mind and explain her decision.

CT274
Burlin, Robert B. 'The Art of Chaucer's Franklin,' *Neophilologus* 51 (1967) 55-73
Burlin suggests that the Franklin is not quite at home with the easy *gentilesse* he affects and that he praises Dorigen, who is dissatisified with reality, because he too is dissatisfied.

CT275
David, Alfred. 'Sentimental Comedy in the *Franklin's Tale,*' *Annuale mediaevale* 6 (1965) 19-27
David sees the Franklin as a bourgeois sentimentalist.

CT276
Gaylord, Alan T. 'The Promises in *The Franklin's Tale,*' *ELH* 31 (1964) 331-65
Gaylord argues that *FranklT* reveals the Franklin's imperfect grasp of *gentilesse.*

CT277
Golding, M.R. 'The Importance of Keeping "trouthe" in *The Franklin's Tale,*' *MAE* 39 (1970) 306-12
Golding argues that the ending of the tale validates not only the individual virtue of keeping *trouthe,* but also the social virtue of keeping mutual *trouthe* as the basis of marriage.

CT278
Gray, Paul Edward. 'Synthesis and the Double Standard in the *Franklin's Tale,*' *TSLL* 7 (1965-6) 213-24
Gray argues that *FranklT* undercuts the Franklin's ideal of marriage by revealing that its apparently successful synthesis of courtly love and Christian marriage is a dichotomy.

CT279
Tatlock, John Strong Perry. 'Astrology and Magic in Chaucer's *Franklin's Tale*' in *Anniversary Papers by Colleagues and Pupils of George Lyman Kittredge* [no ed.] (Boston and London 1913) 339-50
Tatlock demonstrates that the clerk of *FranklT* shows familiarity with medieval astrology and magic.

Fragment VI
(*PhysT, PardT*)

CRITICAL STUDIES

CT280
Barney, Stephen A. 'An Evaluation of the *Pardoner's Tale*' in Faulkner **CT306**, 83-95
Barney suggests that the Pardoner appropriates for his own superbly-told tale certain themes and elements used very ineptly in *PhysT*.

CT281
Beidler, Peter G. 'The Pairing of the *Franklin's Tale* and the *Physician's Tale*,' *ChauR* 3 (1968-9) 275-9
Beidler argues that FragVI follows FragV because *PhysT* is designed as a contrast to *FranklT*; it is a story about a heroine who is strong where Dorigen is weak.

CT282
Hanson, Thomas B. 'Chaucer's Physician as Storyteller and Moralizer,' *ChauR* 7 (1972-3) 132-9
Hanson argues that *PhysT* is the work of a man who does not understand his own material, and that the tale is linked to *PardT* through the words of the Host, who also misunderstands it.

THE PHYSICIAN'S TALE

Editions

Robinson **M30**, 145-7 (text); 726-8, 894 (notes). Skeat **M31**, IV, 290-98 (text); V, 290-64 (notes).

Sources and Analogues

CT283

Lancashire, Anne. 'Chaucer and the Sacrifice of Isaac,' *ChauR* 9 (1974-5) 320-26

Lancashire suggests that Chaucer drew on Genesis and on medieval dramatic accounts of the sacrifice of Isaac for the death of Virginia.

CT284

Shannon, Edgar F. 'The *Physician's Tale*' in Bryan and Dempster **CT8,** 398-408

Shannon discusses the question of what sources, other than the *Roman de la rose* and Livy, Chaucer used for the tale; he prints selections from Livy, the brief version of the story from the *Roman,* and portions of the *De virginibus* of St. Ambrose. On the complex issue of the sources of *PhysT* see Livy **M268** and the comments there.

CT285

Waller, Martha S. 'The *Physician's Tale:* Geoffrey Chaucer and Fray Juan García de Castrojeriz,' *Speculum* 51 (1976) 292-306

Waller points out that nearly all the features of *PhysT* not found in Livy or the *Roman de la rose* appear in the *Regimiento de príncipes* of García de Castrojeriz, and she suggests that Chaucer knew it.

CT286

Young, Karl. 'The Maidenly Virtues of Chaucer's Virginia,' *Speculum* 16 (1941) 340-49

Young gives a convincing argument for the *De eruditione filiorum nobilium* of Vincent of Beauvais as the source for the description of the virtues of Virginia, *PhysT* 35-120. For an edition of the work see **M308**.

Critical Studies

See Ussery **CT89,** 119-42 for the relation of the teller and his tale.

CT287

Hoffman, Richard L. 'Jephthah's Daughter and Chaucer's Virginia,' *ChauR* 2 (1967-8) 20-31

Hoffman shows, with reference to medieval biblical commentaries, that the Physician did not really understand the story of Jephthah, to which he alludes in his tale.

CT288
Longsworth, Robert. 'The Doctor's Dilemma: A Comic View of the
Physician's Tale,' *Criticism* 13 (1971) 223-33
Longsworth suggests that *PhysT* is well suited to its unimaginative
teller; its misunderstood allusions, factual discrepancies, and
conflicting moral advice undercut the Physician's own view of his
tale.
CT289
Middleton, Anne. 'The *Physician's Tale* and Love's Martyrs:
"Ensamples mo than ten" as a Method in the *Canterbury Tales,*'
ChauR 8 (1973-4) 9-32
Middleton suggests that *PhysT* displays, in miniature, the moral
complexity of *CT* as a whole; she argues that Chaucer questions the
validity of Virginius' decision to kill his daughter, while his sources
do not.
CT290
Ramsey, Lee C. ' "The sentence of it sooth is": Chaucer's
Physician's Tale,' *ChauR* (1971-2) 185-97
Ramsey sees the tale as a story about injustice in the broadest
sense; the moral is intentionally false, and the meaning of the tale
lies in the sense of injustice thus aroused.

THE PARDONER'S INTRODUCTION, PROLOGUE, AND TALE

Editions

Robinson **M30**, 148-55 (text); 728-32, 894 (notes). Skeat **M31**, IV
301-19 (text); V, 269-90 (notes). See Havely **CT201** for a student's
edition.

CT291
Brown, Carleton, ed. *Chaucer: The Pardoner's Tale* (Oxford 1935,
many reprints)
Brown gives Skeat's text, with an introduction and notes. He
conjectures that *PardT* was originally a sermon, intended for the
Parson, on the sins of the tavern.
CT292
Coghill, Nevill and Christopher Tolkien, eds. *The Pardoner's Tale*

(London 1958, many reprints)
This student's edition has an introduction and notes.
CT293
Spearing, A.C., ed. *The Pardoner's Prologue and Tale* (Cambridge 1965)
This student's edition includes an introduction, notes, and glossary.

Sources and Analogues

Prologue

CT294
Dempster, Germaine. 'The *Pardoner's Prologue*' in Bryan and Dempster **CT8**, 409-14
Dempster compares the *Prologue* to the speeches of Faux-Semblant in the *Roman de la rose,* and prints three early analogues.
CT295
Patterson, Lee W. 'Chaucerian Confession: Penitential Literature and the Pardoner,' *Medievalia et humanistica* n.s. 7 (1976) 153-73
Patterson shows that themes from penitential literature pervade both *Prologue* and *Tale*.

Tale

See Lowes **M155**, 113-17 for the oaths in *PardT*.

CT296
Bushnell, Nelson Sherwin. 'The Wandering Jew and *The Pardoner's Tale*,' *SP* 28 (1931) 450-60
Bushnell discusses the origins of the legend of the Wandering Jew and compares Chaucer's Old Man to 13th-century descriptions of the legendary figure.
CT297
Kittredge, George Lyman. 'Chaucer and Maximianus,' *American Journal of Philology* 9 (1888) 84-5
Kittredge notes similarities between the speech of the Old Man and the first of the six elegies of Maximianus on impotent old age. For an edition, see E. Baehrens, *Poetae Latini minores* vol. V

(Leipzig 1883) 313-48.
CT298
Tupper, Frederick. 'The *Pardoner's Tale*' in Bryan and Dempster
CT8, 415-38
Noting that no direct source is known, Tupper prints excerpts
from numerous analogues in novelle, exempla, and plays.

Critical Studies

See Miller **CT86** for the theme of the scriptural eunuch and its
significance for the tale. See Kittredge **CrS50**, 211-18 for an
influential early interpretation.

Prologue

CT299
Beichner, Paul E., CSC. 'Chaucer's Pardoner as Entertainer,' *MS*
25 (1963) 160-72
Beichner argues that the Pardoner is trying to entertain the
pilgrims by speaking humorously, though truthfully, about his
dishonest practices.
CT300
Halverson, John. 'Chaucer's Pardoner and the Progress of
Criticism,' *ChauR* 4 (1970-71) 184-202
Halverson surveys criticism from 1940-69. See **CT301** for a
review of earlier criticism.
CT301
Sedgewick, G.G. 'The Progress of Chaucer's Pardoner, 1880-
1940,' *MLQ* 1 (1940) 431-58
Sedgewick gives a historical survey of criticism, rejects
Kittredge's analysis of the Pardoner's benediction, and suggests
that the Pardoner is portrayed as tormented by his inability to
resist evil. For a survey of later criticism see Halverson **CT300**.
CT302
Steadman, John M. 'Chaucer's Pardoner and the *thesaurus
meritorium,*' *ELN* 3 (1965-6) 4-7
Steadman notes that the irony of the tale is heightened by the
nature of the Pardoner's occupation: the man who makes a living
selling indulgences, which derive from the theory of the *thesaurus*

meritorium, tells a tale about earthly treasure.

Tale

See Barney **CT280** for the Pardoner's use of themes from *PhysT.*

CT303
Adelman, Janet. ' "That we may leere som wit",' in Faulkner
CT306, 96-106
Adelman suggests that the *Tale* is a parody in that its elements
are 'literal versions of spiritual facts': the man named Death, the
false Trinity of the three *riotours*, and so on.

CT304
David, Alfred. 'Criticism and the Old Man in Chaucer's
Pardoner's Tale,' *CE* 27 (1965-6) 39-44
David analyses the Old Man as a many-faceted symbol, and
provides a useful review of criticism on him.

CT305
Dean, Christopher. 'Salvation, Damnation, and the Role of the
Old Man in the *Pardoner's Tale*,' *ChauR* 3 (1968-9) 44-9
Dean shows that the Old Man is depicted as the opposite of the
three revellers and suggests that he represents the mercy and
justice of God.

CT306
Faulkner, Dewey R., ed. *Twentieth-Century Interpretations of the
'Pardoner's Tale': A Collection of Critical Essays* (Englewood
Cliffs, N.J. 1973)
This collection includes modern critical essays and brief extracts
from earlier, influential interpretations, such as Kittredge **CrS50**,
211-18.

CT307
Steadman, John M. 'Old Age and *contemptus mundi* in
The Pardoner's Tale,' *MÆ* 33 (1964) 121-30; repr. in
Faulkner **CT306**, 70-82
Steadman argues, citing analogues, that the Old Man represents
old age and is also associated with wisdom; as a figure of
wisdom, he foresees the consequences of touching the gold,
avoids it, and warns the revellers against it.

Fragment VII
(*ShipT, PrT, Thop, Mel, MkT, NPT*)

CRITICAL STUDIES

CT308
Gaylord, Alan T. '*Sentence* and *solaas* in Fragment VII of the
Canterbury Tales: Harry Bailly as Horseback Editor,' *PMLA* 82
(1967) 226-35
Gaylord suggests that the tales of FragVII, including *Thop,* are
linked by the thematic significance of the terms *sentence* and *solaas,*
especially as used by the Host.

CT309
Hemingway, Samuel B. 'Chaucer's Monk and Nun's Priest,' *MLN*
31 (1916) 479-83
Hemingway suggests that Chauntecleer's pomposity and the moral
stories he tells are meant to remind the reader of the Monk.

CT310
Strange, William C. 'The *Monk's Tale:* A Generous View,' *ChauR* 1
(1966-7) 167-80
Strange suggests that the Monk's series of tragedies reflect a
number of different views of Fortune; he also discusses the connection between *MkT* and *NPT.*

CT311
Tupper, Frederick. 'The Bearings of the *Shipman's Prologue,*' *JEGP*
33 (1934) 352-72
Tupper argues that the endlink of *MLT* is the prologue to *ShipT*
and that FragVII was designed to follow FragII. See Furnivall **CT6**
and Keiser **CT316**.

CT312
Watson, Charles S. 'The Relationship of the *Monk's Tale* and the
Nun's Priest's Tale,' *Studies in Short Fiction* 1 (1963-4) 277-88
Watson shows how the two tales work together; he also discusses
the role of *NPT* in *CT* as a whole.

THE SHIPMAN'S TALE

Editions

Robinson **M30**, 156-60 (text); 732-4, 895 (notes). Skeat **M31**, IV, 165-79 (text); V, 165-72 (notes).

Sources and Analogues

CT313
Copland, Murray. 'The *Shipman's Tale:* Chaucer and Boccaccio,' *MÆE* 35 (1966) 11-28
Copland compares *ShipT* to *Decameron* 8, 1 and 2; he discusses the importance of the narrator and interprets the tale as a satire on the effects of commercial success.
CT314
Spargo, John Webster. 'The *Shipman's Tale*' in Bryan and Dempster **CT8**, 439-46
Noting that the actual source of *ShipT* is not known, Spargo argues that it is a fabliau; he prints the closest analogues, *Decameron* 8, 1, and Sercambi's *Novella* 19, along with an outline of the tale-type.
CT315
_____ *Chaucer's 'Shipman's Tale': The Lover's Gift Regained.* Folk-lore Fellows' Communications no. 91 (Helsinki 1930)
This is the basic study of the analogues of *ShipT*.

Critical Studies

See also Copland **CT313**; see Richardson **CT36**, 100-22 for a study of image clusters in the tale.

CT316
Keiser, George R. 'Language and Meaning in Chaucer's *Shipman's Tale*,' *ChauR* 12 (1977-8) 147-61
Keiser examines the characters' use of language, especially of oaths, and shows that it is similar to the language of the Man-of-Law's Endlink. He therefore argues for the 'Bradshaw shift'; see Furnivall **CT6** and Tupper **CT311**.
CT317
Lawrence, William W. 'Chaucer's *Shipman's Tale*,' *Speculum* 33 (1958) 56-68
Lawrence suggests, following earlier critics, that the tale was originally intended for the Wife of Bath; he concludes that Chaucer

changed his mind, but left the inconsistencies for future revision.
CT318
Silverman, Albert H. 'Sex and Money in Chaucer's *Shipman's Tale*,'
PQ 32 (1953) 329-36
Starting with the pun on 'paye' in line 424, Silverman traces the
development of the theme of the commercialization of marriage.
See Richardson **CT36**, 100-22.
CT319
Sullivan, Hazel. 'A Chaucerian Puzzle, Part I: The Puzzle' in *A
Chaucerian Puzzle and Other Medieval Essays*, ed. Natalie Grimes
Lawrence and Jack A. Reynolds. University of Miami Publications
in English and American Literature 5 (Coral Gables, Fla. 1961) 1-12
Sullivan argues, against the prevailing critical view, that *ShipT* was
not originally intended for the Wife of Bath. She suggests that the
problem of the feminine pronouns at the tale's beginning disappears
if lines 5-19 are inserted after 172 as part of the merchant's wife's
speech.

THE PRIORESS'S PROLOGUE AND TALE

Editions

Robinson **M30**, 161-4 (text); 734-6, 895 (notes). Skeat **M31**, IV, 180-
88 (text); V, 173-81 (notes).

CT320
Winny, James, ed. *The Prioress' Prologue and Tale* (Cambridge 1975)
This student's edition has an introduction, notes, and glossary.
CT321
Winstanley, Lilian, ed. *Chaucer: The Prioress's Tale, The Tale of Sir
Thopas* (Cambridge 1922)
This is a student's edition with introduction, notes, and glossary.

Sources and Analogues

CT322
Brown, Carleton. *A Study of the Miracle of Our Lady Told by
Chaucer's Prioress*. Chaucer Society 2nd ser. 45 (London 1910)

Brown analyses the miracle and prints texts of its known English
analogues.
CT323
_____ 'The *Prioress's Tale*' in Bryan and Dempster **CT8**, 447-85
Brown lists all known MSS of the miracle and discusses the relation-
ships among its three versions, Groups A, B, and C; he shows that
Chaucer's source must have belonged to Group C and prints all
known C versions, noting that Chaucer's immediate source is
unknown.
CT324
Wenk, J.C. 'On the Sources of *The Prioress's Tale*,' *MS* 17 (1955)
214-19
Wenk suggests that Chaucer was inspired by the liturgy of the Feast
of the Holy Innocents, and compares *PrT* to *ParsT* and *SecNT*.

Critical Studies

CT325
Beichner, Paul E., CSC. 'The Grain of Paradise,' *Speculum* 36 (1961)
302-7
Beichner suggests that the *greyn* placed on the boy's tongue is the
spice called 'grain of paradise,' which would be symbolically
appropriate.
CT326
Frank, Hardy Long. 'Chaucer's Prioress and the Blessed Virgin,'
ChauR 13 (1978-9) 346-62
Drawing on the literature of devotion to the Virgin, Frank argues
that the Prioress closely resembles the image of Mary in this
tradition in being stereotypically feminine, whimsical, capricious,
emotional, irrational, and unconventional; he maintains that the
anti-Semitism of *PrT* is also a feature of some Marian legends.
CT327
Ridley, Florence H. *The Prioress and the Critics.* University of
California English Studies 30 (Berkeley and Los Angeles 1965)
In this brief and balanced discussion, Ridley re-examines the
evidence for anti-Semitic feeling in Chaucer's day and concludes
that the anti-Semitism of *PrT* reflects the view common in the
period, and that the Prioress herself is depicted as a good-hearted
but naïve woman. See Schoeck **CT329**.

CT328
Russell, G.H. 'Chaucer: The *Prioress's Tale*' in *Medieval Literature and Civilization: Studies in Memory of G.N. Garmonsway,* ed. D.A. Pearsall and R.A. Waldron (London 1969) 211-27
Russell sees the tale as a genuine, sensitive, and carefully-wrought expression of devotion.

CT329
Schoeck, Richard J. 'Chaucer's Prioress: Mercy and Tender Heart,' *The Bridge: A Yearbook of Judaeo-Christian Studies* [Seton Hall University] 2 (1956) 239-55; rev. and repr. in Schoeck and Taylor **CrS15**, I, 245-58
Arguing that Chaucer is condemning the Prioress's anti-Semitism, Schoeck cites contemporary sources, including papal letters, which show that anti-Semitism was not approved officially by the Church.

THE PROLOGUE AND TALE OF SIR THOPAS

Editions

Robinson **M30**, 164-7 (text); 736-40, 895 (notes). Skeat **M31**, IV, 189-96 (text); V, 182-200 (notes). See Winstanley **CT321** for a student's edition.

Sources and Analogues

CT330
Loomis, Laura Hibbard. 'Chaucer and the Auchinleck MS: *Thopas* and *Guy of Warwick*' in *Essays and Studies in Honor of Carleton Brown* [no ed.] (New York 1940) 111-28
On the basis of close textual comparison Loomis argues that Chaucer probably had the Auchinleck MS copy (Edinburgh, National Library, Advocates MS. 19.2.1) of *Guy of Warwick* in hand when he composed *Thop.* See also Loomis **CT268**.

CT331
_____ '*Sir Thopas*' in Bryan and Dempster **CT8**, 486-559
Loomis gives a brief introduction to the problem of sources and provides over sixty pages of extracts from romance analogues to the tale, for such motifs as 'The Hero Rides' and 'The Hero in Love.'

Critical Studies

See Gaylord **CT308** for the place of *Thop* in FragVII; see Winstanley **CT321**, lxviii-lxxvii for the theory that *Thop* is an attack on Flemish knighthood.

CT332
Brewer, Derek.'The Arming of the Warrior in European Literature and Chaucer' in Vasta and Thundy **CrS18**, 221-43
Brewer surveys the long tradition of the arming topos and argues that in mocking this topos Chaucer is also mocking the whole tradition of formal aggrandizement of fighting.
CT333
Burrow, J.A. *'Sir Thopas:* An Agony in Three Fits,' *RES* n.s. 22 (1971) 54-8
Burrow suggests, with supporting MS evidence, that the tale is divided into three fits (712-832, 833-90, and 891-918), according to a progressive diminution of material.
CT334
Camden, Carroll, Jr. 'The Physiognomy of Thopas,' *RES* 11 (1935) 326-30
Camden compares the description of Thopas with extracts from medieval physiognomic lore and argues that he is portrayed as a coward.
CT335
Conley, John. 'The Peculiar Name *Thopas,' SP* 73 (1976) 42-61
Conley gives information on the medieval symbolism of the topaz, suggesting that the use of Thopas as a name is probably meant to reflect the primary meaning, 'brightest of all gems.'
CT336
Gaylord, Alan T. 'Chaucer's Dainty "dogerel": The "elvyssh" Prosody of *Sir Thopas,' Studies in the Age of Chaucer* 1 (1979) 83-104
Pointing out that the first recorded use of the term *doggerel* is Harry Bailly's description of *Thop,* Gaylord describes the verse as provoking an ambivalent response: what seems luxuriously bad from one perspective seems brilliantly comic from another.
CT337
Herben, Stephen J., Jr. 'Arms and Armor in Chaucer,' *Speculum* 12

(1937) 475-87
On the basis of evidence from brasses and from contemporary
literary accounts, Herben argues that Chaucer uses realism, not
satire, in the arming sequence of *Thop.*
CT338
Manly, John Matthews. 'The Stanza-Forms of *Sir Thopas,*' *MP* 8
(1910-11) 141-4
Manly suggests that the eight stanza-forms of *Thop* are all
variations of a single form, and that the use of these stanza-forms is
part of the humour of the tale.
CT339
────── 'Sir Thopas: A Satire,' *E&S* 13 (1928) 52-73
Manly suggests that *Thop* is both a burlesque of medieval metrical
romances and a satire of Flemish manners and attitudes.
CT340
Moore, Arthur K. '*Sir Thopas* as Criticism of Fourteenth-Century
Minstrelsy,' *JEGP* 53 (1954) 532-45
Moore suggests that *Thop* is meant to show Chaucer's contempt for
the uninspired verse of contemporary minstrels.
CT341
Scheps, Walter. '*Sir Thopas:* The Bourgeois Knight, the Minstrel,
and the Critics,' *Tennessee Studies in Literature* 11 (1966) 35-43
Scheps compares the romantic frame with the bourgeois hero.
CT342
Trounce, A. McI. 'The English Tail-Rhyme Romances,' *MÆ* 1
(1932) 87-108, 169-82; 2 (1933) 34-57, 189-93; 3 (1934) 30-50
Trounce argues (pp. 87-93) that *Thop* is not a satire of tail-rhyme
romances as such, but of artificial romantic thought and artificial
style in narrative, traits seldom found in combination in tail-rhyme
romances.

THE PROLOGUE AND TALE OF MELIBEE

Editions

Robinson **M30**, 167-88 (text); 740-45, 895-6 (notes). Skeat **M31**, IV,
197-240 (text); V, 201-23 (notes).

Sources and Analogues

See **M220** for an edition of the Latin source by Albertano da Brescia; see Power **M221** for an English translation of the French version; see Bornstein **CT346** for a close comparison of *Mel* with its French source.

CT343
Severs, J. Burke. 'The Source of Chaucer's *Melibeus*,' *PMLA* 50 (1935) 92-9
Severs shows that the text of Paris, Bibliothèque nationale, MS. Fr. 1165 is closer to the text of Chaucer's source than is the version found in *Le ménagier de Paris*, although it does not account for all of Chaucer's readings; he finds no evidence that Chaucer used the Latin text of Albertano.

CT344
_____ 'The *Tale of Melibeus*' in Bryan and Dempster **CT8**, 560-614
Severs prints his own edition of the French source, *Le Livre de Mellibee et Prudence*, an adaptation of Albertano da Brescia's *Liber consolationis et consilii* made by Renaud de Louhans, using Paris, Bibliothèque nationale, MS. Fr. 1165 as a base text and listing in full the variants of other MSS.

Critical Studies

See Schlauch **M92** for the prose of *Mel.*

CT345
Baum, Paull F. 'Chaucer's Metrical Prose,' *JEGP* 45 (1946) 38-42
Baum notes that the opening paragraphs of *Mel* can be read as decasyllabic verse.

CT346
Bornstein, Diane. 'Chaucer's *Tale of Melibee* as an Example of the *style clergial*,' *ChauR* 12 (1977-8) 236-54
Bornstein gives a brief discussion of the *style clergial* and a detailed comparison of *Mel* with its French source, the translation of Albertano by Renaud de Louhans.

CT347
Owen, Charles A., Jr. 'The *Tale of Melibee*,' *ChauR* 7 (1972-3) 267-80
Owen characterizes *Mel* as a typical medieval allegory and includes useful bibliographical references.

CT348
Stillwell, Gardiner. 'The Political Meaning of Chaucer's *Tale of Melibee*,' *Speculum* 19 (1944) 433-44
Stillwell discusses earlier political interpretations of *Mel* and explains its general political relevance for the period.

CT349
Strohm, Paul. 'The Allegory of the *Tale of Melibee*,' *ChauR* 2 (1967-8) 32-42
Strohm suggests that *Mel* is essentially a book of proverbs contained within a larger framework of moral allegory and he analyses the allegory as a *psychomachia.*

THE MONK'S PROLOGUE AND TALE

Editions

Robinson **M30**, 188-98 (text); 745-50, 896 (notes). Skeat **M31**, IV, 241-68 (text); V, 224-46 (notes).

Sources and Analogues

See **M195** (vol. IX) for a text of Boccaccio's *De casibus virorum illustrium* and **M201** for a translation. See Farnham **Tr37**, 129-72 for the differences between *MkT* and the *De casibus.*

CT350
Aiken, Pauline. 'Vincent of Beauvais and Chaucer's *Monk's Tale*,' *Speculum* 17 (1942) 56-68
Aiken argues that the *Speculum historiale* may have contributed to both the form and the content of *MkT.*

CT351
Babcock, R.W. 'The Mediaeval Setting of Chaucer's *Monk's Tale*,' *PMLA* 46 (1931) 205-13

Babcock discusses the clerical and non-clerical literary traditions behind *MkT* and gives a list of earlier works in the genre.
CT352
Boitani, Piero. 'The *Monk's Tale:* Dante and Boccaccio,' *MAE* 45 (1976) 50-69
Boitani discusses *MkT*'s debt to Dante and Boccaccio, and compares Chaucer's Ugolino and Zenobia stories with the versions in his sources.
CT353
Grennen, Joseph E. ' "Sampsoun" in the *Canterbury Tales:* Chaucer Adapting a Source,' *NM* 67 (1966) 117-22
Grennen shows how Chaucer adapted several versions of the story of Samson and suggests that Sampsoun in *MkT* is a *de casibus* figure and the story is an answer to the Host's jibes about the Monk's potential prowess as a lover.
CT354
Johnson, Dudley R. 'The Biblical Characters of Chaucer's Monk,' *PMLA* 66 (1951) 827-43
Johnson shows that some features of the biblical characters in *MkT* cannot have come from the Vulgate or from Boccaccio, but might have come from the Old French text, the *Bible historiale* of Guyart Desmoulins. Johnson prints the relevant passages of the *Bible historiale*, which has not been edited.
CT355
Pace, George B. 'Adam's Hell,' *PMLA* 78 (1963) 25-35
Pace sets the stories of Lucifer and Adam in the context of medieval traditions about hell.
CT356
Root, Robert K. 'The *Monk's Tale*' in Bryan and Dempster **CT8**, 615-44
Root shows that Chaucer was indebted to Boccaccio's *De casibus virorum illustrium* and to the *de casibus* stories in the *Roman de la rose* for the idea of *MkT;* he prints the relevant sections of the *Roman,* and gives references to and quotations from sources for the individual tragedies.
CT357
Spencer, Theodore. 'The Story of Ugolino in Dante and Chaucer,' *Speculum* 9 (1934) 295-301; repr. in *Theodore Spencer: Selected Essays,* ed. Alan C. Purves (New Brunswick, N.J. 1966) 41-8

Spencer gives a detailed study of the two treatments of the Ugolino story.

Critical Studies

See Strange **CT310** for varying views of Fortune in *MkT.*

CT358
Berndt, David E. 'Monastic *acedia* and Chaucer's Characterization of Daun Piers,' *SP* 68 (1971) 435-50
Berndt gives a useful summary of critical opinion, and suggests that the Monk's particular vice, sloth, is revealed through his tale.
CT359
Kaske, R.E. 'The Knight's Interruption of the *Monk's Tale,*' *ELH* 24 (1957) 249-68
Kaske suggests that the opposition between the Knight and the Monk is based on their different perceptions of the Boethian concept of Fortune.
CT360
Socola, Edward M. 'Chaucer's Development of Fortune in the *Monk's Tale,*' *JEGP* 49 (1950) 159-71
Socola suggests that Chaucer modified materials found in his sources in order to develop the concept of Fortune in *MkT.*

THE NUN'S PRIEST'S PROLOGUE AND TALE

Editions

Robinson **M30**, 198-206 (text); 750-55, 896-7 (notes). Skeat **M31**, IV, 269-89 (text); V, 247-57 (notes).

CT361
Coghill, Nevill and Christopher Tolkien, eds. *The Nun's Priest's Tale* (London 1959, many reprints)
This student's edition has an introduction and notes.
CT362
Hussey, Maurice, ed. *The Nun's Priest's Prologue and Tale* (Cambridge 1965)

This student's edition has an introduction, notes, and glossary.

CT363

Sisam, Kenneth, ed. *The Nun's Priest's Tale* (Oxford 1927; repr. 1933, 1957)

Sisam's edition has an excellent introduction and commentary.

Sources and Analogues

CT364

Aiken, Pauline. 'Vincent of Beauvais and Dame Pertelote's Knowledge of Medicine,' *Speculum* 10 (1935) 281-7

Aiken shows that Pertelote's knowledge of the causes of and antidotes to dreams can be traced to the *Speculum naturale* or the *Speculum doctrinale* of Vincent of Beauvais.

CT365

Brown, Carleton. ' "Mulier est hominis confusio",' *MLN* 35 (1920) 479-82

Brown traces the phrase in line 3164 to the *Speculum historiale* of Vincent of Beauvais, and discusses its later use.

CT366

Gallacher, Patrick. 'Food, Laxatives, and Catharsis in Chaucer's *Nun's Priest's Tale*,' *Speculum* 51 (1976) 49-68

Gallacher sets the medical lore in *NPT* against a wide background of classical and medieval views of diet and catharsis, both scientific and philosophical; he points out that the functions of the body were often seen as analogous to the functions of the soul.

CT367

Hulbert, James R. 'The *Nun's Priest's Tale*' in Bryan and Dempster **CT8**, 645-63

Hulbert prints analogues from the *Roman de Renart* and *Reinhard Fuchs,* and passages from Valerius Maximus which parallel the priest's exempla.

CT368

Levy, Bernard S. and George R. Adams. 'Chauntecleer's Paradise Lost and Regained,' *MS* 29 (1967) 178-92

The study shows how Chaucer uses biblical, patristic, and iconographic material to construct a comic version of the Fall.

CT369

Mann, Jill. 'The *Speculum stultorum* and the *Nun's Priest's Tale*,'

ChauR 9 (1974-5) 262-82

Mann discusses the comic use of beast-fable in the two works, with particular reference to the *Speculum stultorum* of Nigel de Longchamps; see **M311** for an edition of the work.

CT370

Petersen, Kate Oelzner. *On the Sources of 'The Nonne Prestes Tale.'* Radcliffe College Monographs 10 (Boston 1898, repr. New York 1966)

Petersen's monograph is the definitive study of the sources of *NPT,* although some of its conclusions have been modified; see Pratt **CT371-2**.

CT371

Pratt, Robert A. 'Three Old French Sources of the *Nonnes Preestes Tale,*' *Speculum* 47 (1972) 422-44, 646-68

Pratt argues that *NPT*'s sources include *Renart le contrefait,* a little known poem of the early 14th century, as well as Marie de France's fable *Del cok et del gupil* and Branch II of Pierre de St. Cloud's *Roman de Renart.*

CT372

⸺ 'Some Latin Sources of the Nonnes Preest on Dreams,' *Speculum* 52 (1977) 538-70

Pratt examines Chaucer's use of Albertus Magnus' *De somno et vigilia,* Cicero's *De divinatione,* and especially Holkot's commentary on Wisdom, in the *NPT.*

CT373

Steadman, John M. 'Chaunticleer and Medieval Natural History,' *Isis* 50 (1959) 236-44

Steadman argues that Chauntecleer's uxoriousness, regal pride, and choleric temperament are characteristic traits of *gallus domesticus* as described in such works as *De proprietatibus rerum* by Bartholomaeus Anglicus or the *Reductorium morale* of Pierre Bersuire.

CT374

Young, Karl. 'Chaucer and Geoffrey of Vinsauf,' *MP* 41 (1943-4) 172-82

Young discusses the popularity of Geoffrey of Vinsauf's lament for Richard I, to which Chaucer refers in *NPT* 3347-51, the longest of the examples of apostrophe in the *Poetria nova.* He argues that the other examples of apostrophe, especially the addresses for times of prosperity, influenced some of the narrator's moralistic comments

on pride and complacency in *NPT.* For an edition of Geoffrey
see **M309.**

Critical Studies

See McCall **CrS53** on the association of the date May 3 with
irrational love; see Watson **CT312** for the role of *NPT* in FragVII
and the *CT* as a whole; see Curry **CrS35,** 195-240 for the influence
of dream-lore; see Elbow **CrS40,** 95-113 for an analysis of a series
of oppositions in the tale.

CT375
Allen, Judson Boyce. 'The Ironic Fruyt: Chauntecleer as Figura,' *SP*
66 (1969) 25-35
Allen shows that Chaucer's intention in presenting *NPT* as an
allegory with Chauntecleer as cock-preacher must have been
comic; Chauntecleer's appearance, character, and behaviour
consistently undercut a straightforward allegorical interpretation.
CT376
Donaldson, E. Talbot. 'Patristic Exegesis in the Criticism of
Medieval Literature: The Opposition' in Bethurum **CrS1,** 1-26; repr.
in Donaldson **CrS7,** 134-53
Donaldson argues that the interpretation of *NPT* according to the
method of patristic commentary is reductionist and that the
significant feature of the tale is the enormous rhetorical elaboration
of its telling.
CT377
Lenaghan, R.T. 'The Nun's Priest's Fable,' *PMLA* 78 (1963) 300-7
Lenaghan suggests that there are two voices in *NPT:* the voice of
the priest, an accomplished storyteller; and the voice behind the tale
itself, a bumbling rhetorician whose flourishes make the tale
ridiculous.
CT378
Manning, Stephen. 'The Nun's Priest's Morality and the Medieval
Attitude toward Fables,' *JEGP* 59 (1960) 403-16
Manning gives information on the medieval meanings of the word
fabula and on attitudes towards *fabulae.*
CT379
Watkins, Charles A. 'Chaucer's *sweete preest,*' *ELH* 36 (1969)
455-69

Watkins sees the Nun's Priest as an 'unreliable narrator' who is the moral opposite of Chauntecleer.

Fragment VIII
(SecNT, CYT)

CRITICAL STUDIES

CT380
Grennen, Joseph E. 'Saint Cecilia's "Chemical Wedding": The Unity of the *Canterbury Tales*, Fragment VIII,' *JEGP* 65 (1966) 466-81
Grennen discusses parallels and contrasts between the two tales and shows how they unify the fragment.
CT381
Rosenberg, Bruce A. 'The Contrary Tales of the Second Nun and the Canon's Yeoman,' *ChauR* 2 (1967-8) 278-91
Showing that the two tales deal with opposing themes and motifs such as sight and blindness, and revelation and reason, Rosenberg argues that these contrasts unify the fragment.

THE SECOND NUN'S PROLOGUE AND TALE

Editions

Robinson **M30**, 207-13 (text); 755-9, 897 (notes). Skeat **M31**, IV, 509-26 (text); V, 401-13 (notes).

Sources and Analogues

CT382
Gerould, G.H. 'The *Second Nun's Prologue and Tale*' in Bryan and Dempster **CT8**, 664-84
Gerould prints the main source for the Invocation to Mary, St. Bernard's prayer from Canto 33 of Dante's *Paradiso*, and excerpts

from two versions of the story of St. Cecilia which lie behind
Chaucer's version: the short version, as printed in the *Legenda aurea*
of Jacobus de Voragine (as a source for lines 120-357), and the
longer version, as given in a late 15th-century compilation (as a
source for lines 358-553). He notes that more work is needed on MSS
of saints' legends to determine whether Chaucer could have used a
MS which combined the two versions.
CT383
Kölbing, E. 'Zu Chaucers Caecilien-Legende,' *Englische Studien* 1
(1877) 215-48
Kölbing gives a line-by-line comparison of *SecNT* with the *Legenda
aurea* version and with another Latin version which follows the
Greek life by Simeon Metaphrastes; this comparison indicates that
Chaucer used both the *Legenda aurea* version and a Latin version
like the one modelled on Metaphrastes or like the longer version
printed in Gerould **CT382**, both of which derive ultimately from the
early Latin *Acta*. (In German.)
CT384
Reames, Sherry L. 'The Sources of Chaucer's *Second Nun's Tale*,'
MP 76 (1978-9) 111-35
Reames discusses Chaucer's use of sources in *SecNT* and describes
a version of the *Passio S. Caeciliae* that is closer to the text Chaucer
used than any source suggested previously.

Critical Studies

See Howard **CT169** for the place of *SecNT* in the 'Marriage Group';
see Grennen **CT380** and Rosenberg **CT381** for the relation between
SecNT and *CYT*.

CT385
Gardner, William Bradford. 'Chaucer's "unworthy sone of Eve",'
University of Texas: Studies in English 26 (1947) 77-83
Gardner notes that medieval nuns referred to themselves as 'sons of
Eve' when singing the *Salve Regina*, one of the sources of the
Invocacio ad Mariam in the *Prologue;* hence the phrase 'unworthy
sone of Eve' (VIII.62) need not imply that the original speaker of
SecNT was a man.

CT386
Hostia, Sister Mary. 'The Prioress and her Companion,' *CE* 14
(1952-3) 351-2
Hostia compares the two women as revealed in their prologues.
CT387
Peck, Russell A. 'The Ideas of "entente" and Translation in
Chaucer's *Second Nun's Tale*,' *Annuale mediaevale* 8 (1967) 17-37
Peck discusses the language and theology of the poem and relates it
to Chaucer's early work.

THE CANON'S YEOMAN'S PROLOGUE AND TALE

Editions

Robinson **M30**, 213-23 (text); 759-62, 897 (notes). Skeat **M31**, IV,
526-54 (text); V, 414-34 (notes). See also Schmidt **CT50**.

CT388
Hussey, Maurice, ed. *The Canon's Yeoman's Prologue and Tale*
(Cambridge 1965)
This student's edition has an introduction, notes, and glossary.

Sources and Analogues

CT389
Aiken, Pauline. 'Vincent of Beauvais and Chaucer's Knowledge of
Alchemy,' *SP* 41 (1944) 371-89
Aiken cites parallels which suggest that Chaucer drew on the
alchemical chapters of the *Speculum naturale* of Vincent of
Beauvais.
CT390
Duncan, Edgar H. 'The Literature of Alchemy and Chaucer's
Canon's Yeoman's Tale: Framework, Theme, and Characters,'
Speculum 43 (1968) 633-56
Duncan describes some of the alchemical treatises Chaucer might
have known, including those mentioned in *CYT,* and discusses paral-
lel passages.

CT391
Spargo, John Webster. 'The *Canon's Yeoman's Prologue and Tale*' in
Bryan and Dempster **CT8**, 685-98
Spargo discusses the scientific basis for certain alchemical
processes; he prints the decree against alchemy of John XXII and
Petrarch's *De alchimia*, as well as extracts from Gower, Sercambi,
and the *Pretiosa margarita novella* of Petrus Antonius Bonus, as
samples of medieval discussions of alchemy.

Critical Studies

See Muscatine **CrS57**, 213-22 for the relation between *Prologue* and
Tale, and for an interpretation of *CYT* as an attack on the view that
matter is merely something to be manipulated. See Grennen **CT380**
and Rosenberg **CT381** for the relation between *CYT* and *SecNT*.

CT392
Damon, S. Foster. 'Chaucer and Alchemy,' *PMLA* 39 (1924) 782-8
Damon points out that Chaucer was regarded as an expert alchem-
ist by later alchemists, and suggests that the *CYT* was intended to
praise true alchemy while attacking false alchemists.
CT393
Finkelstein, Dorothée. 'The Code of Chaucer's "secree of secrees":
Arabic Alchemical Terminology in *The Canon's Yeoman's Tale*,'
Archiv 207 (1970-71) 260-76
Finkelstein discusses some alchemical topoi of Arabic origin, which
were transmitted in Latin translations of Arabic scientific works,
and which appear in the *CYT*.
CT394
Grennen, Joseph E. 'The Canon's Yeoman and the Cosmic Furnace:
Language and Meaning in the *Canon's Yeoman's Tale*,' *Criticism* 4
(1962) 225-40, 2 pp. of figs.
Grennen discusses alchemical puns and other alchemical references
in the tale and shows that *CYT* is built around the alchemical meta-
phor of the cosmic furnace.
CT395
_____ 'The Canon's Yeoman's Alchemical "Mass",' *SP* 62 (1965)
546-60

Grennen shows that *CYT* has the form of an alchemical treatise, that the two canons probably represent actual mercury and philosophical mercury, and that the transmutation performed by the second canon and the priest is specifically described as a profane Mass.

CT396

———— 'Chaucer and the Commonplaces of Alchemy,' *Classica et mediaevalia* 26 (1965) 306-33
Grennen discusses some alchemical topoi, and shows how they are used in *CYT* with ironic effect.

CT397

Hamilton, Marie P. 'The Clerical Status of Chaucer's Alchemist,' *Speculum* 16 (1941) 103-8
Hamilton shows that the alchemist who joined the pilgrims must have been an Austin canon regular.

CT398

Harrington, David V. 'Dramatic Irony in the *Canon's Yeoman's Tale*,' *NM* 66 (1965) 160-66
Harrington points out that Chaucer emphasizes the covetousness and gullibility of the priest who is duped by the second canon.

CT399

Hartung, Albert E. ' "Pars secunda" and the Development of the *Canon's Yeoman's Tale*,' *ChauR* 12 (1977-8) 111-28
Hartung suggests that 'Pars secunda' was written before 'Pars prima,' and as an occasional piece.

CT400

Herz, Judith Scherer. '*The Canon's Yeoman's Prologue* and *Tale*,' *MP* 58 (1960-61) 231-7
Herz discusses alchemical metaphors and the contrast between romance diction and alchemical realism in the tale.

CT401

Richardson, H.G. 'Year Books and Plea Rolls as Sources of Historical Information,' *Transactions of the Royal Historical Society* ser. 4, 5 (1922) 28-70
Richardson posits (p. 39) a connection between Chaucer and an alchemist called William Shuchirch, canon of the king's chapel at Windsor in 1390, when Chaucer was in charge of repairing the chapel.

Fragment IX
(*MancT*)

THE MANCIPLE'S PROLOGUE AND TALE

Editions

Robinson **M30**, 224-7 (text); 762-5, 897 (notes). Skeat **M31**, IV, 555-66 (text); V, 435-43 (notes).

Sources and Analogues

See Hoffman **CT10** for Chaucer's use of Ovid.

CT402
Cadbury, William. 'Manipulation of Sources and the Meaning of the *Manciple's Tale*,' *PQ* 43 (1964) 538-48
Cadbury shows how Chaucer modified his source materials in his own version.
CT403
Work, James A. 'The *Manciple's Tale*' in Bryan and Dempster **CT8**, 699-722
Work prints Ovid's version of the story along with medieval adaptations from the *Ovide moralisé*, Gower's *Confessio amantis*, Machaut's *Voir-Dit*, and the *Integumenta Ovidii*; he also prints analogues to the non-narrative material.

Critical Studies

CT404
Birney, Earle. 'Chaucer's "gentil" Manciple and his "gentil" Tale,' *NM* 61 (1960) 257-67
Birney argues that *MancT* should be read ironically, as an unsuccessful attempt at a *gentil* tale by a *lewed* man.
CT405
Brodie, Alexander H. 'Hodge of Ware and Geber's Cook: Wordplay in the *Manciple's Prologue*,' *NM* 72 (1971) 62-8
Brodie examines the imagery of the *Prologue*, distinguishing three

areas of wordplay; horsemanship and knighthood, love and drunken-
ness, pallor and death.
CT406
Dean, James. 'The Ending of the *Canterbury Tales,* 1952-1976,'
TSLL 21 (1979) 17-33
Dean surveys recent criticism on *MancT* and discusses its place in
CT.
CT407
Hazelton, Richard. 'The *Manciple's Tale:* Parody and Critique,'
JEGP 62 (1963) 1-31
Hazelton suggests that the tale is comic and parodic and that the
rhetorical flourishes highlight the misplaced moralizing of earlier
versions of the stories, such as Gower's.
CT408
Scattergood, V.J. 'The Manciple's Manner of Speaking,' *Essays in
Criticism* 24 (1974) 124-46
Scattergood suggests that *Prologue* and *Tale* are unified by the
theme of self-control, especially self-control in speech.
CT409
Severs, J. Burke. 'Is the *Manciple's Tale* a Success?' *JEGP* 51 (1952)
1-16
Severs discusses the tale as an exemplum.

Fragment X
(*ParsT,* Chaucer's *Retractation*)

CRITICAL STUDIES

See Baldwin **CT12** for the motif of the heavenly pilgrimage, which
is introduced in the *GenProl* and reappears in FragX; see
Donaldson **M28,** 947-50 and Patterson **CT422** on the place of *ParsT*
and Chaucer's *Retractation* in *CT.*

CT410
Delasanta, Rodney. 'Penance and Poetry in the *Canterbury Tales,*'
PMLA 93 (1978) 240-47
Delasanta argues that *ParsT* is a suitable ending for *CT* and should

not be read ironically; he shows how it fits into the pattern of penitential and eschatological allusion in the *Tales.*

CT411

Madeleva, Sister M., CSC. *A Lost Language and Other Essays on Chaucer* (New York 1951)
Madeleva sees FragX as the fitting culmination of *CT,* arguing (pp. 69-79) that *ParsT* presents confession as the greatest of all solutions for the greatest of all human needs, and (pp. 105-15) that the *Retractation* demonstrates Chaucer's own repentance.

CT412

Tupper, Frederick. 'Chaucer and the Seven Deadly Sins,' *PMLA* 29 (1914) 93-128
Tupper argues that *ParsT* is the culmination of the organizing motif of *CT* as a whole, the seven deadly sins.

THE PARSON'S PROLOGUE AND TALE

Editions

Robinson **M30**, 228-64 (text); 765-72, 897-8 (notes). Skeat **M31**, IV, 567-643 (text); V, 444-74 (notes).

Sources and Analogues

See Bloomfield **B85** for the seven deadly sins, and Pantin **B104**, pt. 5 for English religious manuals.

CT413

Dempster, Germaine. 'The *Parson's Tale*' in Bryan and Dempster **CT8**, 723-60
Dempster summarizes the results of earlier source studies and prints extracts from Raymond of Peñaforte's *Summa casuum penitentiae* and Guilielmus Peraldus' *Summa de vitiis,* the two ultimate sources of *ParsT,* along with short excerpts from two analogues.

CT414

Hazelton, Richard. 'Chaucer's *Parson's Tale* and the *Moralium dogma philosophorum*,' *Traditio* 16 (1960) 255-74
Hazelton juxtaposes parallel passages from the Latin *Moralium* (a

12th-century adaptation of Cicero's *De officiis*), a French translation, and *ParsT* in order to demonstrate the influence of this text as an ultimate source for parts of the section on the *remedia* for the seven sins. For an edition of the text see Holmberg **M247**.

CT415

Kellogg, Alfred L. 'St. Augustine and the *Parson's Tale*,' *Traditio* 8 (1952) 424-30; repr. in Kellogg, *Chaucer, Langland, Arthur: Essays in Middle English Literature* (New Brunswick, N.J. 1972) 343-52

Kellogg suggests that the *Summa de officio sacerdotis* of Richard de Wetheringsett may be the source of *ParsT* 322-49, a passage without known close parallels or source.

CT416

Petersen, Kate Oelzner. *The Sources of the 'Parson's Tale.'* Radcliffe College Monographs 12 (Boston 1901)

Petersen shows that the *Summa casuum penitentiae* of Raymond of Peñaforte and the *Summa de vitiis* of Guilielmus Peraldus are the ultimate sources of *ParsT*.

CT417

Pfander, H.G. 'Some Medieval Manuals of Religious Instruction in England and Observations on Chaucer's *Parson's Tale*,' *JEGP* 35 (1936) 243-58

Pfander describes some manuals and suggests titles worth investigating in the search for immediate sources of *ParsT*.

CT418

Wenzel, Siegfried. 'The Source for the "remedia" of the *Parson's Tale*,' *Traditio* 27 (1971) 433-53

Wenzel prints, from a Latin *Summa de virtutibus*, extracts which are the source of passages in Chaucer's *remedia*. For a restatement of the analysis and an edition of the text with facing translation, see Wenzel, *Summa virtutum de remediis anime*, The Chaucer Library (Athens, Ga. 1984).

CT419

——— 'The Source of Chaucer's Seven Deadly Sins,' *Traditio* 30 (1974) 351-78

Wenzel shows that the treatises *Quoniam* and *Primo*, which derive from Guilielmus Peraldus' *Summa de vitiis*, are closer than Peraldus' own work to the section on sins in *ParsT*.

Critical Studies

See FragX section for studies of *ParsT* in the context of *CT* as a whole.

CT420
Chapman, Coolidge Otis. '*The Parson's Tale:* A Mediaeval Sermon,' *MLN* 43 (1928) 229-34
Chapman discusses medieval sermon structures in *ParsT* and suggests that the long section devoted to the sins reflects the Parson's view that the pilgrims are in need of repentance.

CT421
Dunning, T.P. 'Chaucer's Icarus-Complex: Some Notes on his Adventures in Theology' in *English Studies Today: Third Series,* ed. G.I. Duthie (Edinburgh 1964) 89-106
Dunning shows that the views on marriage expressed in *ParsT* accord generally with those of Aquinas (and with those of Chaucer's ultimate sources), though Chaucer's wording is not always clear.

CT422
Patterson, Lee W. 'The *Parson's Tale* and the Quitting of the *Canterbury Tales,*' *Traditio* 34 (1978) 331-80
Patterson gives a thoughtful and detailed discussion of the genre and structure of *ParsT* and its role in *CT;* he argues convincingly for a late date of composition.

CT423
Peck, Russell A. 'Number Symbolism in the *Prologue* to Chaucer's *Parson's Tale,*' *ES* 48 (1967) 205-15
Peck explores the significance of the numbers mentioned in the first twelve lines of the *Prologue.*

CHAUCER'S *RETRACTATION*

Editions

Robinson **M30,** 265 (text); 772-3, 898 (notes). Skeat **M31,** IV, 644 (text); V, 473-6 (notes).

Analogues

CT424

Sayce, Olive. 'Chaucer's "Retractations": The Conclusion of the *Canterbury Tales* and its Place in Literary Tradition,' *MÆ* 40 (1971) 230-48

Sayce considers the *Retractation* in the context of prologue and epilogue patterns in medieval literature, and argues that it reflects literary tradition rather than Chaucer's personal feelings.

CT425

Tatlock, John S.P. 'Chaucer's *Retractations*,' *PMLA* 28 (1913) 521-9

Tatlock discusses retraction as a medieval tradition and describes the retractions of Augustine, Bede, and Jean de Meun, as a context for *Retr.*

Critical Studies

CT426

Gordon, James D. 'Chaucer's Retraction: A Review of Opinion' in *Studies in Medieval Literature: In Honor of Professor Albert Croll Baugh*, ed. MacEdward Leach (Philadelphia and London 1961) 81-96

Gordon reviews important criticism and shows how discussion has evolved.

CT427

Howard, Donald R. 'Chaucer the Man,' *PMLA* 80 (1965) 337-43; repr. in Cawley **CrS6**, 31-45

Howard sees *Retr* as a genuine and personal expression of repentance; he discusses Chaucer the man in light of this view. See Sayce **CT424** for a contrasting view.

THE BOOK OF THE DUCHESS

Editions

Robinson **M30**, 266-79 (text); 773-8, 898-9 (notes). Skeat **M31**, I, 277-322 (text), 462-95 (notes).

Sources and Analogues

See Muscatine **CrS57**, 98-107 for Chaucer's use of his French sources; Muscatine shows how Chaucer substitutes well-developed characters for personifications in *BD*. See Shannon **M214**, 3-12 for Chaucer's debt to the Roman poets. See Froissart **M158**, Machaut **M164**, and Langlois **M169** for texts of poems which were major sources of **BD**. See Fyler **M282**, 65-81 for Chaucer's adaptation of the Friend's account of the Golden Age in the *Roman de la rose* in order to create a myth to console the Man in Black.

BD1
Dunleavy, Gareth W. 'The Wound and the Comforter: The Consolations of Geoffrey Chaucer,' *Papers on Language and Literature* 3, Supplement (1967) 14-27
Dunleavy gives a brief account of the influence of Boethius' *Consolatio philosophiae* on Chaucer's works and suggests that the narrator functions like Lady Philosophy in the *Consolatio* in guiding the Man in Black to come to terms with his loss by talking out his grief.
BD2
Severs, J. Burke. 'The Sources of *The Book of the Duchess*,' *MS* 25 (1963) 355-62
Severs summarizes and adds evidence to the argument that the anonymous *Songe verte* was a source for the poem; see Wimsatt **BD4** for an opposing view.
BD3
Wimsatt, James I. 'The Apotheosis of Blanche in *The Book of the Duchess*,' *JEGP* 66 (1967) 26-44
Wimsatt shows that the description of the lady echoes descriptions of the Virgin Mary and argues that the references produce a poetic apotheosis of Blanche.

BD4

———— *Chaucer and the French Love Poets: The Literary Background of the 'Book of the Duchess.'* University of North Carolina Studies in Comparative Literature [43] (Chapel Hill 1968) This comprehensive survey of the French poems that influenced the composition of *BD*, particularly the *Roman de la rose* and the poems of Guillaume de Machaut and Jean Froissart, shows in detail what Chaucer borrowed.

Critical Studies

See Bethurum **CrS21** for the contrast between the world of books and the world of love in the poem. See Clemen **CrS32**, 23-66 for a useful general introduction. See Curry **CrS35**, 195-240 for an introduction to the theories of dreams that Chaucer would have known. See Payne **CrS62**, 38-57 for the use of traditional rhetorical devices in the opening lines of the poem.

BD5

Bronson, Bertrand H. '*The Book of the Duchess* Re-opened,' *PMLA* 67 (1952) 863-81; repr. in Wagenknecht **CrS19**, 271-94 In this influential essay, Bronson applies modern psychological theory to the dream sequence and discusses the development of the Dreamer and his tactful consolation of the Man in Black.

BD6

Grennen, Joseph E. ' "Hert-huntyng" in the *Book of the Duchess,*' *MLQ* 25 (1964) 131-9 Grennen connects the hunt for the hart and the hunt for the lady's heart.

BD7

Huppé, Bernard F. and D.W. Robertson, Jr. *Fruyt and Chaf: Studies in Chaucer's Allegories* (Princeton 1963, repr. 1972) 32-100 Interpreting *BD* allegorically, Huppé and Robertson argue that the Dreamer stands for Reason and guides the Knight, who stands for Will, to acceptance of loss and reconciliation with God. For a full statement of this method of interpretation see Robertson **CrS66**.

BD8

Jordan, Robert M. 'The Compositional Structure of the *Book of the*

Duchess,' ChauR (1974-5) 99-117
Arguing that structure is a more important consideration than characterization, Jordan analyses the structure of *BD* as 'inorganic and multiple rather than organic and simple.'

BD9
Lawlor, John. 'The Pattern of Consolation in *The Book of the Duchess,' Speculum* 31 (1956) 626-48; repr. in Schoeck and Taylor **CrS15,** II, 232-60
Lawlor reviews criticism of the poem and suggests that the consolation consists in the Dreamer's recognition and understanding of the extent of the Black Knight's loss.

BD10
Lumiansky, R.M. 'The Bereaved Narrator in Chaucer's *The Book of the Duchess,' Tulane Studies in English* 9 (1959) 5-17
Lumiansky views the suffering of the narrator as a key to the meaning of the poem.

BD11
Palmer, J.J.N. 'The Historical Context of the *Book of the Duchess:* A Revision,' *ChauR* 8 (1973-4) 253-61
Palmer argues persuasively that Duchess Blanche died in 1368, not 1369; the date of the poem's composition can thus be pushed back.

BD12
Peck, Russell A. 'Theme and Number in Chaucer's *Book of the Duchess'* in *Silent Poetry: Essays in Numerological Analysis,* ed. Alastair Fowler (London 1970) 73-115
Peck discusses Chaucer's use of symbolic numbers, especially the number three, and number metaphors.

BD13
Robertson, D.W., Jr. 'The Historical Setting of Chaucer's *Book of the Duchess'* in *Mediaeval Studies in Honor of Urban Tigner Holmes, Jr.,* ed. John Mahoney and John Esten Keller. University of North Carolina Studies in the Romance Languages and Literatures 56 (Chapel Hill 1965) 169-95; repr. in Robertson **CrS67,** 235-56
Robertson develops the approach suggested in Huppé and Robertson **BD7,** and argues that Chaucer adapts the method of Boethius to present a Christian response to death.

BD14
———— 'The *Book of the Duchess'* in Rowland **CrS13,** 403-13
Robertson gives a review of scholarship with selected bibliography.

BD15
Stevens, Martin. 'Narrative Focus in *The Book of the Duchess:* A Critical Revaluation,' *Annuale mediaevale* 7 (1966) 16-32
Stevens sees the Dreamer as the true protagonist of the poem.
BD16
Whitman, F.H. 'Exegesis and Chaucer's Dream Visions,' *ChauR* 3 (1968-9) 229-38
Whitman argues that the poem is a moral allegory.

THE HOUSE OF FAME

Editions

Robinson **M30**, 280-302 (text); 778-88, 899-901 (notes). Skeat **M31**, III, vii-xv (introduction), 1-64 (text), 243-87 (notes).

Sources and Analogues

See McCall **CrS54** for Chaucer's use of classical myth in the poem, and Shannon **M214** for his use of the Roman poets, particularly Virgil. For a text of Virgil's *Aeneid* see **M305**. For Chaucer's use of the *Ovide moralisé* in *HF* see Lowes **M290**. For the reference to Lollius see Kittredge **Tr21** and Pratt **Tr22**. For a text of Dante's *Divina commedia* see **M210**; for studies of its influence on *HF* see Lowes **M205**, Praz **M192**, and Schless **M206**. See Koonce **HF7** and Leyerle **HF8** for critical readings of the poem that offer discussions of Chaucer's creative use of his sources.

HF1
Bennett, J.A.W. *Chaucer's Book of Fame: An Exposition of 'The House of Fame'* (Oxford 1968)
In this masterly book-length commentary Bennett elucidates the complex literary tradition which lies behind the text; of particular interest is the iconographical material on Venus and Aeolus.
HF2
Berry, Reginald. 'Chaucer's Eagle and the Element Air,' *UTQ* 43 (1974) 285-97, 6 pls.
Berry sketches the iconographical tradition of the eagle as a symbol of the element air. The article expands on Leyerle **HF8**.
HF3
Patch, Howard R. 'Chaucer's Desert,' *MLN* 34 (1919) 321-8
After canvassing a variety of possible sources for the image of the desert in *HF*, Patch discusses in detail the resemblances between *HF* and the *Panthère d'amours* attributed to Nicole de Margival (for which see **M167**).

HF4

Sypherd, W.O. *Studies in Chaucer's 'Hous of Fame.'* Chaucer
Society 2nd ser. 39 (London 1907, repr. New York 1965)
After some discussion of Chaucer's dream poetry and the tradition
of the love-vision in Old French, and the relation of *HF* to Dante's
Commedia, Sypherd discusses possible sources for some of the main
topics in *HF:* the discussion of dreams, the invocations, the temple
of Venus, the Eagle and the journey through the upper air, Fame
and the house of tidings.

Critical Studies

See Clemen **CrS32**, 67-121 for an introduction to the poem which
emphasizes its factual, non-allegorical character.

HF5

Bevington, David M. 'The Obtuse Narrator in Chaucer's *House of
Fame,*' *Speculum* 36 (1961) 288-98
Bevington argues that the narrator's progression from fantasy to
experience unifies *HF.*

HF6

Delany, Sheila. *Chaucer's 'House of Fame': The Poetics of Skeptical
Fideism* (Chicago and London 1972)
Delany argues that the poem deliberately presents a series of conflicting theories about such matters as dreams, moral behaviour, the
universe, and literary theory, and that it appeals to faith rather than
to reason in order to reconcile them.

HF7

Koonce, B.G. *Chaucer and the Tradition of Fame: Symbolism in 'The
House of Fame'* (Princeton 1966)
Koonce interprets *HF* according to the exegetical method described
in Robertson **CrS66** and identifies the three parts of the poem as
the Hell, Purgatory, and Paradise of Chaucer's version of the *Divine
Comedy.*

HF8

Leyerle, John. 'Chaucer's Windy Eagle,' *UTQ* 40 (1971) 247-65, 4
pls.
Leyerle discusses the complex ancestry of the eagle and explains the
date of the dream; he finds in the eagle's discourse a statement of

the poem's central theme: secret love is contrary to natural order and will be reported unreliably.

HF9

Manly, John Matthews. 'What is Chaucer's *Hous of Fame?*' in *Anniversary Papers by Colleagues and Pupils of George Lyman Kittredge* [no ed.] (Boston and London 1913) 73-81

This important article shifted critical preoccupation from the poem's complex pattern of sources to its internal structure and meaning.

HF10

Ruggiers, Paul G. 'The Unity of Chaucer's *House of Fame*,' *SP* 50 (1953) 16-29; repr. in Wagenknecht **CrS19**, 295-308 and Schoeck and Taylor **CrS15**, II, 261-74

Ruggiers argues that the vicissitudes of fortune, fame, and love are closely linked in the poem, and that their connection provides its unifying theme.

HF11

Shepherd, Geoffrey T. 'Make Believe: Chaucer's Rationale of Story-telling in *The House of Fame*' in *J.R.R. Tolkien, Scholar and Story-teller: Essays in Memoriam,* ed. Mary Salu and Robert T. Farrell (Ithaca and London 1979) 204-220

Focussing on Chaucer's use of the words *sooth* and *trouthe,* Shepherd argues that a central concern of *HF* is how and why stories are believed.

HF12

Shook, Laurence K. '*The House of Fame*' in Rowland **CrS13**, 414-27

Shook argues that *HF* is an informal *ars poetica* that also discusses speech and sound in their relation to poetic order, and that its treatment of love is really a metaphorical discussion of poetry; Shook includes a selected bibliography of criticism on the poem to 1978.

HF13

Steadman, John M. 'Chaucer's Eagle: A Contemplative Symbol,' *PMLA* 75 (1960) 153-9

Citing numerous sources, Steadman shows that the eagle was a traditional symbol for the flight of thought.

HF14

Wilson, William S. 'The Eagle's Speech in Chaucer's *House of Fame*,' *Quarterly Journal of Speech* 50 (1964) 153-8

Wilson analyses the Ciceronian rhetoric of the eagle's speech.

ANELIDA AND ARCITE

Editions

Robinson **M30**, 303-8 (text); 788-90, 901-2 (notes). Skeat **M31**, I, 365-78 (text), 529-38 (notes).

Sources and Analogues

Anel has no known source, but it parallels Boccaccio's *Teseida* at various points; for these parallels and for the relationship between *Anel* and *KnT* see the notes in Robinson **M30** and Skeat **M31** at the pages listed above. See also Pratt **CT106**. For a text of the *Teseida* see **M195** (vol. II). For the use of Statius see Wise **M302**.

Anel1
Shannon, Edgar F. 'The Source of Chaucer's *Anelida and Arcite*,' *PMLA* 27 (1912) 461-85
Shannon suggests that Chaucer took the outline of the narrative from Ovid's *Heroides,* and the name of his authority, Corinne (*Anel* 21), from the name of Ovid's mistress, Corinna, to whom many of the poems in the *Amores* are addressed.

Critical Studies

See Clemen **CrS32**, 197-209 for an analysis of the poem. See Owen **M88** for a discussion of *Anel* as an experiment in rhyming.

Anel2
Green, A. Wigfall. 'Meter and Rhyme in Chaucer's *Anelida and Arcite*,' *University of Mississippi Studies in English* 2 (1961) 55-63
Green discusses Chaucer's use of internal rhymes, repetition, and stanza linking.

Anel3
Tupper, Frederick. 'Chaucer's Tale of Ireland,' *PMLA* 36 (1921) 186-222

Tupper identifies the characters of *Anel* with historical personages who have similar-sounding names; his view has not been widely accepted.

THE PARLIAMENT OF FOWLS

Editions

Robinson **M30**, 309-18 (text); 791-6, 902-3 (notes). Skeat **M31**, I, 335-59 (text), 505-26 (notes).

PF1
Brewer, D.S., ed. *The Parlement of Foulys.* Nelson's Mediaeval and Renaissance Library (London 1960; repr. 1962, 1964)
This edition, based on Cambridge, University Library, MS. Gg. IV. 27, contains a bibliography, a glossary, copious notes, and translations of passages from the sources.

Sources and Analogues

See Economou **B137**, 125-50 for Chaucer's Goddess Nature and the tradition of Nature in medieval literature. See McCall **CrS54** for Chaucer's use of classical myth, and Shannon **M214** for Chaucer's debts to classical poets. For texts and translations of the *Roman de la rose,* one of the main sources of the poem, see **M169-72**. For texts and translations of two other sources, Macrobius and Alan of Lille, see **M271-2** and **M217-18**. See Robertson **CrS65** for the garden in *PF.* See Boitani **CrS25** for borrowings from the *Teseida.*

PF2
Bennett, J.A.W. *The 'Parlement of Foules': An Interpretation* (Oxford 1957)
Bennett gives an illuminating and learned examination of the sources and literary traditions behind *PF.*

PF3
Brewer, D.S. 'The Genre of the "Parlement of Foules",' *MLR* 53 (1958) 321-6
Brewer surveys and evaluates the role of the love-vision and the *demande d'amour* traditions in *PF.*

PF4
Chamberlain, David S. 'The Music of the Spheres and *The*

Parlement of Foules,' ChauR 5 (1970-71) 32-56
Chamberlain discusses the references to music and their probable sources.
PF5
Loomis, Dorothy Bethurum. 'The Venus of Alanus de Insulis and the Venus of Chaucer' in *Philological Essays: Studies in Old and Middle English Language and Literature in Honour of Herbert Dean Meritt,* ed. James L. Rosier (The Hague 1970) 182-95
Loomis compares and contrasts the two images of Venus.
PF6
Pelen, Marc M. 'Form and Meaning of the Old French Love Vision: The *Fableau dou dieu d'amors* and Chaucer's *Parliament of Fowls,'* *Journal of Medieval and Renaissance Studies* 9 (1979) 277-305
Pelen places the love-vision in an intellectual and poetic tradition and uses as examples the *Fableau* and *PF.*

Critical Studies

See Bennett **PF2** for a critical reading of the poem against the traditions from which it arises, and see Pearsall and Salter **B151** for Chaucer's use of the traditional visionary landscape. See Bethurum **CrS21** for a discussion of the role of the narrator. Clemen **CrS32**, 122-69 provides an excellent general introduction. See Curry **CrS35**, 195-240 for theories of dreams Chaucer would have known; Hieatt **CrS44**, 78-84 argues that dream logic is an important unifying element. Huppé and Robertson **BD7**, 104-48 argue that the poem is an allegory in which selfish love is condemned. See Hieatt **CT114** for a comparison of *PF* with *KnT.* Muscatine **CrS57**, 115-263 describes the *PF* as an illustration of the comically contradictory variety of human attitudes towards love.

PF7
Baker, Donald C. 'The *Parliament of Fowls'* in Rowland **CrS13**, 428-45
Baker summarizes the major critical approaches to the poem and provides a bibliography of criticism to 1978.
PF8
Bethurum, Dorothy. 'The Center of the *Parlement of Foules'* in

Essays in Honor of Walter Clyde Curry [no ed.]. Vanderbilt Studies
in the Humanities 2 (Nashville 1954) 39-50
Bethurum shows that the garden and the idea of love it represents
are central to *PF,* and she argues against critics who try to distort
the poem to make it conform to their own ideas of unity.
PF9
Braddy, Haldeen. 'The *Parlement of Fowles:* A New Proposal,'
PMLA 46 (1931) 1007-19; repr. in Braddy, *Geoffrey Chaucer:
Literary and Historical Studies* (Port Washington, N.Y. and London
1971) 3-15
Braddy provides evidence and arguments for his view that *PF* deals
with the negotiations for a marriage between Richard II and Marie
of France. The article is a summary of *Chaucer's Parlement of
Foules in its Relation to Contemporary Events* (Lancaster, Pa. 1932,
rev. ed. New York 1969). The first ed. was also published as pt. II of
Three Chaucer Studies by Russell Krauss, Haldeen Braddy, and C.
Robert Kase (New York 1932) 1-101, separately paged.
PF10
Bronson, Bertrand H. *In Appreciation of Chaucer's 'Parlement of
Foules.'* University of California Publications in English 3, no. 5
(Berkeley 1935)
Bronson emphasizes the ironic element in *PF* and provides an
introduction to some puzzling features of the poem.
PF11
Cawley, Arthur C. 'Chaucer's Valentine: The *Parlement of Foules*'
in Cawley **CrS6,** 125-39
Cawley makes a close examination of the garden in *PF;* compare
Bennett **PF2,** ch. 2.
PF12
Cowgill, Bruce Kent. 'The *Parlement of Foules* and the Body
Politic,' *JEGP* 74 (1975) 315-35
Cowgill presents a convincing analysis of the role of Scipio in the
poem.
PF13
Everett, Dorothy. 'Chaucer's Love-Visions, with Particular
Reference to the *Parlement of Foules*' in Everett, *Essays on Middle
English Literature,* ed. Patricia M. Kean (Oxford 1955, repr. 1959)
97-114
Everett argues that *PF* must be read in the context of 14th-century
French court poetry.

PF14
Frank, Robert Worth, Jr. 'Structure and Meaning in the *Parlement of Foules*,' *PMLA* 71 (1956) 530-39
Frank shows that three different attitudes towards love are discussed and compared in *PF*.

PF15
Hutchinson, Judith. 'The *Parliament of Fowls* a Literary Entertainment?' *Neophilologus* 61 (1977) 143-51
Hutchinson suggests that Chaucer encourages his audience to expect a valentine poem, and then frustrates its expectations.

PF16
Lumiansky, Robert M. 'Chaucer's *Parlement of Foules:* A Philosophical Interpretation,' *RES* 24 (1948) 81-9
Lumiansky interprets the poem as an examination of true and false felicity; he gives a bibliography and a summary of the major critical theories to 1947.

PF17
McCall, John P. 'The Harmony of Chaucer's Parliament,' *ChauR* 5 (1970-71) 22-31
McCall argues that the poem is a conscious interweaving of conflicting elements and ideas.

PF18
McDonald, Charles O. 'An Interpretation of Chaucer's *Parlement of Foules*,' *Speculum* 30 (1955) 444-57
McDonald suggests that the poem is a survey of various kinds of love and is unified by the idea and the figure of Nature.

PF19
Owen, Charles A., Jr. 'The Role of the Narrator in the *Parlement of Foules*,' *CE* 14 (1953) 264-9
Owen discusses the narrator as lover, reader, and dreamer.

PF20
Stillwell, Gardiner. 'Unity and Comedy in Chaucer's *Parlement of Foules*,' *JEGP* 49 (1950) 470-95
After a comparison of the text with the sources and analogues, Stillwell concludes that *PF* is a comedy of medieval manners and ideas adapted to the framework of a love-vision, and that it is unlikely to have been meant as a compliment to individual persons.

BOECE

This work is a translation of the *Consolatio philosophiae* of Boethius.

Editions

Robinson **M30**, 309-84 (text); 797, 903-5 (notes). Skeat **M31**, II, vii-xlviii (introduction), 1-151 (text), 419-60 (notes). Skeat gives a list of Chaucer's borrowings from Boethius, with line references; his notes on the translation are much more extensive than Robinson's.

For editions and modern translations of the source, see **M232-3** and **M235-6**.

Sources

See **M237** for a French translation by Jean de Meun which Chaucer probably used in addition to the Latin original; see **M232** for an edition of the Latin text.

Bo1
Lowes, John Livingston. 'Chaucer's Boethius and Jean de Meun,' *Romanic Review* 8 (1917) 383-400
Lowes shows that Chaucer made use of the Old French translation of the *Consolatio* by Jean de Meun. This source accounts for Chaucer's translation of the Latin metres into prose and for his use of the French form *Boece*.

Bo2
Petersen, Kate O. 'Chaucer and Trivet,' *PMLA* 18 (1903) 173-93
Petersen shows that Chaucer used the Latin commentary of Nicholas Trivet in his translation of the *Consolatio;* see Jourdain **M238** for an account of the commentary, which has not been edited.

Studies

See Barrett **M239** for an introduction to Boethius and his era; see
Courcelle **M240** and Patch **M242** for his influence on the Middle
Ages. Patch also discusses Boethius' influence upon Chaucer. See
Jefferson **M241**, 1-46 for a detailed study of Chaucer's method of
translation.

Bo3
Fischer, Olga. 'A Comparative Study of Philosophical Terms in
the Alfredian and Chaucerian Boethius,' *Neophilologus* 63 (1979)
622-39
On the basis of her comparative study, Fischer demonstrates that
Chaucer often used loanwords from French which would have been
unfamiliar to his contemporaries when there were available English
words for the concepts he needed.

TROILUS AND CRISEYDE

Editions

Robinson **M30**, 449-564 (text); 922-52, 1023-30 (notes). Skeat **M31**, II, xlix-lxxx (introduction), 153-417 (text), 461-506 (notes).

Tr1
Root, Robert Kilburn, ed. *The Book of Troilus and Criseyde* (Princeton and London 1926)
This edition includes an introduction and detailed notes, but lacks a glossary.
Tr2
――――― *The Textual Tradition of Chaucer's 'Troilus.'* Chaucer Society 1st ser. 99 (London 1916; repr. 1945, 1967)
Root argues that MS evidence shows at least two distinct versions of the poem; the conclusions and the resulting text are controversial.
Tr3
Windeatt, Barry. 'The Text of the *Troilus*' in Salu **Tr59**, 1-22
Windeatt re-examines Root's influential view (**Tr2**) that there were two distinct authorial versions of *Tr* and argues that the MSS show Chaucer continued to work on the poem over an extended period of time, revising and adding material from other sources; he concludes that *Tr*, unlike *LGWProl*, did not exist in two distinct versions.

Sources and Analogues

Tr is based on Boccaccio's *Il filostrato;* see **M195** (vol. II) for an edition and **M203** for a translation. For the influence of the *Roman de la rose* see Cipriani **M178** and Fansler **M180**. For the influence of Ovid see Shannon **M214**. For a discussion of the influence of the tradition of *concordia discors* see Rowe **Tr57**, and for the influence of the apotheosis tradition see Steadman **Tr64**.

GENERAL STUDIES

Tr4
Gordon, R.K., ed. and trans. *The Story of Troilus as Told by Benoît de Sainte-Maure, Giovanni Boccaccio, Geoffrey Chaucer, and Robert Henryson* (London 1934, repr. New York 1964); repr. as Medieval Academy Reprints for Teaching 2 (Toronto, Buffalo, London 1978)
Gordon includes a brief introduction to each work; the translation from Benoît includes only those few excerpts that bear directly on the story of Troilus; see Mieszkowski **Tr6** for discussion of passages from Benoît omitted here.

Tr5
Kaske, R.E. 'The Aube in Chaucer's *Troilus*' in Schoeck and Taylor **CrS15**, II, 167-79
Kaske suggests that Chaucer put a medieval *aube* tradition to comic use in *Tr* III.1415-1533.

Tr6
Mieszkowski, Gretchen B. 'The Reputation of Criseyde 1155-1500,' *Transactions of the Connecticut Academy of Arts and Sciences* 43 (1971) 71-153
Mieszkowski shows that Criseyde was regarded as fickle in love throughout the tradition of her story. Criseyde's character was thus given more favourable treatment by Chaucer than by other medieval authors both before and after him.

Tr7
Rollins, Hyder E. 'The Troilus-Cressida Story from Chaucer to Shakespeare,' *PMLA* 32 (1917) 383-429
Rollins concludes that Shakespeare somewhat restores Criseyde's character from its degeneration, evident in Henryson's many 16th-century followers, such as Turberville and Gascoigne.

Tr8
Young, Karl. *The Origin and Development of the Story of Troilus and Criseyde.* Chaucer Society 2nd ser. 40 (London 1908, repr. New York 1968)
Young traces the development of the story from Dares and Dictys through Benoît and Guido to Boccaccio and Chaucer.

BEAUVEAU, SENESCHAL OF ANJOU

Tr9
Pratt, Robert A. 'Chaucer and *Le Roman de Troyle et de Criseida*,'
SP 53 (1956) 509-39
Although the date of *Le Roman de Troyle et de Criseida* by
Beauveau, Seneschal of Anjou, is uncertain, Pratt argues that
Chaucer made use of this French translation of Boccaccio's work
and lists parallel readings with *Tr*.

BENOIT DE SAINTE-MORE [Benoît de Sainte-Maure]

For an edition of Benoît's *Roman de Troie* see **M152**; for a partial
translation in prose, see Gordon **Tr4**.

BOCCACCIO, GIOVANNI

For the text of the *Filostrato* and for other studies of Chaucer's
use of Boccaccio in *Tr*, see **M195-6, M203**, and especially
Wright **M197**, 59-101.

Tr10
Lewis, C.S. 'What Chaucer Really Did to *Il filostrato*,' *E&S* 17
(1932) 56-75; repr. in Schoeck and Taylor **CrS15**, II, 16-33 and in
Barney **Tr27**, 37-54
In this influential essay, Lewis shows how Chaucer used rhetoric,
the courtly love tradition, and the idea of *sentence* to change the
Renaissance flavour of Boccaccio's poem back to a medieval one.
Tr11
Meech, Sanford B. *Design in Chaucer's 'Troilus'* (Syracuse 1959)
Meech's close textual analysis, based on detailed comparison of *Tr*
with the *Filostrato*, is full of valuable insights, but offers little sense
of the overall design of the poem.
Tr12
Rossetti, Wm. Michael, trans. and intro. *Chaucer's 'Troylus and
Cryseyde' (from the Harl. MS. 3943) Compared with Boccaccio's
'Filostrato.'* 2 pts. Chaucer Society 1st ser. 44, 65 (London 1873,

1883)
Rossetti prints the two texts side by side, translating in full the *Filostrato* passages used by Chaucer in *Tr* and summarizing the others briefly; his translations of the Italian are not entirely reliable.

BOETHIUS, ANICIUS MANLIUS SEVERINUS

For a text of the *Consolatio philosophiae* see **M232**; for Chaucer's translation see **Bo1-3**; see Jefferson's **M241**, 120-33 for the influence of the *Consolatio* on *Tr*.

Tr13
Eldredge, Laurence. 'Boethian Epistemology and Chaucer's *Troilus* in the Light of Fourteenth-Century Thought,' *Mediaevalia* 2 (1976) 49-75
Eldredge argues that Troilus' views on free will and necessity would have been familiar to Chaucer's contemporaries.

Tr14
Gaylord, Alan T. 'Uncle Pandarus as Lady Philosophy,' *Papers of the Michigan Academy of Science, Arts, and Letters* 46 pt. 3 (1961) 571-95
Gaylord compares the speeches of Pandarus with those of Lady Philosophy in Boethius' *Consolatio philosophiae* and suggests that Chaucer depicts the advice of Pandarus to Troilus as a parody of the advice of Lady Philosophy to Boethius.

Tr15
McCall, John P. 'Five-Book Structure in Chaucer's *Troilus*,' *MLQ* 23 (1962) 297-308
McCall suggests that Chaucer imitated in *Tr* the five-book structure of the *Consolatio philosophiae* and created a formal and thematic design which reflects the ordered argument of Lady Philosophy while inverting the dramatic movement.

COLONNE, GUIDO DELLE [Guido de Columnis]

For an edition and translation of Guido's *Historia destructionis Troiae* see **M250-51**.

Tr16
Benson C. David. ' "O nyce world": What Chaucer Really Found in Guido delle Colonne's History of Troy,' *ChauR* 13 (1978-9) 308-15
Benson gives a clear analysis of the distinctive features of Guido's history and argues that Guido's historical pessimism and his distinctive narrator were influences on *Tr;* see also Benson **M252**.
Tr17
Hamilton, George L. *The Indebtedness of Chaucer's 'Troilus and Criseyde' to Guido delle Colonne's 'Historia Trojana.'* Columbia University Studies in Romance Philology and Literature [5] (New York 1903)
Hamilton discusses all the borrowings from Guido, giving the English and Latin text of each passage; he includes a summary of critical opinion on Chaucer's sources for *Tr,* from Gower to 1900.

DARES PHRYGIUS and DICTYS CRETENSIS

Tr18
Frazer, R.M., Jr., trans. *The Trojan War: The Chronicles of Dictys of Crete and Dares the Phrygian.* Indiana University Greek and Latin Classics (Bloomington and London 1966)
Chaucer refers to Dares and Dictys in *Tr* I.146 as the ultimate sources, together with Homer, for the story of Troy. As Frazer points out in his introduction, Dares and Dictys were regarded in the Middle Ages as more historical than Homer, since they were believed to be eye-witness accounts of the war from the Trojan and Greek viewpoints. There is little evidence to suggest that Chaucer knew these texts directly, however, and they are best regarded as analogues rather than as sources for *Tr.* Chaucer's reference to Dares in *Tr* V.1770-71, as Root **Tr20** points out, is based on the version of Dares by Joseph of Exeter. Frazer's translation is based on *Daretis Phrygii de excidio Troiae historia,* ed. Ferdinandus Meister (Leipzig 1873) and *Dictys Cretensis ephemeridos belli Troiani libri,* ed. Werner Eisenhut (Leipzig 1958). A revised edition of *Dictys,* ed. Werner Eisenhut (Leipzig 1973), appeared after Frazer's translation was published.

GUILLAUME DE MACHAUT

See **M164-5** for editions of his works.

Tr19

Wimsatt, James. 'Guillaume de Machaut and Chaucer's *Troilus and Criseyde*,' *MAE* 45 (1976) 277-92
Wimsatt argues that Machaut's lay 'Mireoir amoureux' is probably the nearest thing to a single source for Antigone's song in *Tr*; he discusses other possible influences of Machaut on the characterization of Troilus and on Chaucer's use of the language of love throughout the poem; for an edition of Machaut's poem see **M165**, II, 362-70.

JOSEPH OF EXETER [Joseph Iscanus]

For an edition and translation see **M265-6**.

Tr20

Root, Robert Kilburn. 'Chaucer's Dares,' *MP* 15 (1917-18) 1-22
Root demonstrates that Chaucer drew on Joseph's verse adaptation of Dares rather than on Dares himself.

'LOLLIUS'

Tr21

Kittredge, George Lyman. 'Chaucer's Lollius,' *Harvard Studies in Classical Philology* 28 (1917) 47-133
Kittredge shows why Chaucer cited the fictional Lollius as a source, and concludes that he must have derived the name from a misreading of Horace, *Epistles* 1. 2.1-2, which he could have known from a quotation in the *Policraticus* of John of Salisbury; see further Pratt **Tr22**.

Tr22

Pratt, Robert Armstrong. 'A Note on Chaucer's Lollius,' *MLN* 65 (1950) 183-7

Pratt cites two MSS of the *Policraticus* which contain, in the lines quoted from Horace, precisely the variants suggested by Kittredge **Tr21**; one MS adds to the text in the *Policraticus* the statement that Lollius wrote a history of the Trojan War.

PAMPHILUS DE AMORE

For an edition and translation see **M291-2**.

Tr23

Garbáty, Thomas Jay. 'The *Pamphilus* Tradition in Ruiz and Chaucer,' *PQ* 46 (1967) 457-70

Garbáty lists parallels between *Tr* and *Pamphilus,* a medieval Latin comedy which Chaucer mentions in *FranklT* 1110 and *Mel* 1556.

PETRARCA, FRANCESCO [Petrarch]

Tr24

Thomson, Patricia. 'The "Canticus Troili": Chaucer and Petrarch,' *Comparative Literature* 11 (1959) 313-28

Thomson discusses Chaucer's translation (*Tr* I.400-20) of Petrarch's Sonnet 88 (In Vita), 'S'amor non è,' in considerable detail.

Critical Studies

See Donaldson **M28** for a perceptive introduction to the poem; see Elbow **CrS40**, 49-72 for an analysis of the conflict between free will and necessity and its Boethian background; see Kelly **B47**, 217-44 for the argument that Troilus and Criseyde marry clandestinely. Kittredge **CrS50** argues that *Tr* should be viewed as the first modern novel. Lewis **B181** discusses the influence of the *Roman de la rose* and suggests that Criseyde is motivated by fear and by concern for her reputation. Payne **CrS62**, 472-502 discusses six rhetorical methods Chaucer uses to elaborate the *Filostrato,* with particular attention to his use of figurative elaboration. Robertson **CrS66**, 472-502 argues that *Tr* is a tale of idolatrous love set against a background of Boethian philosophy and claims that both Chaucer and his audience would have condemned the two main characters of the poem. Curry **CrS35**, 241-98 (repr. in Schoeck and Taylor **CrS15**, II, 34-70) argues from astrological references that the notion of destiny pervades *Tr;* he also argues that the epilogue is in contradiction with the poem as a whole, a point disputed by Donaldson **Tr32**, Dronke **Tr34**, and others.

Tr25
Aers, David. 'Criseyde: Woman in Medieval Society,' *ChauR* 13 (1978-9) 177-200
Drawing on the social history of Power **B56**, Aers argues that in *Tr* Chaucer uses the romance genre and the conventions of courtly literature to explore the anomalies between literary convention and social reality for aristocratic women.

Tr26
Barney, Stephen A. 'Troilus Bound,' *Speculum* 47 (1972) 445-58
Barney shows the importance of the imagery of binding in the poem, especially as a poetic means of suggesting order.

Tr27
Barney, Stephen A., ed. *Chaucer's 'Troilus': Essays in Criticism* (Hamden, Conn. 1980)
Barney prints a collection of modern critical essays, some reprinted, some written for the collection.

Tr28
Bloomfield, Morton W. 'Distance and Predestination in *Troilus and Criseyde,*' *PMLA* 72 (1957) 14-26; repr. in Schoeck and Taylor **CrS15**, II, 196-210; in Bloomfield **CrS2**, 200-16; and in Barney **Tr27**, 75-90
Bloomfield explores the tension between the narrator's foreknowledge of the historical events he relates and his sympathies for his characters; as the events reach their inevitable outcome, the narrator distances himself from the action.

Tr29
Covella, Sister Frances Dolores. 'Audience as Determinant of Meaning in the *Troilus,*' *ChauR* 2 (1967-8) 235-45
Covella argues that there are two epilogues at the end of *Tr*: one contained in lines 1751-85, addressed to the courtly audience who might have listened to the poem, and another, immediately

following, addressed to the general reader.

Tr30

David, Alfred. 'Chaucerian Comedy and Criseyde' in Salu **Tr59**,
90-104

David discusses the distinctively Chaucerian sense of humour that
characterizes Chaucer's portrait of Criseyde.

Tr31

Denomy, Alexander J., CSB. 'The Two Moralities of Chaucer's
*Troilus and Criseyde,' Proceedings and Transactions of the Royal
Society of Canada* 44 ser. 3, sec. 2 (1950) 35-46; repr. in Schoeck
and Taylor **CrS15**, II, 147-59

Denomy argues that the epilogue of *Tr* was appended for fear of
ecclesiastical censure, since without it the poem might have been
read as a celebration of illicit love.

Tr32

Donaldson, E. Talbot. 'The Ending of Chaucer's *Troilus*' in *Early
English and Norse Studies Presented to Hugh Smith in Honour of His
Sixtieth Birthday*, ed. Arthur Brown and Peter Foote (London 1963)
26-45; repr. as 'The Ending of *Troilus,*' in Donaldson **CrS7**, 84-101
and in Barney **Tr27**, 115-30

Donaldson argues that Chaucer's ending is in keeping with his
'poetry of complex significance.'

Tr33

_____ 'Criseide and her Narrator' in Donaldson **CrS7**, 65-83

Donaldson gives a close analysis of the narrator's attitude towards
Criseyde.

Tr34

Dronke, Peter. 'The Conclusion of *Troilus and Criseyde,' MAE* 23
(1964) 47-52

Dronke suggests, on the basis of comparison with passages in
Dante, Boccaccio, and Boethius, that the conclusion of *Tr* is an
integral part of the poem and does not invalidate the view of human
love expressed in Bk. III.

Tr35

Dunning, T.P. 'God and Man in *Troilus and Criseyde*' in *English and
Medieval Studies Presented to J.R.R. Tolkien,* ed. Norman Davis and
C.L. Wrenn (London 1962) 164-82

Dunning argues that because *Tr* is a poem in praise of love, the
divine perspective in the epilogue is consistent with the poem as a
whole.

Tr36
Erzgräber, Willi. 'Tragik und Komik in Chaucers *Troilus and Criseyde*' in *Festschrift für Walter Hübner,* ed. Dieter Riesner and Helmut Gneuss (Berlin 1964) 139-63
Erzgräber argues that fate and character are equally responsible for the tragic outcome of the story and that tragedy and comedy are interwoven throughout the poem, in ironic contrast.

Tr37
Farnham, Willard Edward. 'Falls of Princes: Chaucer and Lydgate' in Farnham, *The Medieval Heritage of Elizabethan Tragedy* (Berkeley 1936) 137-60
Farnham analyses the tragic elements in *Tr* and *MkT* with reference to Boccaccio's *De casibus virorum illustrium.*

Tr38
Gaylord, Alan T. 'Friendship in Chaucer's *Troilus,*' *ChauR* 3 (1968-9) 239-64
Gaylord surveys a variety of medieval ideas of friendship and their treatment in *Tr.*

Tr39
Gordon, Ida L. *The Double Sorrow of Troilus: A Study of Ambiguities in 'Troilus and Criseyde'* (London 1970)
Gordon emphasizes the ambiguities and complexities of the poem.

Tr40
Green, Richard F. 'Troilus and the Game of Love,' *ChauR* 13 (1978-9) 201-20
Green studies the game of love-talking in the poem and sets it in the context of social and literary conventions of the period.

Tr41
Howard, Donald R. 'Experience, Language, and Consciousness: *Troilus and Criseyde,* II, 596-931' in *Medieval Literature and Folklore Studies: Essays in Honor of Francis Lee Utley,* ed. Jerome Mandel and Bruce A. Rosenberg (New Brunswick, N.J. 1970) 173-92; repr. in Barney **Tr27,** 159-80
Howard traces the progress of Criseyde's decision to love Troilus, bringing in psycholinguistics, oral tradition, and folklore as bases for his argument.

Tr42
Kiernan, K.S. 'Hector the Second: The Lost Face of Troilustratus,' *Annuale mediaevale* 16 (1975) 52-62
Kiernan shows that Troilus is subtly and sometimes unfavourably

compared to Hector throughout the poem.

Tr43

Kirby, Thomas A. *Chaucer's 'Troilus': A Study in Courtly Love.*
Louisiana State University Studies 39 (Baton Rouge 1940; repr.
Gloucester, Mass. 1958)
Kirby discusses the development of courtly love and Chaucer's use
of the courtly love tradition in characterization. On this tradition
see **B173-90**.

Tr44

Kittredge, George Lyman. *The Date of Chaucer's 'Troilus' and Other
Chaucer Matters.* Chaucer Society 2nd ser. 42 (London 1909, for
1905)
Kittredge shows that *Tr* was written later than Gower's *Mirour de
l'omme* and Chaucer's *HF,* and points out that Criseyde, as a
character, originates in a misreading by Benoît of Dares and Dictys;
on Criseyde's character see also Mieszkowski **Tr6**.

Tr45

Leyerle, John. 'The Heart and the Chain' in *The Learned and the
Lewed: Studies in Chaucer and Medieval Literature,* ed. Larry D.
Benson. Harvard English Studies 5 (Cambridge, Mass. 1974) 113-45;
repr. in Barney **Tr27**, 181-209
Leyerle identifies the 'poetic nucleus' of *Tr* as the heart and
discusses its connection with the central themes and action of the
poem, love and change.

Tr46

Lowes, John Livingston. 'The Date of Chaucer's *Troilus and
Criseyde,*' *PMLA* 23 (1908) 285-306
Lowes offers evidence to support a date in the early 1380s.

Tr47

Lumiansky, R.M. 'The Function of the Proverbial Monitory
Elements in Chaucer's *Troilus and Criseyde,*' *Tulane Studies in
English* 2 (1950) 5-48
Lumiansky examines Chaucer's use of proverbial monitory
elements in *Tr,* material that is absent from the sources, and
concludes that Chaucer used these elements for characterization
and dramatic development.

Tr48

McAlpine, Monica. *The Genre of 'Troilus and Criseyde'* (Ithaca and
London 1978)
McAlpine analyses the poem as a tragedy.

Tr49

McCall, John P. 'The Trojan Scene in Chaucer's *Troilus*,' *ELH* 29 (1962) 263-75

McCall shows that the fortunes of Troilus are presented in the poem as analogous to the fortunes of Troy.

Tr50

_____ '*Troilus and Criseyde*' in Rowland **CrS13**, 446-63

McCall provides a critical review of scholarship and a selective bibliography to 1978.

Tr51

McKinnell, John. 'Letters as a Type of the Formal Level in *Troilus and Criseyde*' in Salu **Tr59**, 73-89

Setting the letters in *Tr* in the context of medieval theory and practice of letter-writing, McKinnell argues that Chaucer's modifications of the letters in the *Filostrato* are extensive, and that their function in the work is often altered from their source in Boccaccio.

Tr52

Manlove, Colin. ' "Rooteles moot grene soone deye": The Helplessness of Chaucer's Troilus and Criseyde,' *E&S* n.s. 31 (1978) 1-22

Manlove argues that the lovers doom their love by cutting themselves off from the world.

Tr53

Mehl, Dieter. 'The Audience of Chaucer's *Troilus and Criseyde*' in Rowland **CrS14**, 173-89; repr. in Barney **Tr27**, 211-29

Mehl makes a sensitive examination of the poet's rhetorical manipulation of his audience.

Tr54

Patterson, Lee W. 'Ambiguity and Interpretation: A Fifteenth-Century Reading of *Troilus and Criseyde*,' *Speculum* 54 (1979) 297-330

Patterson provides an *editio princeps* of a portion of a treatise for women religious which quotes a stanza from *Tr* and makes explicit reference to the poem; he sets the discussion of love and of *Tr* in the treatise in the context of similar medieval accounts of love and friendship.

Tr55

Price, Thomas R. '*Troilus and Criseyde:* A Study in Chaucer's Method of Narrative Construction,' *PMLA* 11 (1896) 307-22

This early essay remains valuable as a perceptive general discussion of the dramatic quality of *Tr*, which Price likens to a 19th-century play.

Tr56

Robertson, D.W., Jr. 'Chaucerian Tragedy,' *ELH* 19 (1952) 1-37; repr. in Schoeck and Taylor **CrS15**, II, 86-121
Robertson argues that the tragedy of Troilus is a repetition of the fall of Adam.

Tr57

Rowe, Donald W. *O Love! O Charite! Contraries Harmonized in Chaucer's 'Troilus'* (Carbondale and Edwardsville, Ill. 1976)
Rowe sets the poem in the tradition of *concordia discors,* the view of God's creation as a harmony of contraries.

Tr58

Salter, Elizabeth. '*Troilus and Criseyde:* A Reconsideration' in Lawlor **B180**, 86-106
Salter presents an intelligent examination of the difficulties Chaucer encountered in dealing with his material.

Tr59

Salu, Mary, ed. *Essays on 'Troilus and Criseyde.'* Chaucer Studies 3 (Cambridge and Totowa, N.J. 1979; repr. 1982)
Salu prints a collection of critical essays written for the volume.

Tr60

Sams, Henry W. 'The Dual Time-Scheme in Chaucer's *Troilus,*' *MLN* 56 (1941) 94-100; repr. in Schoeck and Taylor **CrS15**, II, 180-85
Sams shows that there are two concurrent time-schemes in *Tr,* one provided by the formal dates which extend over several years, and the other by a seasonal imagery which seems to extend over a single year.

Tr61

Shepherd, G.T. '*Troilus and Criseyde*' in Brewer **CrS4**, 65-87
Shepherd views *Tr* as 'a romance in a tragic mode' which adopts conventions of romances designed to be read aloud.

Tr62

Smyser, H.M. 'The Domestic Background of *Troilus and Criseyde,*' *Speculum* 31 (1956) 297-315
Smyser shows that the domestic scenes in *Tr* fit a typical medieval

house; he discusses the lack of privacy characteristic of medieval
life and of the households described in *Tr.*
Tr63
Stanley, E.G. 'Stanza and Ictus: Chaucer's Emphasis in *Troilus and
Criseyde*' in Esch **CrS9**, 123-48
Stanley argues that the last line of each stanza, and within that line
the metrically stressed syllable preceding the caesura, are of
particular importance in *Tr.*
Tr64
Steadman, John M. *Disembodied Laughter: 'Troilus' and the
Apotheosis Tradition. A Reexamination of Narrative and Thematic
Contexts.* (Berkeley, Los Angeles, London 1972)
Steadman gives background on the tradition behind the epilogue
and analysis of the epilogue in relation to *Tr* as a whole.
Tr65
Wimsatt, James I. 'Medieval and Modern in Chaucer's *Troilus and
Criseyde*,' *PMLA* 92 (1977) 203-16
Wimsatt offers a balanced discussion of the use of epic, romance,
philosophical narrative, and realism in *Tr.*
Tr66
Windeatt, Barry. ' "Love that oughte ben secree" in Chaucer's
Troilus,' *ChauR* 14 (1979-80) 116-31
Windeatt offers many detailed analyses of Chaucer's changes of
Boccaccio which emphasize the sharply-felt distinction between
public and private worlds in *Tr.*

THE LEGEND OF GOOD WOMEN

Editions and Textual Studies

Robinson **M30**, 480-518 (text); 839-54, 912-15 (notes). Skeat **M31**, III, xvi-lvi (introduction), 65-174 (text), 288-351 (notes).

LGW1
Amy, Ernest F. *The Text of Chaucer's 'Legend of Good Women'* (Princeton 1914, repr. New York 1965)
Amy presents an authoritative study of the MSS.

Sources and Analogues

For a general discussion of the sources of *LGW* see Root **CrS68**, 135-42. For texts of Ovid's *Metamorphoses* and *Heroides,* two of the most important sources, see **M280-81**. The *Metamorphoses* is a source for four of the legends: Thisbe (4.55-166), Hypsipyle and Medea (7), Ariadne (7.456-8, 8.6ff.), and Philomela (4.424ff.). The *Heroides* is a source for five of the legends: Dido (7), Hypsipyle and Medea (6, 12), Ariadne (10), Phyllis (2), and Hypermnestra (14). For Chaucer's use of the *Ovide moralisé* in *Philomela* and *Ariadne,* see Lowes **M290**.

See **M195** and **M201-2** for texts and translations of two other important sources: Boccaccio's *De casibus virorum illustrium* and *De mulieribus claris.*

See **M158** and **M164** for texts of French poems by Froissart and Machaut which influenced the *Prologue.*

See Lowes **M154** for the influence of Deschamps' *Miroir de mariage;* see McCall **CrS54** for the influence of the traditions of the pagan gods; see Shannon **M214** for the influence of the Roman poets, especially Ovid.

For a text of Guido delle Colonne's *Historia destructionis Troiae,* the main source for the legend of Hypsipyle and Medea, see **M250**; for a text of Virgil's *Aeneid,* the source of the legend of Dido, see **M305**. The main source for the legend of Lucrece is Ovid, *Fasti* 2.685-852 (see **M279**).

LGW2

Aiken, Pauline. 'Chaucer's *Legend of Cleopatra* and the *Speculum historiale,' Speculum* 13 (1938) 232-6

Aiken shows that Chaucer's version of the Cleopatra story is closer to the one in the *Speculum historiale* of Vincent of Beauvais than to the one in Florus' *Epitome rerum Romanorum,* the supposed source.

LGW3

Estrich, Robert M. 'Chaucer's Prologue to the *Legend of Good Women* and Machaut's *Le Jugement dou Roy de Navarre,' SP* 36 (1939) 20-39

Estrich argues that the *Jugement* is more likely to be the principal source for the incident of the poet's defence to the God of Love than Deschamps' *Lai de Franchise,* as suggested by Lowes **LGW5**.

LGW4

Lossing, Marian. 'The Prologue to the *Legend of Good Women* and the *Lai de Franchise,' SP* 39 (1942) 15-35

Lossing questions the identification of the *Lai de Franchise* as a source for *LGWProl,* as suggested by Lowes **LGW5**.

LGW5

Lowes, John L. 'The Prologue to the *Legend of Good Women* as Related to the French *marguerite* Poems and the *Filostrato,' PMLA* 19 (1904) 593-683

Lowes shows, in great detail, that *LGWProl* borrows from Machaut's *Dit de la marguerite,* Froissart's *Dittié de la flour de la marguerite,* and Boccaccio's *Filostrato;* on the basis of the dating of these poems, he argues that B(F) is the earlier version of the *Prologue.* He also argues that Deschamps' *Lai de Franchise* was a source for the *Prologue,* but that argument is disputed by Estrich **LGW3** and Lossing **LGW4**.

LGW6

———— 'The Two Prologues to the *Legend of Good Women:* A New Test' in *Anniversary Papers by Colleagues and Pupils of George Lyman Kittredge* [no ed.] (Boston and London 1913) 95-104

Lowes shows that the B(F) version of *LGWProl* reveals marks of revision, while the A(G) version does not.

LGW7

Meech, Sanford Brown. 'Chaucer and an Italian Translation of the *Heroides,' PMLA* 45 (1930) 110-28

Meech shows that Chaucer used an Italian translation of the

Heroides as an additional source for the legends of Hypermnestra, Phyllis, Medea, and Dido.

LGW8

———— 'Chaucer and the *Ovide moralisé* — A Further Study,' *PMLA* 46 (1931) 182-204

In a continuation of Lowes **M290**, Meech shows that Chaucer drew on the *Ovide moralisé* for the legend of Ariadne, thus refuting the claim of Shannon **M214** that the only sources for this legend were Ovid and Boccaccio's *De genealogia deorum.*

LGW9

Tatlock, John S.P. 'Chaucer and the *Legenda aurea*,' *MLN* 45 (1930) 296-8

Tatlock shows that Chaucer drew on the *Legenda aurea* for the legend of Lucrece.

LGW10

Young, Karl. 'The *Dit de la harpe* of Guillaume de Machaut' in *Essays in Honor of Albert Feuillerat,*' ed. Henri M. Peyre (New Haven 1943) 1-20

Young shows that the *Dit de la harpe* was not a direct source for *LGWProl,* despite the appearance of the image of the harp in lines 89-93; he gives the text of the *Dit* and discusses the larger tradition it reflects as an influence on Chaucer.

Critical Studies

See Middleton **CT289** for a comparison of the poetic methods of *LGW* and *CT;* Spearing **CrS70**, 101-10 for a discussion of the *Prologue* in the tradition of medieval dream-poetry; and Payne **CrS63** for *LGW* and Chaucer's poetics.

LGW11

Brown, Carleton. 'The Date of Prologue F to the *Legend of Good Women,*' *MLN* 58 (1943) 274-8

Brown points out that, if Alceste is to be identified with Joan of Kent, then the *Prologue* must have been written in 1385 rather than 1386, and could not have been borrowed from the *Lai de Franchise*; cf. Galway **LGW15**.

LGW12

Fisher, John H. 'The Revision of the Prologue to the *Legend of Good Women:* An Occasional Explanation,' *South Atlantic Bulletin* 43 pt. 4 (1978) 75-84

Fisher suggests that *LGWProl,* first written in honour of Queen Anne, was revised on the occasion of Richard II's marriage to Princess Isabel of France (1396).

LGW13

―――― 'The *Legend of Good Women*' in Rowland **CrS13**, 464-76

Fisher reviews scholarship on *LGW* and supplies a selective bibliography to 1978.

LGW14

Frank, Robert Worth, Jr. *Chaucer and 'The Legend of Good Women'* (Cambridge, Mass. 1972)

Frank analyses narrative technique in an attempt to assess the role of *LGW* in Chaucer's development as a narrative poet.

LGW15

Galway, Margaret. 'Chaucer's Sovereign Lady: A Study of the Prologue to the *Legend* and Related Poems,' *MLR* 33 (1938) 145-99

Galway identifies the Alceste of *LGWProl,* and other female characters in Chaucer, with Princess Joan of Kent. Alceste has also been identified with Queen Anne; see Robinson **M30**, 840 for other identifications that have been proposed.

LGW16

Goddard, H.C. 'Chaucer's *Legend of Good Women,*' *JEGP* 7, pt. 4 (1908) 87-129; 8 (1909) 47-111

Goddard suggests that *LGW* may be a satire on the standards upheld in the legends themselves.

LGW17

Griffith, D.D. 'An Interpretation of Chaucer's *Legend of Good Women*' in *The Manly Anniversary Studies in Language and Literature* [no ed.] (Chicago 1923) 32-41

Griffith examines the religious motifs of the F-version of the *Prologue* in an interpretation of *LGW* as a legend of Cupid's saints.

LGW18

Koonce, B.G. 'Satan the Fowler,' *MS* 21 (1959) 176-84

Koonce applies traditional exegesis of the biblical image of the fowler to the fowler image in *LGWProl.*

LGW19
Lowes, John Livingston. 'Is Chaucer's *Legend of Good Women* a
Travesty?' *JEGP* 8 (1909) 513-69
Arguing against the view of Goodard **LGW16** that *LGW* is satirical,
Lowes defends his own position by discussing the work's sources
and tradition.
LGW20
_____ 'The Prologue to the *Legend of Good Women* Considered in
its Chronological Relations,' *PMLA* 20 (1905) 749-864
By studying the sources of and the relations among *HF, Bo, PF, Tr,*
and *LGW,* Lowes discusses the chronology of *LGW* and of the two
versions of the *Prologue.*
LGW21
Payne, Robert O. 'Making his own Myth: The Prologue to
Chaucer's *Legend of Good Women,*' *ChauR* 9 (1974-5) 197-211
Payne argues that *LGWProl* is the final version of the poem which
Chaucer had been trying to write in *BD, PF,* and *HF.*
LGW22
Schofield, William Henry. 'The Sea-Battle in Chaucer's "Legend of
Cleopatra",' in *Anniversary Papers by Colleagues and Pupils of
George Lyman Kittredge* [no ed.] (Boston and London 1913) 139-52
Schofield compares the sea battle in the 'Legend of Cleopatra' with
other accounts of medieval naval warfare, especially with those by
Froissart, to demonstrate the medieval realism of the action.

SHORT POEMS

This section includes the short poems known to be Chaucer's, and those poems classified by Robinson **M30** as 'Short Poems of Doubtful Authorship.'

Editions

Robinson **M30**, 519-43, 854-67, 915-20 (texts); 303-8, 788-90, 901-2 (notes). Skeat **M31**, I, 20-92 (introduction); 261-76, 323-34, 360-64, 379-416 (texts); 452-61, 495-504, 526-8, 538-68 (notes).

SP1
Koch, John, ed. *Geoffrey Chaucers kleinere Dichtungen nebst Einleitung, Lesarten, Anmerkungen, und einem Wörterverzeichnis.* Englische Textbibliothek 18 (Heidelberg 1928, repr. 1947) Koch provides textual notes, variant readings, and a table of early editions and MSS showing which of the short poems are included.

Textual Studies

See Brusendorff **M40**, 178-295 for a discussion of the MSS and the MS tradition of the short poems.

SP2
Doyle, A.I. and George B. Pace. 'A New Chaucer Manuscript,' *PMLA* 83 (1968) 22-34
Doyle and Pace describe a rediscovered MS now in the Coventry Record Office and formerly known only from a 17th-century catalogue; it is the fourth largest extant collection of Chaucer's short poems. The authors transcribe the poems and collate them against Robinson's text, proposing a number of new readings.
SP3
_____ 'Further Texts of Chaucer's Minor Poems,' *Studies in Bibliography: Papers of the Bibliographical Society of the University of Virginia* 28 (1975) 41-61

Doyle and Pace provide a description, introduction, and transcriptions of the Melbourne MS *ABC;* Nottingham, University Library, MS. ME LM 1 *Truth;* and Oxford, Bodleian Library Fairfax MS. 16 *Against Women Inconstant.*

SP4
Pace, George Blocker. 'Four Unpublished Chaucer Manuscripts,' *MLN* 63 (1948) 457-62
Pace prints and discusses unpublished MSS of *Truth* (London, British Library, Additional MS. 36983 and Cambridge, Magdalene College, Pepys MS. 2006), *Lak of Stedfastnesse* (Dublin, Trinity College, MS. 432), and *Complaint of Chaucer to His Purse* (Cambridge, Caius College, MS. 176).

Critical and Source Studies of More Than One Poem

See Moore **M50** for Chaucer's lost lyrics, and Robbins **CrS64** for the argument that Chaucer's lost early poems were written in French. See Clemen **CrS32**, 170-97 for analysis of *An ABC, The Complaint unto Pity, A Complaint to his Lady,* and *The Complaint of Mars.* Studies relating the short poems to events in Chaucer's life are listed under **M106-33**. For analysis of *The Complaint of Mars, The Complaint of Venus,* and *The Complaint unto Pity* see Norton-Smith **CrS60**.

SP5
Dean, Nancy. 'Chaucer's *Complaint,* a Genre descended from the *Heroides,' Comparative Literature* 19 (1967) 1-27
Distinguishing two types of complaint, the public lament deriving from the *planctus* and the personal lament deriving from Ovid's *Heroides,* Dean discusses the relationship of Chaucer's complaint to the Ovidian tradition.

SP6
Green, A. Wigfall. 'Chaucer's Complaints: Stanzaic Arrangement, Meter, and Rhyme,' *University of Mississippi Studies in English* 3 (1962) 19-34
Green makes a detailed study of rhyme-words and metrics, comparing Chaucer's poems to the French complaint genre.

SP7
Reiss, Edmund. 'Dusting Off the Cobwebs: A Look at Chaucer's
Lyrics,' *ChauR* 1 (1966-7) 55-65
Reiss examines the use of language in *An ABC* and *To
Rosemounde,* revealing the skilful opposition of subject and speaker
in the former and the bantering tone of the latter.
SP8
Robbins, Rossell Hope. 'The Lyrics' in Rowland **CrS13**, 380-402
Robbins discusses the body of Chaucer's lyrics in connection with
their sources and analogues in contemporary lyric forms of the
time, both French and English; he includes a selected bibliography.
SP9
Wimsatt, James I. 'Guillaume de Machaut and Chaucer's Love
Lyrics,' *MÆ* 47 (1978) 66-87
Wimsatt argues that, with the exception of the *Complaint of Venus,*
all of Chaucer's independent love-lyrics are based on poems of
Guillaume de Machaut.

Studies of Individual Poems

Only those poems which have been the subject of significant studies
are listed here. The poems are listed alphabetically, according to
Robinson's (**M30**) version of their titles; textual, critical, and source
studies of each poem are grouped together.

THE COMPLAINT OF CHAUCER TO HIS PURSE

SP10
Ferris, Sumner. 'The Date of Chaucer's Final Annuity and of the
"Complaint to his Empty Purse",' *MP* 65 (1967-8) 45-52
Ferris makes a careful examination of the documents relating to
Chaucer's annuity, in connection with the request for money made
in the poem; he concludes that the annuity was not granted until
February 1400 although the document was antedated to October
1399.
SP11
Pace, George B. 'The Text of Chaucer's *Purse,*' *Studies in*

Bibliography: Papers of the Bibliographical Society of the University of Virginia 1 (1948-9) 103-21
Pace provides a detailed textual analysis.
SP12
Scott, Florence R. 'A New Look at "The Complaint of Chaucer to his Empty Purse",' *ELN* 2 (1964) 81-7
Scott relates the poem to the political circumstances surrounding it and describes Chaucer as an astute courtier who took advantage of his political position on the acceptance of Henry of Lancaster as king.

THE COMPLAINT OF MARS

See Wood **CrS73**, 103-60 for a detailed discussion in light of the astrological references.

SP13
Braddy, Haldeen. 'Chaucer and Graunson: The Valentine Tradition,' *PMLA* 54 (1939) 359-68; revised in **M160**
Braddy discusses the influence of the valentine tradition on the *Complaint of Mars.*
SP14
Hultin, Neil C. 'Anti-courtly Elements in Chaucer's *Complaint of Mars,'* *Annuale mediaevale* 9 (1968) 58-75
Hultin discusses anti-courtly elements and critical attitudes towards courtly love.
SP15
Manly, John Matthews. 'On the Date and Interpretation of Chaucer's *Complaint of Mars,'* [Harvard] *Studies and Notes in Philology and Literature* 5 (1896) 107-26
Manly analyses the astrological elements.
SP16
Merrill, Rodney. 'Chaucer's *Broche of Thebes:* The Unity of "The Complaint of Mars" and "The Complaint of Venus",' *Literary Monographs* 5 (1973) 1-61
Basing his argument on MS evidence, Merrill shows that the convention of modern editors of printing the two complaints as separate

works obscures the fact that they are presented as a single work, *The Broche of Thebes,* in a number of early MSS.

SP17
Stillwell, Gardiner. 'Convention and Individuality in Chaucer's *Complaint of Mars,' PQ* 35 (1956) 69-89
Stillwell sees the poem as a synthesis of the various traditional forms on which it draws; he includes a history of critical opinion.

THE COMPLAINT OF VENUS

See Merrill **SP16** for the convincing argument that the *Complaint of Venus* and the *Complaint of Mars* are to be read as a single poem.

THE COMPLAINT UNTO PITY

SP18
Nolan, Charles J., Jr. 'Structural Sophistication in "The Complaint unto Pity",' *ChauR* 13 (1978-9) 363-72
Drawing on parallels with legal bills, Nolan argues that the poem represents an attempt to blend the amorous and legal traditions of complaint.

SP19
Pittock, Malcolm. 'Chaucer: *The Complaint unto Pity,' Criticism* 1 (1959) 160-68
Pittock gives a close reading of the poem.

THE FORMER AGE

SP20
Norton-Smith, J. 'Chaucer's *Etas prima,' MÆ* 32 (1963) 117-24
Norton-Smith examines *The Former Age* in the context of Chaucer's 'Boethian' poems.

SP21
Pace, George B. 'The True Text of *The Former Age,' MS* 23 (1961) 363-7

Pace gives textual evidence in support of Brusendorff's theory
(see **M40**) that *The Former Age* was never finished but was copied by
a scribe from one of the poet's drafts.
SP22
Schmidt, A.V.C. 'Chaucer and the Golden Age,' *Essays in Criticism*
26 (1976) 99-115
Schmidt gives a thorough analysis of *The Former Age.*

FORTUNE

SP23
Wimsatt, James I. 'Chaucer, Fortune, and Machaut's "Il m'est
avis",' in Vasta and Thundy **CrS18**, 119-31
Wimsatt argues that Machaut's balade is a main source for *Fortune*
as well as the source for the image of Fortune as 'monstre' in *BD*
628.

LAK OF STEDFASTNESSE

SP24
Cross, J.E. 'The Old Swedish *Trohetsvisan* and Chaucer's *Lak of
Stedfastnesse* — A Study in a Mediaeval Genre,' *Saga-Book of the
Viking Society for Northern Research* 16 (1962-5) 283-314
Cross discusses both poems as examples of the moralizing
complaint.
SP25
Holt, Lucius Hudson. 'Chaucer's *Lac of Stedfastnesse,' JEGP* 6
(1907) 419-31
Holt gives a stemma and a text which he compares with Skeat's.
SP26
Pace, George B. 'Chaucer's *Lak of Stedfastnesse,' Studies in Bibliog-
raphy: Papers of the Bibliographical Society of the University of
Virginia* 4 (1951-2) 105-22
Pace presents a new text, based partly on an 18th-century transcrip-
tion of the burnt London, British Library, MS. Cotton Otho A. XVIII,
and he establishes the priority of certain distinctive readings,
including 'wed thi folk' at line 28.

LENVOY DE CHAUCER A BUKTON

SP27
Kuhl, Ernest P. 'Chaucer's "My Maistre Bukton",' *PMLA* 38 (1923) 115-32
Kuhl summarizes the available evidence and decides in favour of Peter Bukton of Yorkshire over Robert Bukton of Suffolk as the Bukton addressed in the poem.

LENVOY DE CHAUCER A SCOGAN

SP28
David, Alfred. 'Chaucer's Good Counsel to Scogan,' *ChauR* 3 (1968-9) 265-74
David suggests that *Scog* is a moral balade rather than a begging poem.

SP29
French, Walter H. 'The Meaning of Chaucer's *Envoy to Scogan*,' *PMLA* 48 (1933) 289-92
French suggests that *Scog* is a diplomatic refusal to write a poem which Scogan had requested.

SP30
Lenaghan, R.T. 'Chaucer's *Envoy to Scogan:* The Uses of Literary Conventions,' *ChauR* 10 (1975-6) 46-61
Lenaghan discusses affinities between *Scog* and similar poems by Deschamps and Machaut, showing that all three derive from a court culture.

MERCILES BEAUTE

SP31
Lowes, John Livingston. 'The Chaucerian *Merciles Beaute* and Three Poems of Deschamps,' *MLR* 5 (1910) 33-9
Lowes examines the relationship between *Merciles Beaute* and Deschamps' chanson baladée (no. 541), *marguerite* balade (no. 540), and rondeau, 'Puis qu'Amour ay servi trestout mon temps' (no. 570).

PROVERBS

SP32
Pace, George B. 'The Chaucerian *Proverbs,*' *Studies in Bibliography: Papers of the Bibliographical Society of the University of Virginia* 18 (1965) 41-8
Pace provides detailed textual analysis and concludes that the *Proverbs* were probably ascribed to Chaucer in their MS archetype.

TO ROSEMOUNDE

SP33
Kökeritz, Helge. 'Chaucer's *Rosemounde,*' *MLN* 63 (1948) 310-18
Kökeritz provides helpful textual and explanatory notes.
SP34
Vasta, Edward. '*To Rosemounde*: Chaucer's "gentil" Dramatic Monologue' in Vasta and Thundy **CrS18**, 97-113
On the basis of a close reading, Vasta argues that the poem is a multi-layered satire of the style and content of conventional medieval love-poetry, appropriately addressed to a 'rose of the world.'

TRUTH

SP35
Rickert, Edith. ' "Thou Vache",' *MP* 11 (1913-14) 209-25
Rickert suggests that 'thou Vache' in *Truth*, line 22, refers to Sir Philip de la Vache, the Lollard knight who was the son-in-law of Chaucer's friend Sir Lewis Clifford.

A TREATISE ON THE ASTROLABE

For the nature and use of an astrolable see Hartner **B230**. For Chaucer's astronomical and astrological references see Curry **CrS35**, Grimm **B229**, North **B231**, Smyser **B236**, and Wood **CrS73**. For medieval astronomy in general see Orr **B232**, Wedel **B237**, and the general studies listed in the section on science, **B211-23**. For *De sphaera*, a medieval astronomical textbook which Chaucer knew, see Sacrobosco **M296** and Veazie **M297**.

Editions

Robinson **M30**, 544-63 (text); 867-72, 921-3 (notes). Skeat **M31**, III, lvii-lxxx (introduction); lxxxi-lxxxvi (plates); 175-232 (text); 233-42, 352-69 (notes).

Astr1
Pintelon, P. *Chaucer's Treatise on the Astrolabe, MS. 4862-4869 of the Royal Library in Brussels.* Rijksuniversiteit te Gent, Werken uitgegeven door Faculteit van de Wysbegeerte en Letteren, 89e Aflevering (Antwerp 1940)
In addition to a facsimile of fols. 75r-96v, which contain pt. I and forty conclusions from pt. II of *Astr*, Pintelon provides a discussion of the twenty-five MSS, an analysis of grammatical structure, and an account of the characteristic features of the prose.
Astr2
Skeat, Walter W., ed. *A Treatise on The Astrolabe, addressed to his son Lowys, by Geoffrey Chaucer. A.D. 1391.* EETS e.s. 16 (London 1872; repr. 1880, 1928, 1967, 1968)
This volume, Skeat's first edition of *Astr*, contains an introduction and notes along with the Latin text of pt. II of Messahala's [Māshā' allāh's] *Operatio astrolabii*, Chaucer's source for part of the work. The edition of *Astr* printed in Skeat **M31** has a shorter introduction and lacks the Messahala text, but the notes from the earlier edition are there revised and corrected.

Sources

One of Chaucer's main sources for *Astr* was a Latin treatise by Messahala [Māshā' allāh]; for a text see Skeat **Astr2**.

Astr3
Gunther, Robert William Theodore. *Chaucer and Messahalla on the Astrolabe.* Early Science in Oxford 5 (Oxford 1929, repr. 1967)
Gunther gives a collotype facsimile of Cambridge, University Library, MS. Ii. 3. 3., Messahala's *Compositio et operatio astrolabii,* along with an English translation of the work.

Astr4
Harvey, S.W. 'Chaucer's Debt to Sacrobosco,' *JEGP* 34 (1935) 34-8
Harvey shows, quoting parallel passages, that Chaucer drew directly on the *De sphaera* of Johannes de Sacrobosco for *Astr.*

Astr5
Masi, Michael. 'Chaucer, Messahala, and Bodleian Selden Supra 78,' *Manuscripta* 19 (1975) 36-47
Masi suggests that Chaucer knew and used Oxford, Bodleian Library, MS. Selden Supra 78 (S.C. 3466), a collection of astronomical treatises which includes Messahala's *De compositione et utilitate astrolabii.*

Studies

See Schlauch **M92**, 143-7 for a study of the prose structure of *Astr,* and Schlauch **M93** for a contrast between the prose of *Astr* and of *Boece* and *Melibee.*

Astr6
Eisner, Sigmund. 'Building Chaucer's Astrolabe,' *Journal of the British Astronomical Association* 86 (1975-6) 18-29, 125-32, and 219-27
Eisner gives instructions for the making of an astrolabe and suggests that Chaucer's treatise becomes easier to understand with a working model in hand.

Astr7
Madeleva, Sister M., CSC. 'A Child's Book of Stars' in Madeleva, *A Lost Language and Other Essays on Chaucer* (New York 1951) 87-100
Madeleva gives a brief, general account of the work.

THE ROMAUNT OF THE ROSE

Though this partial Middle English translation of the *Roman de la rose* is usually printed in editions of the complete works of Chaucer, the attribution is by no means certain (see the section Authorship, below). However, we have Chaucer's own testimony (*LGW* F329) that he translated the poem, and it undoubtedly influenced his work heavily. For this reason a bibliography on the French poem is included in the section on French sources and influences, **M168-88**; see that section for editions, modern translations, and studies of the *Roman* itself. The studies listed below deal with the Middle English translation.

Editions

Robinson **M30**, 566-637 (text); 872-82, 924-8 (notes). Skeat **M31**, I, 93-259 (text), 417-51 (notes). Both editions print the text from the unique MS; Skeat's is collated with Thynne's edition, and he includes the French text corresponding to Fragment A and a glossary.

Rom1
Sutherland, Ronald, ed. *The Romaunt of the Rose and Le Roman de la rose: A Parallel-Text Edition* (Berkeley and Los Angeles 1968) Sutherland prints the text side by side with the most probable source lines in selected MSS of the *Roman,* with emendations and notes on textual variants at the back of the book. His introduction discusses the groups of MSS of the *Roman* used for the *Romaunt.* He concludes, with some earlier scholars, that Fragment A is Chaucer's work, that B and C are the work of a northerner, and that the translations were linked and revised by a third hand.

Authorship

See Brusendorff **M40**, 296-425 for the fullest statement of the view that Chaucer wrote all three of the surviving fragments of the *Romaunt;* Brusendorff argues that the three fragments of a

translation by Chaucer were written down, from memory, by a
northern scribe in the early 15th century; see Sutherland **Rom1** for a
review of the MS evidence and the conclusion that only Fragment A
is Chaucer's.

Rom2
Kittredge, George Lyman. 'The Authorship of the English *Romaunt
of the Rose*,' [Harvard] *Studies and Notes in Philology and Literature*
1 (1892) 1-65
Kittredge concludes that the *Romaunt* is not Chaucer's, with the
possible exception of the first 1700 lines.

Studies

See Cipriani **M178** for an account of the influence of the *Roman de
la rose* on Chaucer. See Fansler **M180** for an assessment of the
relative influence of the two parts of the *Roman de la rose* on
Chaucer.

THE EQUATORIE OF THE PLANETIS

The unique MS of the *Equatorie of the Planetis* was discovered in 1951, and ascribed to Chaucer largely on the strength of the appearance in one of its astronomical tables of the phrase 'Radix Chaucer,' in a hand which may be the poet's. This attribution is greatly disputed. See the introduction in Price **Eq1** below.

Editions

See Fisher **M29**, 935-48.

Eq1
Price, Derek J., ed. *The Equatorie of the Planetis,* with a linguistic analysis by R.M. Wilson (London 1955)
Price's edition of Cambridge, University Library, Peterhouse MS. 75.i includes an introduction discussing the question of authorship, notes, extensive background material, and a linguistic analysis. See the review by Roland M. Smith, *JEGP* 57 (1958) 533-7, for the problems concerning the attribution to Chaucer.

Sources

For the astronomical background, see the headnote to the section under *Astr.*

Eq2
Kennedy, E.S. 'A Horoscope of Messehalla in the Chaucer Equatorium Manuscript,' *Speculum* 34 (1959) 629-30
Kennedy notes that the horoscope on fol. 64v is a version of one computed by Messahala; he also identifies the source of the Latin text which accompanies the horoscope.

Studies

See Schlauch **M93**, 147-8 and 162-3 for a brief discussion of the langauge of the work.

Eq3
Herdan, G. 'Chaucer's Authorship of the *Equatorie of the Planetis:*
The Use of Romance Vocabulary as Evidence,' *Language* 32 (1956)
254-9
Herdan calculates that the percentage of romance words (both
French and Latin) in *Eq* is typical of Chaucer's other works of comparable length, and he offers this as further evidence for Chaucer's
authorship. Herdan also argues that the percentage of romance
words in Chaucer's works is a logarithmic function of text length.
See also Mersand **M86**.

III
Backgrounds

The highly selective list of books and articles presented here has
been assembled to provide a basic guide for the various backgrounds of Chaucer's work. Included are standard works on the
14th
century, especially on 14th-century England. Some specialized
studies are also included in subjects such as astronomy, where
Chaucer had special interest and knowledge. Where several titles
might have been chosen, preference has been given to recent work
in order to provide relatively current information about the bibliography in the subject covered. Emphasis is needed on the fact that
Part III has been compiled as a guide to background reading on
Chaucer, not as an independent guide for the subjects treated.

BIBLIOGRAPHY

B1
Farrar, Clarissa P. and Austin P. Evans. *Bibliography of English Translations from Medieval Sources.* [Columbia University] Records of Civilization, Sources and Studies 39 (New York 1946)
Farrar and Evans list translations published through 1942; for translations published subsequently, see Ferguson **B2**.

B2
Ferguson, Mary Anne Heyward. *Bibliography of English Translations from Medieval Sources, 1943-1967.* [Columbia University] Records of Civilization, Sources and Studies 88 (New York and London 1974)
Ferguson continues the work of Farrar and Evans **B1**; for translations published 1968-72, see *Manuscripta;* for translations after 1972, see "Bibliography of Editions and Translations in Progress" compiled by Louis L. Gioia and published at the end of the first issue of each annual volume of *Speculum.*

B3
Graves, Edgar B., ed. *A Bibliography of English History to 1485 based on 'The Sources and Literature of English History from the Earliest Times to about 1485'* by Charles Gross. Issued under the sponsorship of The Royal Historical Society, The American Historical Association, and The Mediaeval Academy of America (Oxford and New York 1975)
This revision of the great bibliography of Charles Gross is indispensable for the study of all aspects of early English history.

B4
Guth, DeLloyd J. *Late-medieval England, 1377-1485.* Conference on British Studies Bibliographical Handbook (Cambridge, London, New York, Melbourne 1976)
Like Wilkinson **B5**, this study provides a supplement to Graves **B3**.

B5
Wilkinson, Bertie. *The High Middle Ages in England, 1154-1377.* Conference on British Studies Bibliographical Handbook (Cambridge, London, New York, Melbourne 1978)
Wilkinson is somewhat broader in scope than Graves **B3** and includes material on art and literary history.

CHAUCER'S WORLD

The works listed in this section are handbooks and collections of essays or contemporary documents prepared specifically to be companions to the study of Chaucer and other writers of his time. The title of this section is taken from Rickert **B13**, one of the best of the works on the subject.

For a mixed collection which includes contemporary writing, essays on 14th-century literature, and introductions to various aspects of late medieval culture, see Newstead **CrS11**.

B6
Ackerman, Robert W. *Backgrounds to Medieval English Literature* (New York and Toronto 1966)
Ackerman sketches in general terms the social and religious background of the Middle Ages.

B7
Brewer, Derek. *Chaucer in his Time* (London 1963, repr. 1965; repr. Westport, Conn. 1977)
Basing his account on quotations from primary sources, Brewer provides a sketch of the general culture of Chaucer's times; his chapters on home life, growing up, and court life are especially useful.

B8
Brewer, Derek, ed. *Geoffrey Chaucer.* Writers and their Background (London 1974; Athens, Ohio 1975)
This collection includes essays by different authors on various aspects of 14th-century culture. 'Gothic Chaucer,' the opening paper (pp. 1-32) by Brewer himself, is an able and stimulating essay on Chaucer's relation to his culture and its literary tradition. The other essays are listed in the appropriate sub-sections of this bibliography.

B9
Coulton, G.G. *Chaucer and his England* (London 1908; 8th ed. with new bibliography by T.W. Craik 1950; repr. 1952, 1963)
Coulton offers an entertaining, illustrated account of the social background of Chaucer's life and poetry; the work is now somewhat out of date.

B10
Hussey, Maurice. *Chaucer's World: A Pictorial Companion* (London

and New York 1968)
This volume is a pictorial companion to Hussey et al. **CrS45.**

B11
Loomis, Roger Sherman. *A Mirror of Chaucer's World* (Princeton 1965)
Loomis offers well-chosen illustrations, with commentaries, of various aspects of Chaucer's life and works, such as the Chaucer portraits, MS illuminations from the *Roman de la rose,* the wheel of Fortune, and London Bridge.

B12
Miller, Robert P., ed. *Chaucer: Sources and Backgrounds* (New York 1977)
Miller provides translations of extracts from medieval texts, some of which Chaucer knew and used; the others, selected to illustrate aspects of medieval thought, are grouped under such categories as 'The Antifeminist Tradition,' 'The Three Estates,' and 'Modes of Love.'

B13
Rickert, Edith, comp., with Clair C. Olson and Martin M. Crow, eds. *Chaucer's World* (New York and London 1948, repr. 1964)
This collection of extracts, in translation, from contemporary documents, is designed to illustrate 14th-century life and is arranged under such headings as 'London Life,' 'Education,' and 'Careers.'

FINE ARTS

For a discussion of aesthetics in late medieval thought see de Bruyne **B88.** For a convenient collection of excellent reproductions of late medieval art see Evans **B40.**

Visual Arts

BIBLIOGRAPHY

B14
Ehresmann, Donald L. *Fine Arts: A Bibliographic Guide to Basic Reference Works, Histories, and Handbooks* (Littleton, Colo. 1975; 2nd ed. 1979)

This comprehensive work covers architecture, sculpture, and painting; the most directly useful sections are ch. 6 on iconography and Section II of ch. 8 on the medieval period, arranged by country.

STUDIES

See Jordan **CrS46** for an attempt to connect the Gothic style in architecture with a Chaucerian aesthetic; see Mathew **B182** for the importance of the decorative arts in the courtly culture of Richard II.

B15
Braun, Hugh. *An Introduction to English Mediaeval Architecture* (London 1951, 2nd ed. 1968)
Most of the work is topically arranged by type of building; there are copious illustrations, a glossary of technical terms, and an index.
B16
Evans, Joan. 'Chaucer and Decorative Art,' *RES* 6 (1930) 408-12
Evans argues that Chaucer used themes from decorative art in his verse.
B17
_____ *Pattern: A Study of Ornament in Western Europe from 1180-1900,* vol. I (Oxford 1931)
This volume of Evans' comprehensive survey deals with the 13th through the 15th centuries; it is lavishly illustrated.
B18
_____ *English Art 1307-1461.* Oxford History of English Art 5, gen. ed. T.S.R. Boase (Oxford 1949)
Evans' detailed study of late medieval English art includes a bibliography and many fine black and white plates.
B19
Harvey, John. *The Mediaeval Architect* (London 1972)
Harvey gives an account of the theory and practice of architecture with an emphasis on the principles of design; he includes copious quotations from original sources, primarily English, French, and Latin, and an appendix of sources on style and symbolism.
B20
Kolve, V.A. 'Chaucer and the Visual Arts' in Brewer **B8**, 290-320

Kolve offers a stimulating and interesting analysis of Chaucer's visual imagination.
B21
Norris, Herbert. *Costume and Fashion,* vol. II: *Senlac to Bosworth, 1066-1485* (London, Toronto, New York 1927)
Norris offers detailed accounts, based on literary sources and on the visual arts, of materials and methods of making clothing; the discussion is arranged by period and within each period by social class.
B22
Pickering, F.P. *Literature and Art in the Middle Ages* (orig. German ed. Berlin 1966; Coral Gables, Fla. 1970; repr. London 1970)
Pickering analyses the difficulties of comparing literature and art; he suggests that the comparison is best made of specific motifs, such as Fortune's wheel, rather than of general style, such as 'gothic.'
B23
Platt, Colin. *The Atlas of Medieval Man* (London 1979)
Platt's illustrated atlas is concerned primarily with architecture and art, from the 11th century to the 15th. Its five chapters, on each of these five centuries, are divided into sections on historical context and material culture, and are accompanied by maps. Platt balances presentation of the art of Western Europe during its medieval period with presentation of contemporary artistic activity in other parts of the world, including Eastern Europe, the Near East, India, South-East Asia, the Far East, and the Americas. For the 14th century, see pp. 143-93.
B24
Rickert, Margaret. *Painting in Britain: The Middle Ages.* Pelican History of Art (London 1954, 2nd ed. 1965)
This survey includes a chapter, 'The International Style (1350-ca. 1420)' (pp. 146-79), which characterizes the style and discusses its sources; the work includes 200 pages of plates.
B25
Salter, Elizabeth. 'Medieval Poetry and the Visual Arts,' *E&S* n.s. 22 (1969) 16-32
In this cautionary essay on the difficulties of comparing literature and art, Salter discusses some areas in which comparisons might be valuable; she finds similarities between the problems of a poet who must balance drama and narrative in a work like *CT* and a MS

illuminator whose pictures must fit the text, balance the page, and please his patron.

B26

Salzman, L.F. *Building in England down to 1540: A Documentary History* (Oxford 1952, repr. 1967; repr. Millwood, N.Y. 1979)
Drawing on contemporary documentary evidence, Salzman discusses the attitudes of medieval builders and writers towards the buildings of the age. The work is topically arranged according to materials and methods of construction; it includes a valuable running account of the medieval technical terminology of the building trades as well as an Appendix with excerpts from primary sources describing medieval buildings.

B27

Schiller, Gertrud. *Ikonographie der christlichen Kunst*, 4 vols. in 5 (Gütersloh 1966-79; 2nd ed. of vols. I-II, 1969); *Registerbeiheft*, comp. Rupert Steiner (Gütersloh 1980); trans. of vols. I-II (2nd ed.) as *Iconography of Christian Art* by Janet Seligman (Greenwich, Conn. 1971-2)
Schiller studies the origins, development, and significance of individual pictorial themes, focussing on the life of Christ (vol. I), the Passion (II), the Resurrection (III), the Church (IV.1), and Mary (IV.2). A running theme is the process of secularization of iconography in the late Middle Ages. The work includes a thematic index and an index of biblical and legendary texts cited; more than one-third of each volume is devoted to plates.

B28

Stone, Lawrence. *Sculpture in Britain: The Middle Ages.* Pelican History of Art [29] (London and Baltimore 1955, 2nd ed. 1972)
Stone offers a discussion of changes in style and subject with some account of symbolism. Two chapters are directly relevant to the study of Chaucer: 'Sculpture of the Decorated Period (1275-1350)' (pp. 129-76) and 'The Reaction (1350-1410)' (pp. 177-94). There are 191 pages of plates.

B29

Tristram, E.W. *English Wall Painting of the Fourteenth Century*, ed. Eileen Tristram (London 1955)
Tristram gives a description and analysis of many individual paintings with special attention to frequently recurring allegories and

moralities and frequent references to parallels in literature; the apparatus includes a catalogue of wall-paintings, a list of subject paintings, an iconographic list, and 64 plates.

MUSIC

Bibliography

B30
Hughes, Andrew. *Medieval Music: The Sixth Liberal Art.* Toronto Medieval Bibliographies 4 (Toronto 1974, rev. ed. 1980)
This comprehensive, annotated bibliography is topically arranged and includes an index of subjects; the sections on philosophy and speculative theory, iconography, music in everyday life, and the lyric are of special interest.

Studies

See Chamberlain **PF4** for music in the *PF,* and Stevens **B190** for the importance of music at court.

B31
Bukofzer, Manfred F. 'Speculative Thinking in Mediaeval Music,' *Speculum* 17 (1942) 165-80
Bukofzer provides an introduction to some important topics in medieval musical theory, especially the classifications of music, the Pythagorean doctrine of numerical proportions, and the tendency towards interpolation as commentary.

B32
The New Oxford History of Music, vol. III: *Ars nova and the Renaissance, c. 1300-1450,* ed. Dom Anselm Hughes and Gerald Abraham (London and New York 1960)
This collaborative history of musical composition and performance includes three chapters especially relevant here: 'English Church Music in the Fourteenth Century' (Frank L. Harrison, pp. 82-106), 'Popular Secular Music in England' (Manfred F. Bukofzer, 107-33),

and 'Musical Instruments' (Gerald Hayes, 466-502).
B33
Olson, Clair C. 'Chaucer and the Music of the Fourteenth Century,'
Speculum 16 (1941) 64-91
Olson provides an introduction to medieval musical terminology
and examines the references to music in Chaucer's works.
B34
Reese, Gustave. *Music in the Middle Ages: With an Introduction on
the Music of Ancient Times* (New York 1940, repr. 1968)
The study is arranged chronologically within the basic divisions into
monody and polyphony; the chapter 'Polyphony in the British Isles
from the 12th Century to the Death of Dunstable' (pp. 387-424) is
of special interest.
B35
Wilkins, Nigel. *Music in the Age of Chaucer.* Chaucer Studies 1
(Cambridge, Woodbridge, Suffolk, and Totowa, N.J. 1979)
Wilkins offers an introduction to 14th-century music designed for
readers of Chaucer; he includes a chapter on Chaucer's references
to music.

ECONOMIC, POLITICAL, AND SOCIAL BACKGROUND

General Historical Studies

See **CT69-98** for studies dealing with the historical origins of
Chaucer's portraits of the Canterbury pilgrims.

B36
Armitage-Smith, Sydney. *John of Gaunt* (London 1904, repr. New
York 1964)
Although later scholarship has added and modified some details,
this monumental narrative biography is still valuable for the mass of
detailed information it offers concerning Chaucer's great patron.
B37
Bean, J.M.W. 'Plague, Population, and Economic Decline in
England in the Later Middle Ages,' *Economic History Review* 2nd
ser. 15 (1962-3) 423-37
Bean argues that general assumptions about the economic decline

caused by the plague may be misleading, because different areas reacted differently to onslaughts of the plague after 1348.
B38
Crump, C.G. and E.F. Jacob, eds. *The Legacy of the Middle Ages* (Oxford 1926, rev. ed. 1932; repr. 1938, 1943, 1948, 1951, 1962) This illustrated collection (41 plates) includes introductory essays on a variety of subjects: the Christian life (F.M. Powicke, pp. 23-57), architecture (W.R. Lethaby, 59-91), sculpture (Paul Vitry, 93-121), decorative and industrial arts (Marcel Aubert, 123-46), Latin literature (Claude Jenkins, 147-72), vernacular literature (Cesare Foligno, 173-95), handwriting (E.A. Lowe, 197-226), philosophy (C.R.S. Harris, 227-53), education (J.W. Adamson, 255-85), the position of women (Eileen Power, 401-33), economic activity of towns (N.S.B. Gras, 435-64), royal power and administration (Charles Johnson, 465-504), political thought (E.F. Jacob, 505-33). A distinctive feature of the book is the very full treatment of law: customary law (Paul Vinogradoff, 287-319), canon law (Gabriel Le Bras, 321-61), Roman law (Ed. Meynial, 363-99).
B39
Du Boulay, F.R.H. *The Age of Ambition: English Society in the Late Middle Ages* (London 1970)
Starting from the view that social and economic decline in this period was less widespread than previously thought, Du Boulay provides a discussion of such major social issues as class, marriage and sex, household and family, and attitudes to authority, among others. Much of the evidence cited is from the 15th century, but the book provides an excellent overview of Chaucer's times.
B40
Evans, Joan, ed. *The Flowering of the Middle Ages* (London 1966)
This lavishly illustrated volume includes 631 illustrations, 192 in colour, and essays, designed for a general audience, dealing with a variety of topics: medieval society (Christopher Brooke, pp. 11-40), the monastic world (George Zarnecki, 41-80), architecture (John Harvey, 81-132), court life (Christopher Hohler, 133-78), universities (Richard Hunt, 179-202), death (T.S.R. Boase, 203-44), trade (Donald King, 245-80), the craftsman (Andrew Martindale, 281-314), the end of the Middle Ages (Joan Evans, 315-41). The essay by Boase has been enlarged and published separately as *Death in the Middle Ages: Mortality, Judgment, and Remembrance,* Library of

Medieval Civilization (New York and London 1972).
B41
Henisch, Bridget Ann. *Fast and Feast: Food in Medieval Society* (University Park, Pa. and London 1976)
Henisch assembles and arranges topically a large collection of references to food in order to illustrate the complexity of medieval practices and attitudes towards food; most of the examples are from English sources of the 13th-15th centuries.
B42
Holmes, George. *The Later Middle Ages: 1272-1485.* Thomas Nelson and Sons, A History of England vol. 3, gen. eds. Christopher Brooke and Denis Mack Smith (Edinburgh 1962, rev. ed. 1967; repr. 1970, 1974)
This introductory survey is topically arranged within two broad divisions into the periods 1272-1361 and 1361-1485; it includes a selected bibliography.
B43
Huizinga, J. *The Waning of the Middle Ages: A Study of the Forms of Life, Thought, and Art in France and the Netherlands in the Dawn of the Renaissance,* trans. F. Hopman (orig. Dutch ed. 1919; English trans. of 2nd ed. 1924, repr. Garden City, N.Y. 1954)
Huizinga's influential study attempts to synthesize the style of late medieval culture as a whole; his thesis that the period represents a decline of chivalry, especially as it applies to England, has been challenged by others; see Benson and Leyerle **B175** for a review of this issue. The translation omits some of the valuable apparatus in the original edition.
B44
Hutchison, Harold F. *The Hollow Crown: A Life of Richard II* (London 1961)
Hutchison summarizes for the general reader the results of modern research and presents Richard II and his reign as 'a mirror to chivalry in brilliant decline.'
B45
Jones, Richard H. *The Royal Policy of Richard II: Absolutism in the Later Middle Ages.* Studies in Medieval History 10 (Oxford 1968)
Jones attempts to deduce Richard II's theory of sovereignty from his actions as king; the work serves as an excellent introduction to the

various meanings of 'sovereignty' in Chaucer's time.
B46
Jusserand, J.J. *English Wayfaring Life in the Middle Ages,* trans. Lucy
Toulmin Smith (1st French ed. Paris 1889; rev. and enlarged Eng.
ed. New York and London 1920, 4th ed. 1950; many reprints)
Although out of date, the work is a lively discussion of the state of
roads in medieval England and of the sorts of laymen and religious
who travelled them. Of particular interest is the account of
'Pilgrims and Pilgrimages' (pt. III, ch. 3). See also Hall **B93**.
B47
Kelly, Henry Ansgar. *Love and Marriage in the Age of Chaucer*
(Ithaca and London 1975)
On the basis of an examination of canon law, the medieval practice
of clandestine marriage, and his own interpretations of writings on
mysticism and of the medieval poetry of Chaucer and Gower and
their sources, Kelly argues that medieval lovers favoured marriage
and did not consider sexual passion incompatible with virtue; he
argues for a re-evaluation of the views of Lewis **B181**.
B48
Leyerle, John, ed. and intro. 'Five Papers on Marriage in the Middle
Ages,' *Viator* 4 (1973) 413-501
The essays written for this volume cover topics on women and
marriage; those of most direct relevance here are on the power to
choose a marriage partner (John T. Noonan, pp. 419-34), on
clandestine marriage and Chaucer's *Troilus* (Henry Ansgar Kelly,
435-57), and on medieval medical and scientific views of women
(Vern L. Bullough, 485-501). Kelly's essay is reprinted in **B47**.
B49
Lloyd, T.H. *The English Wool Trade in the Middle Ages* (Cambridge,
London, New York, Melbourne, 1977)
Lloyd traces the economic and political history of the growth and
decline of the English wool trade in the 13th through the 15th
centuries.
B50
McFarlane, K.B. *The Nobility of Later Medieval England: The Ford
Lectures for 1953 and Related Studies* [ed. J.P. Cooper and J.
Campbell] (Oxford 1973, repr. 1980)
This important collection of essays, edited after McFarlane's death,

is largely based on the study of genealogical and topographical records and the private accounts of noble families for the light they cast on political history. Of the eight items included, three are of most direct relevance here: The Ford Lectures, in six parts with four appendices, on 'The English Nobility, 1290-1536' (pp. 1-141); 'The Education of the Nobility in Later Medieval England' (228-47); and 'The English Nobility in the Later Middle Ages' (268-78).

B51
McKisack, May. *The Fourteenth Century, 1307-1399.* Oxford History of England 5 (Oxford 1959)
McKisack's study is the standard political history of the period; it includes full bibliographies, emphasizing the primary sources.

B52
Mullett, Charles F. *The Bubonic Plague in England: An Essay in the History of Preventive Medicine* (Lexington, Ky. 1956)
In a chapter surveying the effects of the Black Death (pp. 12-42), Mullett argues that in almost any of the 320 years from 1348-1668 some community suffered, and considerable regions were devastated on several occasions.

B53
Myers, A.R. *England in the Late Middle Ages.* Pelican History of England 4 (Harmondsworth and Baltimore 1952, 8th ed. 1971)
This brief survey combines a narrative of the political history of the period with separate chapters on the economic and social history, religious and educational movements, and the arts; it includes a book list, topically arranged.

B54
Postan, M.M. *The Medieval Economy and Society: An Economic History of Britain in the Middle Ages* (London 1972, repr. Harmondsworth and Baltimore 1975)
This survey discusses the medieval English economy and relates it to village and manorial society, towns, and trade.

B55
Power, Eileen E. *Medieval People* (London 1924, 10th ed. rev. 1963)
Power presents social history in the form of biographical studies of six representative figures: Bodo, a peasant; Marco Polo; a prioress; a Paris housewife; a merchant of the staple in the 15th century; and a clothier. The revised edition includes a preface by M.M. Postan

and an additional chapter on the last years of the Roman Empire.
See **M221**.
B56
_____ *Medieval Women,* ed. M.M. Postan (Cambridge, London,
New York, Melbourne 1975)
Power's study of medieval ideas about women was assembled
posthumously by M.M. Postan, who supplies the notes and
bibliography; it focusses mainly on the Church and the aristocracy
and explores the inconsistencies in the conflict between theory and
social reality.
B57
Robertson, D.W., Jr. 'Some Disputed Chaucerian Terminology,'
Speculum 52 (1977) 571-81; repr. in Robertson **CrS67**, 291-301
Robertson examines some recent work in social and economic
history to show how it casts light on the portraits in *GenProl.*
B58
Tuchman, Barbara W. *A Distant Mirror: The Calamitous 14th
Century* (New York 1978)
A popular book written by a non-specialist for the general reader,
this is primarily a political and military history, based on
contemporary chronicles and focussed on the conflict between
ideals and practices, a conflict which Tuchman sees as
characteristic of the period.
B59
Tuck, Anthony. *Richard II and the English Nobility* (London 1973,
repr. 1974)
Tuck traces the shifting alliances among the nobility and the
changing relationships between Richard II and the magnates; he
offers valuable insights into the political situation in which Chaucer
was involved for much of his life.
B60
Ziegler, Philip. *The Black Death* (New York 1969, repr. Harmondsworth and Baltimore 1970)
Ziegler's study is addressed to a general audience; its discussion of
the impact of the plague on England (pp. 117-86), and four
concluding chapters on various aspects of the effects of the plague
(202-80), are of special interest.

Studies of Selected Topics

THE HUNDRED YEARS WAR

B61

Allmand, C.T., ed. *Society at War: The Experience of England and France during the Hundred Years War* (Edinburgh 1973)
This collection of documents in translation illustrates the progress and effects of the war.

B62

Barnie, John. *War in Medieval English Society: Social Values and the Hundred Years War 1337-99* (London 1974)
Barnie emphasizes the role and importance of chivalric ideals in French and English society of the period.

B63

Froissart, Sir John [Jean]. *The Chronicles of England, France, and Spain,* H.P. Dunster's condensation of Thomas Johnes's version, intro. Charles W. Dunn (New York 1961)
This account of the Hundred Years War is by a contemporary chronicler whose poems were known to Chaucer. See **M158**.

B64

Palmer, J.J.N. *England, France, and Christendom, 1377-99* (London 1972)
Palmer discusses political events as they relate to the Hundred Years War; the work provides a useful background for Chaucer's diplomatic career.

B65

Perroy, Edouard. *The Hundred Years War,* trans. W.B. Wells (orig. French ed. Paris 1945; Eng. trans., ed. with intro. David C. Douglas, London 1951; repr. New York 1961, 1965)
Perroy combines military, social, and constitutional history in an illuminating narrative account. The introductory essay by Douglas (pp. ix-xxvi) provides a convenient summary of the main events and their significance.

LAW

See Kelly **B47** for contemporary laws relating to marriage and courtship.

B66
Alford, John A. 'Literature and Law in Medieval England,' *PMLA* 92 (1977) 941-51
Alford discusses some representative examples of the influence of legal language and legal thought on literature; he gives extended accounts of the Anglo-Norman *Château d'amour,* the harrowing of hell in *Piers Plowman,* and the metaphorical uses of marriage law in *Pearl* and in the religious lyric 'Quia amore langueo.'

B67
Harding, Alan. *The Law Courts of Medieval England.* Historical Problems, Studies and Documents 18 (London and New York 1973) 32-123, 162-93
Harding provides a brief introduction to the subject, accompanied by illustrative documents.

B68
Helmholz, R.H. *Marriage Litigation in Medieval England* (London and New York 1974)
Helmholz describes various aspects of marriage litigation, as illustrated from some of the surviving records of ecclesiastical courts.

B69
Holdsworth, W.S. *A History of English Law.* 16 vols. (London 1909-52; 7th ed. rev. A.L. Goodhart and H.G. Hanbury, with introductory essays and additions by S.B. Chrimes, 1956-66) vols. I-III
This monumental work combines topical and chronological arrangements: after an analysis of the nature and origins of the English judicial system (vol. I), Holdsworth gives an account of Anglo-Saxon law and medieval common law (vol. II); in vol. III, he examines selected topics important in the medieval period: the rules of law, land law, crime and torts, contracts, statutes, succession to chattels, and legal procedure. The work is useful as a source of detailed information on the meaning and significance of Chaucer's legal references and terminology.

B70
Kiralfy, A.K.R. and Gareth H. Jones, eds. *Selden Society: General Guide to the Society's Publications* (London 1960)
The Selden Society has published editions of many early English legal texts in use during the 14th century; the introductions are valuable for their elucidations of legal terms and concepts important in each text. This work gives detailed summaries of each volume. For Selden Society publications after 1961, it should be supplemented by the Society's handbook, *Publications, List of Members.*

LONDON

B71
Bird, Ruth. *The Turbulent London of Richard II* (London 1949)
Bird gives a detailed account of the social, economic, and political history of late 14th-century London, with an emphasis on the shifting political alliances of the time.
B72
Myers, A.R. *London in the Age of Chaucer.* Centers of Civilization Series 31 (Norman, Okla. 1972; 4th repr. 1974)
Myers describes London life, its customs, laws, social conditions, and government. He includes a selected bibliography, topically arranged, and a map of the city in Chaucer's time.
B73
Robertson, D.W., Jr. *Chaucer's London.* New Dimensions in History, Historical Cities (New York, London, Sydney, Toronto 1968)
Robertson's study is designed primarily for the reader of Chaucer; it includes a walking tour of the city, a brief chronicle of events, an account of city customs, and a discussion of London as an intellectual centre together with many interpolated references suggesting connections between these topics and Chaucer's works.
B74
Thrupp, Sylvia L. *The Merchant Class of Medieval London: 1300-1500* (Chicago 1948, repr. Ann Arbor 1962)
Thrupp provides a detailed account of a group of powerful London merchants with whom Chaucer was associated.

THE PEASANTS' REVOLT

See Gower **M147** for an account of the Peasants' Revolt by a
contemporary witness and friend of Chaucer.

B75
Dobson, R.B., comp. *The Peasants' Revolt of 1381* (London, New
York, Toronto, Melbourne 1970; 2nd ed. 1983)
The volume contains an excellent introduction, a chronology of the
revolt and its antecedents, a selection of illustrative documents in
translation, and a bibliography.

B76
Hilton, Rodney. *Bond Men Made Free: Medieval Peasant Movements
and the English Rising of 1381* (London 1973)
This Marxist interpretation places the revolt in the general context
of European peasant movements.

B77
Réville, André. *Le Soulèvement des travailleurs d'Angleterre en 1381*,
ed. Ch. Petit-Dutaillis. Mémoires et documents publiées par la
Société de l'Ecole des chartes 2 (Paris 1898)
Although long out of print, Réville's study is still a standard work
on the subject, largely because it is based on a wealth of archival
materials including judicial records, diplomatic records, and
unedited chronicles; a number of the most important documents are
printed in an Appendix. Petit-Dutaillis contributes a long and
helpful introduction (pp. xix-cxxxvi).

EDUCATION AND THE UNIVERSITIES

See Bennett **CT13** for Oxford and Cambridge in Chaucer's time,
Plimpton **M139** for illustrations of the school-books in use in
Chaucer's time, Severs **CT38** for Chaucer's clerks, and McFarlane
B50, 228-47 for an account of the kind of education available to the
nobility in Chaucer's time.

B78
Jacob, E.F. 'English University Clerks in the Later Middle Ages:
The Problem of Maintenance,' *Bulletin of the John Rylands Library*

29 (1946) 304-25; rev. and repr. in Jacob, *Essays in the Conciliar Epoch,* 3rd rev. ed. (Manchester 1963) 207-22
Jacob presents numerous examples from contemporary documents which illustrate the economic difficulties of university clerks.
B79
Leff, Gordon. *Paris and Oxford Universities in the Thirteenth and Fourteenth Centuries: An Institutional and Intellectual History.* New Dimensions in History, Essays in Comparative History (New York, London, Sydney 1968)
Leff treats the main intellectual and doctrinal developments at Paris and Oxford within the context of their universities.
B80
Orme, Nicholas. *English Schools in the Middle Ages* (London 1973)
Orme discusses the curriculum, various kinds of schools and their patrons, and traces the development of schools from the 12th century to the Elizabethan period.
B81
Paetow, Louis John. *The Arts Course at Medieval Universities with Special Reference to Grammar and Rhetoric.* University Studies of the University of Illinois 3, no. 7 (Champaign-Urbana 1910) 491-624; also printed separately (Champaign, Ill. 1910) 1-134
Focussing primarily on French universities, especially Paris and Toulouse, in the period 1150-1350, Paetow examines the neglect of the classics and the study of grammar and rhetoric, in an attempt to determine 'the aim and object and general trend of the actual instruction which was given'; he argues that his conclusions shed light on Oxford and Cambridge as well. The bibliography, pp. 603-24 (113-34), remains of particular value.
B82
Rashdall, Hastings. *The Universities of Europe in the Middle Ages,* vol. III: *English Universities — Student Life* (Oxford 1895; 2nd ed. rev. F.M. Powicke and A.B. Emden 1936, repr. 1942)
Rashdall gives a detailed account of life and learning at the various colleges of Oxford and Cambridge universities; most relevant here are the discussions of university and church relations (pp. 114-40), studies at Oxford (140-68), and the place of Oxford in medieval thought (236-73).
B83
Thompson, James Westfall. *The Medieval Library* (Chicago 1939; repr. with supplement by Blanche B. Boyer, New York and London

1967)

In Thompson's chronological survey, the chapter 'English Libraries in the Fourteenth and Fifteenth Centuries' brings together what has been discovered about their contents, and discusses the sources available for further research; the concluding four chapters discuss topics important to the medieval period as a whole: scriptoria, library administration and the care of books, the book trade and book prices, and the transmission of MSS.

INTELLECTUAL, PHILOSOPHICAL, AND RELIGIOUS BACKGROUND

General Studies

B84

Ackerman, Robert W. 'Chaucer, the Church, and Religion' in Rowland **CrS13**, 21-41

Drawing on a wide variety of recent scholarship on the Church and on Chaucer, Ackerman concludes that Chaucer's work gives some evidence of interest in the religious ideas and issues of his day but very little certain indication of his own personal beliefs; he includes a selected bibliography.

B85

Bloomfield, Morton W. *The Seven Deadly Sins: An Introduction to the History of a Religious Concept, with Special Reference to Medieval English Literature* (East Lansing, Mich. 1952; repr. 1967)

Bloomfield's definitive study of the seven capital sins in their literary tradition includes useful background material on the concepts of sin, penitence, and penance, and on the evolution of penitential literature.

B86

_____ 'Fourteenth-Century England: Realism and Rationalism in Wyclif and Chaucer,' *English Studies in Africa* 16 (1973) 59-70

Bloomfield discusses rationalist elements in Chaucer's works, their relation to Chaucer's own kind of literary realism, and their relation to 14th-century thought.

B87

Bruyne, Edgar de. *Etudes d'esthetique médiévale.* 3 vols. (Bruges 1946)

This monumental study includes a wealth of quotations from original sources illustrating medieval views on a variety of topics in aesthetic theory: the sources of aesthetic theory, the basic principles, the various kinds of aesthetic systems, views of the aesthetic experience, the nature of art, and the fine arts.

B88

———— *The Esthetics of the Middle Ages,* trans. Eileen B. Hennessey (New York 1969)

This translation is based on an abridged version of **B87**, *L'Esthetique du moyen âge* (Louvain 1947), which includes the main topics but omits many of the quotations from original sources.

B89

Carlyle, R.W. and A.J. Carlyle. *A History of Mediaeval Political Theory in the West.* 6 vols. (New York, Edinburgh, London 1903-36, repr. 1950; repr. New York 1950, 1953)

Focussing primarily on the ideas of justice and law in political philosophy, Carlyle and Carlyle cover the period from the 2nd to the 17th centuries; of particular relevance here is vol. VI on political theory from 1300 to 1600, but the other volumes are also useful in tracing the range of meaning associated with such ideas as sovereignty and natural law.

B90

Copleston, Frederick, S.J. *A History of Philosophy,* vol. II: *St. Augustine to Scotus;* vol. III: *Ockham to Suarez* (London 1947, many reprints)

Copleston focusses on important figures in the philosophy of medieval Christendom, summarizing and evaluating their main ideas; many lesser figures receive brief mention. Full indices, cross-references, and selected bibliographies make the work useful as a standard reference.

B91

Gilson, Etienne. *The Spirit of Mediaeval Philosophy (Gifford Lectures 1931-1932),* trans. A.H.C. Downes (London and New York 1936, repr. New York 1940 and London 1950)

Gilson maintains that the Middle Ages shared a coherent Christian philosophy, and in a series of essays, topically arranged, he analyses some of the fundamental attitudes and assumptions involved.

B92

———— *A History of Christian Philosophy in the Middle Ages* (New

York 1955)
Gilson's magisterial survey of the period from the 2nd through the
15th centuries is arranged chronologically by individual figures and
includes notes and bibliographies; a main theme is the assimilation
and adaptation of topics and concepts from Greek philosophy to
Christian thought.

B93
Hall, D.J. *English Mediaeval Pilgrimage* (London 1965)
Hall offers information on pilgrimage in Chaucer's time and
includes a chapter on the shrine of Thomas à Becket at Canterbury.
See also Jusserand **B46**.

B94
Jacob, E.F. 'Christian Humanism in the Late Middle Ages'
in *Europe in the Late Middle Ages*, ed. J.R. Hale, J.R.L. Highfield,
and B. Smalley (London 1965) 437-65
Jacob discusses the 14th- and early 15th-century humanists' interest
in Plato and the Fathers, especially Augustine.

B95
Knowles, David. *The Religious Orders in England.* 3 vols.
(Cambridge 1948-59)
In vol. II, which covers 1350 through the 15th century, Knowles
focusses on selected, hitherto less-explored topics: the diffusion of
Ockhamism in the English universities, conflicts and controversies
between monks and friars, and the literary work and controversial
interests of university monks. He discusses Chaucer specifically in
the context of contemporary criticism of religious (pp. 90-114),
noting the surprising 'moderation of tone' in his poetry, and he
includes an appendix (pp. 365-6) on Chaucer's Monk.

B96
_____ *The Evolution of Medieval Thought* (London 1962)
Knowles presents the history of medieval philosophy as a
continuation of Greek thought enriched by Christian teaching; his
account of the 14th century focusses on the aftermath of Aristotle,
Duns Scotus and Henry of Ghent, William of Ockham, and
nominalism.

B97
Ladner, Gerhart B. '*Homo viator:* Mediaeval Ideas on Alienation
and Order,' *Speculum* 42 (1967) 233-59
Ladner discusses the pervasive medieval idea of man as a wayfarer

towards a divine order and explores the relationship between these ideas of order and alienation in literature and philosophy.
B98
Leff, Gordon. *Bradwardine and the Pelagians: A Study of 'De causa Dei' and its Opponents.* Cambridge Studies in Medieval Life and Thought n.s. 5 (Cambridge 1957)
This specialist work on Bradwardine is useful for background to Chaucer's mention of Bradwardine (*NPT* 3242) in connection with the problem of foreordination and free will; see also Oberman **B102** and Robson **B107**.
B99
_____ *Medieval Thought: St. Augustine to Ockham*
(Harmondsworth and Baltimore 1958; repr. 1962, 1965, 1968, 1970)
Leff emphasizes variety and change in the ongoing effort in medieval philosophy to harmonize reason and faith. He divides his history into three sections, each preceded by a brief account of the main historical developments: 400-1000, 1000-1300, and 1300-1350. The section on the 14th century focusses on the conflict between scepticism and authority.
B100
_____ *The Dissolution of the Medieval Outlook: An Essay on Intellectual and Spiritual Change in the Fourteenth Century* (New York 1976)
In a topically arranged interpretive essay, Leff documents the increasing pluralism in 14th-century thought in a large number of fields, including philosophy, theology, the study of nature, and spiritual life.
B101
McFarlane, K.B. *John Wycliffe and the Beginnings of English Nonconformity* (London 1952, repr. 1966)
McFarlane discusses Wyclif's thought in the context of contemporary Oxford scholasticism and sketches the beginning of the Lollard movement.
B102
Oberman, H.A. *Archbishop Thomas Bradwardine, a Fourteenth Century Augustinian: A Study of his Theology in its Historical Context* (Utrecht 1957)
The main focus of Oberman's study is Bradwardine's views on

determinism in the context of contemporary theology; the study includes a chapter on contemporary doctrinal developments. See also Leff **B98**.

B103

_____ 'Fourteenth-Century Religious Thought: A Premature Profile,' *Speculum* 53 (1978) 80-93

Oberman stresses the diversity of views in the period and maintains that the most important sources of inspiration were St. Bonaventure and the Franciscan tradition; the main themes in the period are the new authority granted to 'experience' and 'simplicity.'

B104

Pantin, W.A. *The English Church in the Fourteenth Century: Based on the Birkbeck Lectures, 1948* (London 1955; repr. Toronto, Buffalo, London, 1980)

Pantin focusses on selected topics, arranged in three main sections: 'Church and State,' 'Intellectual Life and Controversy,' and 'Religious Literature.'

B105

Peck, Russell A. 'Chaucer and the Nominalist Questions,' *Speculum* 53 (1978) 745-60

Peck discusses Chaucer's theory of knowledge in relation to late medieval nominalism; footnotes provide bibliography on recent scholarship on nominalism.

B106

Rand, Edward Kennan. *Founders of the Middle Ages* (Cambridge, Mass. 1928; repr. New York 1957)

In a series of essays, Rand discusses the relations between the Church and pagan culture; the character and influence of St. Ambrose, St. Jerome, and Boethius; the 'new poetry,' the 'new education,' and St. Augustine and Dante. These essays were originally delivered as lectures to a general audience, and they are lucid introductions to these topics.

B107

Robson, J.A. *Wyclif and the Oxford Schools: The Relation of the 'Summa de ente' to the Scholastic Debates at Oxford in the Later Fourteenth Century* (Cambridge 1961)

Robson discusses Wyclif's metaphysics in the context of philosophical trends at Oxford during the period; of special interest to students of Chaucer is his comparison of Wyclif's and Bradwardine's views on free will and predestination; see also Leff **B98** and Oberman **B102**.

B108
Schlauch, Margaret. 'Chaucer's Doctrine of Kings and Tyrants,' *Speculum* 20 (1945) 133-56
Schlauch places Chaucer's references to rulers against a background of medieval political theory.

B109
Shepherd, Geoffrey. 'Religion and Philosophy in Chaucer' in Brewer **B8**, 262-89
Shepherd attempts to recreate a sense of the climate of thought in Chaucer's time, giving a brief account of the important issues and devoting an extensive section to Wyclif; he argues that Chaucer was little interested in most religious doctrinal controversies, but that his works do give evidence of interest in two philosophical problems current in the period: the certainty of knowledge and the relations among free will, foreknowledge, and grace.

B110
Southern, R.W. *Western Society and the Church in the Middle Ages.* Pelican History of the Church 2 (Harmondsworth and Baltimore 1970)
Southern's study combines topical and chronological arrangements; after a brief outline of the main features of the institutional history of the Church, he devotes chapters to the Eastern and Western churches, the papacy, the episcopacy, and the religious orders.

B111
Taylor, Henry Osborn. *The Mediaeval Mind: A History of the Development of Thought and Emotion in the Middle Ages.* 2 vols. (London 1911; 4th ed. 1925, repr. Cambridge, Mass. 1949)
Taylor's wide-ranging work is descriptive rather than analytical; it offers many summaries and paraphrases from medieval texts and concludes with consideration of the intellectual interests of the 12th and 13th centuries.

B112
Thompson, A. Hamilton. *The English Clergy and their Organization in the Later Middle Ages: The Ford Lectures for 1933* (Oxford 1947, repr. 1966)

Thompson includes chapters on the episcopate, diocesan administration, cathedral and collegiate churches, parish clergy, chantries, and monasteries.

B113
Ullmann, Walter. *A History of Political Thought: The Middle Ages.* Pelican History of Political Thought (Harmondsworth and Baltimore 1965, repr. 1968); reissued as *Medieval Political Thought* (Harmondsworth and Baltimore 1975)
Drawing on a variety of sources as well as abstract political theories, Ullmann traces the development of various views of the nature and locus of political authority; he adopts a chronological order and focusses the discussion on selected concepts rather than on the work of individual thinkers.

B114
_____ *The Individual and Society in the Middle Ages* (Baltimore 1966)
Ullmann traces the history of a political idea: the development from the concept of the individual as subject to the concept of the individual as citizen.

Anthologies of Religious and Philosophical Texts

See Colledge **B193** for selections from the English mystics.

B115
Hudson, Anne, ed. *Selections from English Wycliffite Writings* (London, New York, Melbourne 1978)
Hudson provides examples of Wycliffite polemic and excerpts from the Wycliffite Bible, topically arranged with useful notes and glossary.

B116
Hyman, Arthur and James J. Walsh, eds. *Philosophy in the Middle Ages: The Christian, Islamic, and Jewish Traditions* (New York, Evanston, London, 1967; repr. Indianapolis 1973, 1974)
This collection is especially useful for its full selections from the Islamic and Jewish traditions; it includes brief introductions and a selected bibliography.

B117
McKeon, Richard Peter, ed. and trans. *Selections from Medieval Philosophers.* 2 vols. (London 1928, New York 1929-30)
McKeon gives representative selections, with introductions.
B118
Wippel, John F. and Allan B. Wolter, eds. *Medieval Philosophy from St. Augustine to Nicholas of Cusa* (New York 1969)
The works included in this collection were chosen to illustrate the important philosophical issues of the period covered, but some of the extracts are obscure and difficult for the non-specialist. Short introductions and bibliographies are given for each section.

Preaching, the Bible, and the Liturgy

PREACHING

B119
Caplan, Harry. *Of Eloquence: Studies in Ancient and Mediaeval Rhetoric,* ed. and intro. Anne King and Helen North (Ithaca and London 1970)
This collection of Caplan's previously published essays includes several of particular interest to students of medieval sermon literature; see 'A Late Mediaeval Tractate on Preaching' (ch. III, pp. 40-78; includes translation), 'Rhetorical Invention in Some Mediaeval Tractates on Preaching' (IV, 79-92), 'The Four Senses of Scriptural Interpretation and the Mediaeval Theory of Preaching' (V, 93-104), 'Classical Rhetoric and the Mediaeval Theory of Preaching' (VI, 105-34), and ' "Henry of Hesse" on the Art of Preaching' (VII, 135-59; includes text and translation).
B120
Charland, Th.-M., OP. *Artes praedicandi: Contribution à l'histoire de la rhétorique au moyen âge,* intro. M.-D. Chenu. Publications de l'Institut d'études médiévales d'Ottawa 7 (Paris and Ottawa 1936)
Charland gives a detailed account of authors and MSS and of the development of the theory together with editions of treatises by Robert of Basevorn and Thomas Walleys.

THE BIBLE

B121
Deanesly, Margaret. *The Lollard Bible and Other Medieval Biblical Versions* (Cambridge 1920, repr. 1966)
Deanesly discusses early Bible translations and analyses the state of popular knowledge of the Bible before the appearance of the Wycliffite translations; she argues that lay people's knowledge of Scripture derived chiefly from sermons.

B122
Lampe, G.W.H., ed. *The Cambridge History of the Bible*, vol. II: *The West from the Fathers to the Reformation* (Cambridge 1969)
This collection includes the following articles of particular interest to students of Chaucer: 'The Bible in the Medieval Schools' (Beryl Smalley, pp. 197-220), 'The "People's Bible": Artists and Commentators' (R.L.P. Milburn, 280-308), 'English Versions of the Scriptures before Wyclif' (Geoffrey Shepherd, 362-86), and 'The Wycliffite Versions' (Henry Hargreaves, 387-414).

B123
Lubac, Henri de, SJ. *Exégèse médiévale: Les quatres sens de l'écriture.* 2 pts. in 4 vols. Collection Théologie, Etudes publiées sous la direction de la Faculté de Théologie S.J. de Lyon-Fourvière 41 [pt. 1, vols. I-II], 42 [pt. 2, vol. I], 59 [pt. 2, vol. II] (Paris 1959-64)
After tracing the origins and development of medieval traditions of exegesis, de Lubac adopts an arrangement by topics: the tradition of the relation between the two testaments, the tradition of the four senses of Scripture, the relation between symbolism and allegory, and exegesis in the scholastic period.

B124
Owst, G.R. *Preaching in Medieval England: An Introduction to Sermon Manuscripts of the Period c. 1350-1450.* Cambridge Studies in Medieval Life and Thought [1] (Cambridge 1926)
In this pioneering study, Owst argues for the importance of sermon MSS to the student of medieval literature and history.

B125
———— *Literature and Pulpit in Medieval England: A Neglected Chapter in the History of English Letters and of the English People* (Cambridge 1933, 2nd rev. ed. Oxford and New York 1961)
Quoting at length from numerous unpublished sermons, Owst shows

that Chaucer and his contemporaries drew extensively on popular homiletic tradition.

B126
Smalley, Beryl. *The Study of the Bible in the Middle Ages* (Oxford 1941; 2nd ed. 1952, repr. 1964)
Smalley traces the development of biblical exegesis from the Fathers to the friars, stopping at 1300. She deals exclusively with the learned and scholarly rather than the lay approach to the Bible, touching on such subjects as the compilation of the Ordinary Gloss and the development of different schools of exegesis.

B127
Wenzel, Siegfried. 'Chaucer and the Language of Contemporary Preaching,' *SP* 73 (1976) 138-61
Wenzel discusses a number of story plots, specific images, and technical terms which Chaucer borrowed from contemporary sermon literature.

THE LITURGY

B128
Pfaff, Richard W. *Medieval Latin Liturgy: A Select Bibliography.* Toronto Medieval Bibliographies 9 (Toronto, Buffalo, London 1982)
Pfaff provides sections (among others) on the Mass, the Daily Office, the Occasional Offices, liturgical year and observances, and English liturgy.

LITERARY BACKGROUND

Bibliography

See **M7-9** for annual bibliographies of work on medieval literature.

B129
Fisher, John H., ed. *The Medieval Literature of Western Europe: A Review of Research, mainly 1930-1960.* Modern Language Association of America (London and New York 1966, repr. 1968)
This volume is a collection of bibliographical essays, each

concentrating on the literature of a single language, including an essay on 'Middle English Literature to 1400' by Robert W. Ackerman (pp. 73-123, Chaucer section 110-22).

General Studies

B130
Bédier, Joseph. *Les Fabliaux: Etudes de littérature populaire et d'histoire littéraire du moyen âge* (Paris 1893, 6th ed. 1964)
In this important early study of the fabliaux, Bédier argues that they were written for a bourgeois audience; contrast Nykrog **B148**.
B131
Bennett, H.S. *Chaucer and the Fifteenth Century*. Oxford History of English Literature 2, pt. I (Oxford 1947, rev. ed. 1948; many reprints) 1-95
After a brief characterization of the age and an overview of religion in the period, Bennett describes the life and works of Chaucer, giving examples of what he considers the typical characteristics of his style and thought.
B132
Blake, Norman. *The English Language in Medieval Literature* (London, Melbourne, Toronto, and Totowa, N.J. 1977)
Blake discusses a variety of ways in which the nature of the English language in the Middle Ages may have affected the character of the literature; after a brief account of the literary and linguistic backgrounds, he discusses a variety of topics: word formation, wordplay, parody, themes, syntax, and levels of discourse.
B133
Bolgar, R.R. *The Classical Heritage and its Beneficiaries* (London 1954); repr. as *The Classical Heritage and its Beneficiaries from the Carolingian Age to the End of the Renaissance* (New York 1964)
Bolgar gives a general introductory survey to the history of classical studies in the period; Appendix II presents in tabular form the date and language of translations from Greek and Latin classics before 1600.
B134
Bolton, W.F., ed. *The Middle Ages.* [Sphere] History of Literature in the English Language 1 (London 1970) 67-402

The volume provides an introduction to a variety of topics in
Middle English literature: early literature, alliterative poetry,
Chaucer (pp. 159-262), late popular poetry, courtly poetry, and
prose.
B135
Chaytor, H.J. *From Script to Print: An Introduction to Medieval
Vernacular Literature* (Cambridge 1945, repr. New York 1967)
Chaytor provides a thoughtful examination of the differences
between literatures produced in the age of MS and in the age of
print.
B136
Cottle, Basil. *The Triumph of English, 1350-1400* (London 1969)
Cottle's introduction to English writings produced between 1350
and 1400 includes short texts and translations.
B137
Economou, George D. *The Goddess Natura in Medieval Literature*
(Cambridge, Mass. 1972)
Economou examines the image of nature in the *Consolatio
philosophiae* of Boethius, the *De mundi universitate* of Bernard
Silvestris, the *Planctus naturae* and *Anticlaudianus* of Alan of Lille,
the *Roman de la rose,* and *PF.*
B138
Gradon, Pamela. *Form and Style in Early English Literature* (London
1971)
Using as examples passages from Chaucer as well as from a wide
variety of other medieval texts, Gradon applies a structural
approach in linguistics to a study of selected aspects of the relation
of language to style and form.
B139
Highet, Gilbert. *The Classical Tradition: Greek and Roman
Influences in Western Literature* (New York and London 1949, 3rd
rev. ed. 1953; repr. New York 1957, 1967)
Highet outlines the influence of the classics on vernacular literatures
from 700-1949; the most useful sections here are his introductory
discussion of the transmission of the classical tradition to the
Middle Ages (pp. 1-14) and his accounts of classical influences on
medieval French literature (48-69), on Dante (70-80), on Petrarch
(81-8), on Boccaccio (89-93), and on Chaucer (93-103).

B140
Jackson, W.T.H. *The Literature of the Middle Ages* (New York and London 1960, 3rd repr. 1962)
Jackson's introductory study treats medieval literature in all languages as a unit; after introductory chapters on the influence of the classics, the motives of authors, the character of the medieval audience and the variety of literary types, Jackson discusses the romance, the *chanson de geste*, the Germanic epic, the medieval lyric, the drama, and the beast epic; the work includes a chronology and a selected bibliography.

B141
Jauss, Hans Robert. 'Form und Auffassung der Allegorie in der Tradition der *Psychomachia* (von Prudentius zum ersten *Romanz de la Rose*)' in *Medium aevum vivum: Festschrift für Walther Bulst*, ed. Jauss and Dieter Schaller (Heidelberg 1960) 179-206
Jauss shows that the distinction between allegory and symbol is a purely modern one.

B142
_____ 'Entstehung und Strukturwandel der allegorischen Dichtung' in Jauss, ed. *La Littérature didactique, allégorique, et satirique.* 2 vols., pt. VI of *Grundriss der romanischen Literaturen des Mittelalters*, gen. eds. Jauss and Erich Köhler, with Jean Frappier, Martin de Riquer, and Aurélio Roncaglia (Heidelberg 1968-70) I, 146-244; II, 203-80 (bibliography)
Jauss provides a thorough, detailed analysis of the evolution of allegorical poetry. Students who can read French but not German will find much of Jauss's work discussed in Jung **B143**.

B143
Jung, Marc-René. *Etudes sur la poème allégorique en France au moyen âge.* Romanica Helvetica 82 (Bern 1971)
Jung sets the *Roman de la rose* in the tradition of allegorical poetry in France and offers a reconsideration of the nature and significance of allegory.

B144
Lehmann, Paul. *Die Parodie im Mittelalter: Mit 24 ausgewahlten parodistischen Texten*, 2nd rev. ed. (Stuttgart 1963)
Lehmann defines and classifies medieval modes of parody and sketches the history of parody from the 11th to the 15th century;

most of his examples are from Latin texts, twenty-four of which are printed in the volume.

B145

Lewis, C.S. *The Discarded Image: An Introduction to Medieval and Renaissance Literature* (Cambridge 1964, repr. 1967)

In this important study, Lewis describes the image of the universe bequeathed by late antiquity to medieval poets; the impact of this tradition on Chaucer is a central concern.

B146

McPeek, James A.S. 'Chaucer and the Goliards,' *Speculum* 26 (1951) 332-6

McPeek discusses the resemblances between the *Apocalypsis Goliae*, the *Magister Golias de quodam abbate*, and *FrT, SumT*, and *PardT*.

B147

Muscatine, Charles. 'The Social Background of the Old French Fabliaux,' *Genre* 9 (1976-7) 1-19

Muscatine continues the work of Bédier **B130** and Nykrog **B148** on the origins and audience of Old French fabliaux and concludes that 'we cannot speak of simple homogeneous social classes nor of simple social attitudes.'

B148

Nykrog, Per. *Les Fabliaux: Etude d'histoire littéraire et de stylistique médiévale* (Copenhagen 1957; repr. Geneva 1973)

In a thorough study of the genre, Nykrog argues that the fabliau audience was as likely to have been aristocratic as bourgeois; for a contrasting view, see Bédier **B130**.

B149

Patch, Howard R. *The Goddess Fortuna in Mediaeval Literature* (Cambridge, Mass. 1927; repr. New York 1967, 1974)

Patch makes a thorough analysis of the figure and role of Fortuna in medieval literature, including material on the philosophy of Fortuna, her functions and cults, dwelling-place, and wheel.

B150

———— *The Other World: According to Descriptions in Medieval Literature* (Cambridge, Mass. 1950; repr. New York 1970)

Patch analyses the literature of visions, journeys to paradise, descriptions of heaven and hell, romance, and allegory as descriptions of 'the other world.'

B151
Pearsall, Derek and Elizabeth Salter. *Landscapes and Seasons of the Medieval World* (London 1973)
Pearsall and Salter trace changing images of nature in visual art and literature from Homer through the late medieval period; in ch. IV, 'The Enclosed Garden,' they give some account of garden imagery in *Rom* (pp. 83-96), *PF* (94-100, 193-4), *MerchT* (100-2), and *FranklT* (99-100). The printing of the plates is uneven and some are badly inked.

B152
Peter, John. *Complaint and Satire in Early English Literature* (Oxford 1956)
Peter devotes the first four chapters to medieval complaint, a mode he distinguishes from the satire characteristic of the Renaissance; he argues that Chaucer created his own tradition of satire, in contrast to the impersonal and conceptual complaint of his time. For a contrary view that emphasizes Chaucer's indebtedness to medieval complaint see Mann **CT53**.

B153
Piehler, Paul. *The Visionary Landscape: A Study in Medieval Allegory* (London 1971, repr. Montreal 1971)
Piehler studies the development of the landscape imagery of the medieval visionary allegory; after an introductory account of the nature of allegory and the character of central images in visionary allegories, he discusses individual works and authors: Boethius, Alan of Lille, John of Hauville's *Architrenius,* the *Roman de la rose,* the *Divina commedia,* and the *Pearl.* The work includes a chapter offering an archetypal description of these landscape images.

B154
Smalley, Beryl. *English Friars and Antiquity in the Early Fourteenth Century* (Oxford 1960)
Smalley discusses the literary work of a group of little-known learned English friars and their use of classical literature. See also Allen **B160**.

B155
Tristram, Philippa. *Figures of Life and Death in Medieval English Literature* (London 1976)
Using examples from visual art as well as from a wide variety of 14th- and 15th-century texts, Tristram discusses some themes

common in the work of Chaucer and his contemporaries, such as youth, age, the seasons, Fortune, and the figure of Death.
B156
Tuve, Rosemond. *Allegorical Imagery: Some Medieval Books and their Posterity* (Princeton 1966)
Tuve discusses a variety of kinds of allegory; she devotes a special section (pp. 233-83) to allegorical interpretations imposed on the *Roman de la rose* by such writers as Marot and Molinet, pointing out their distortions of the text and adding her own interpretation of the allegorical reading intended by Jean de Meun, whose continuation she sees as a discussion of misdirected love.
B157
Woolf, Rosemary. *The English Religious Lyric in the Middle Ages* (London 1968)
Woolf offers a wealth of detailed analysis of religious lyrics from the 13th through the 15th centuries, organized according to their principal subjects: the Passion, Death, the Virgin and her joys.

Studies of Selected Topics

MEDIEVAL RHETORIC AND POETICS

Bibliography

B158
Murphy, James J. *Medieval Rhetoric: A Select Bibliography.* Toronto Medieval Bibliographies 3 (Toronto and Buffalo 1971)
Murphy's bibliography covers rhetoric from the 5th to the early 15th century and includes a section on rhetorical works from the ancient world in use during this period. Separate sections are devoted to each of the important arts of language: the art of preaching, the art of letter-writing, grammar, and university disputation. The emphasis is on editions and translations of primary sources and on the basic secondary works in each area.
B159
Payne, Robert O. 'Chaucer and the Art of Rhetoric' in Rowland **CrS13**, 42-64
Payne gives a succinct review of scholarship on medieval rhetoric

and Chaucer's rhetoric, with a useful bibliography.

Studies

See Payne **CrS62** for an important and influential study of Chaucer's rhetoric. See Robertson **CrS66** for the controversial argument that medieval poetry was meant to be interpreted by the methods applied to scripture. See Caplan **B119** and Charland **B120** for the rhetoric of preaching.

B160
Allen, Judson Boyce. *The Friar as Critic: Literary Attitudes in the Later Middle Ages* (Nashville, Tenn. 1971)
Allen discusses the literary theories of the 14th-century 'classicizing friars' first studied by Smalley **B154**.

B161
Atkins, J.W.H. *English Literary Criticism: The Medieval Phase* (London 1943, repr. 1952)
Atkins' general history begins with the Anglo-Saxon grammarians and ends with Caxton and Skelton.

B162
Auerbach, Erich. *Mimesis: The Representation of Reality in Western Literature,* trans. Willard R. Trask (orig. German ed. Berne 1946; trans. Princeton, N.J. 1953)
An extremely important and influential book, Auerbach's study examines 'the representation of reality' in selections from works of Western literature from the *Odyssey* to *To the Lighthouse;* various medieval works, including the *Song of Roland* and the *Divina commedia*, are discussed.

B163
———— *Literary Language & its Public in Late Latin Antiquity and in the Middle Ages,* trans. Ralph Manheim (orig. German ed. Berne 1958; trans. London and New York 1965)
A supplement to *Mimesis* **B162**, this book concentrates on the literature of the period 600-1100, which was neglected in the earlier work.

B164
Baldwin, Charles S. *Medieval Rhetoric and Poetic (to 1400), Interpreted from Representative Works* (New York 1928; repr.

St. Clair Shores, Mich. 1972)
Baldwin offers a broad survey of rhetorical treatises from the
classical Sophists through the later Middle Ages, summarizing
briefly the major treatises and speculating on their influence; he
includes a helpful synoptic index.
B165
Curtius, Ernst Robert. *European Literature and the Latin Middle
Ages,* trans. Willard R. Trask (orig. German ed. Berne 1948, trans.
New York 1953)
Indispensable to any student of medieval literature, this massive and
learned study traces the development of the idea of literature in
Western literature, including material on literary mannerisms, topoi,
and rhetorical figures. The translation omits some of the valuable
footnotes in the original edition.
B166
Faral, Edmond. *Les Arts poétiques du XIIe et du XIIIe siècle:
Recherches et documents sur la technique littéraire du moyen âge*
(Paris 1924; repr. 1958, 1962)
Faral includes texts of some rhetorical treatises as well as an
influential study of the medieval rhetorical tradition.
B167
Manly, John Matthews. *Chaucer and the Rhetoricians.* The British
Academy Warton Lecture on English Poetry 17, *Proceedings of the
British Academy* 12 (1926) 95-113; also publ. separately (London
1926); repr. in Schoeck and Taylor **CrS15**, I, 268-90
Manly argues that Chaucer knew and used the techniques of
medieval rhetoricians such as Geoffrey of Vinsauf. See
Murphy **B170**.
B168
Middleton, Anne. 'The Idea of Public Poetry in the Reign of
Richard II,' *Speculum* 53 (1978) 94-114
Middleton suggests that the poets of Chaucer's age — pre-
eminently Langland, Gower, and Chaucer himself — wrote about,
and in the context of, a new idea of common good, what Chaucer
calls the "commune profit' (*PF* 75).
B169
Murphy, James J. *Rhetoric in the Middle Ages: A History of
Rhetorical Theory from Saint Augustine to the Renaissance* (Berkeley,
Los Angeles, London 1974)

Murphy divides his history into two parts: a survey of ancient rhetorical theory and its influence in the Middle Ages, and a discussion of the three principal medieval rhetorical genres — *ars poetriae, ars dictaminis,* and *ars praedicandi.*

B170

_____ 'A New Look at Chaucer and the Rhetoricians,' *RES* n.s. 15 (1964) 1-20

Murphy argues that Chaucer could have learned much of his rhetoric from grammatical textbooks, and that there is little evidence for the availability in 14th-century England of the *Poetria nova* of Geoffrey of Vinsauf, his apparent source for passages on rhetoric in *NPT* and *Tr.* See Manly **B167**.

B171

Olson, Glending. 'Deschamps' *Art de dictier* and Chaucer's Literary Environment,' *Speculum* 48 (1973) 714-23

Olson discusses Deschamps' treatise as an example of a non-Augustinian theory of poetry which presents poetry as a kind of 'natural music' designed to delight rather than to teach.

B172

Spitzer, Leo. 'Note on the Poetic and the Empirical "I" in Medieval Authors,' *Traditio* 4 (1946) 414-22

Spitzer examines the use of literary conventions and of unacknowledged sources by a number of medieval authors, and comments that first person narratives are not meant to be empirically true.

THE LITERATURE OF CHIVALRY AND COURTLY LOVE

B173

Andreae Capellani regii Francorum de amore libri tres, ed. E. Trojel (Copenhagen 1892, repr. Munich 1972)

Trojel's edition presents an authoritative text of *De amore,* a prose work of the late 12th century often called by the somewhat misleading title, *The Art of Courtly Love.* Little is known about Andreas beyond what can be learned from his text. The work has been interpreted as evidence that courts of love and a recognized system of aristocratic love existed in 12th-century northern France. For discussion of the text and its historical significance see

Boase **B176**, Lewis **B181**, and Newman **B183**.
B174
Andreas Capellanus on Love, ed. and trans. P.G. Walsh. Duckworth
Classical, Medieval, and Renaissance Editions, gen. ed. Nigel
Wilson (London 1982)
Walsh uses Trojel's text (**B173**) as the basis for his edition. The
introduction gives a good account of current views on *De amore,*
and the facing translation is accurate and clear.
B175
Benson, Larry D. and John Leyerle, eds. *Chivalric Literature: Essays
on Relations between Literature and Life in the Later Middle Ages.*
Studies in Medieval Culture 14 (Kalamazoo 1980, Toronto 1981)
The essays written for this volume illustrate the way in which the
concepts and practice of chivalry developed in a recurrent pattern:
literature influenced social behaviour, which became, in turn, the
subject of further literature. The conclusion is that both chivalry
and chivalric literature reached their most flourishing state in the
15th century.
B176
Boase, Roger. *The Origin and Meaning of Courtly Love: A Critical
Study of European Scholarship* (Manchester and Totowa, N.J. 1977)
The first part of this bibliographical study provides a chronological
survey of critical thinking about courtly love from 1500 to 1975.
The second part is a discussion of current theories about the origins
of courtly love; here the categories used by Boase are 'Hispano-
Arabic,' 'Chivalric-Matriarchal,' 'Crypto-Cathar,' 'Neoplatonic,'
'Bernardine-Marianist,' 'Spring Folk Ritual,' and 'Feudal-
Sociological.' The third part is a discussion of current theories about
the meaning of courtly love; here the categories used by Boase are
'Collective Fantasy,' 'Play Phenomenon,' 'Courtly Experience,'
'Stylistic Convention,' and 'Critical Fallacy.'
B177
Dronke, Peter. *Medieval Latin and the Rise of the European Love-
Lyric.* 2 vols. (Oxford 1965-6, 2nd ed. 1968)
Dronke argues that romantic love was a pervasive and important
theme in medieval as in other literature, even though, as he shows,
courtly love did not exist as a social phenomenon in the form
posited by earlier literary historians; he traces the development of
the theme with erudition and in detail.

B178

Green, Richard Firth. *Poets and Princepleasers: Literature and the English Court in the Late Middle Ages* (Toronto 1980)
Green combines social, economic, intellectual, and literary history in this study of court poets including Chaucer, and the nature and expectations of their audiences.

B179

Holzknecht, Karl Julius. *Literary Patronage in the Middle Ages* (Philadelphia 1923, repr. London 1966)
Holzknecht offers a broad survey of literary patronage and the social and economic conditions behind it; he discusses the work of a large number of court poets and includes Chaucer among them.

B180

Lawlor, John, ed. *Patterns of Love and Courtesy: Essays in Memory of C.S. Lewis* (London 1966; repr. Evanston, Ill. 1966)
These essays deal with love, friendship, and courtesy, as they appear in various works of medieval literature, and many of them use Lewis' *Allegory of Love* (**B181**) as a starting point. Of particular interest to the student of courtly-love literature of the 14th century are 'Dante and the Tradition of Courtly Love' (Colin Hardie, pp. 26-44), 'Ideals of Friendship' (Gervase Mathew, 45-53), 'Courtesy and the *Gawain*-Poet' (D.S. Brewer, 54-85), '*Troilus and Criseyde*: A Reconsideration' (Elizabeth Salter, 86-106) [already listed as **Tr58**], 'Gower's "Honeste Love" ' (J.A.W. Bennett, 107-21), 'On Romanticism in the *Confessio amantis*' (John Lawlor, 122-40), and 'Love and "Foul Delight": Some Contrasted Attitudes' (N.K. Coghill, 141-56).

B181

Lewis, C.S. *The Allegory of Love: A Study in Medieval Tradition* (Oxford 1936, many reprints; paperback repr. 1958)
In this important and extremely influential book, Lewis traces the allegorical love-vision in poetry from the *Roman de la rose* to the *Faerie Queene*, and discusses and defines courtly love. Some of the central points of the book are no longer widely accepted; examples are the distinction Lewis makes between allegory and symbol and his contention that courtly love was always adulterous.

B182

Mathew, Gervase. *The Court of Richard II* (London 1968)
Mathew discusses the culture and society of Richard's court, with

special emphasis on the role of Chaucer and other poets.
B183
Newman, F.X., ed. *The Meaning of Courtly Love*. Papers of the First
Annual Conference of the Center for Medieval and Early
Renaissance Studies, State University of New York at Binghamton,
March 17-18, 1967 (Albany 1968)
The essays in this volume provide a sample of modern views on
courtly love as a critical concept. The titles are as follows: 'Clio and
Venus: An Historical View of Medieval Love' (John F. Benton, pp.
19-42), 'Faith Unfaithful — The German Reaction to Courtly Love'
(W.T.H. Jackson, 55-76), 'The Concept of Courtly Love as an
Impediment to the Understanding of Medieval Texts' (D.W.
Robertson, Jr., 1-18), 'Dante: Within Courtly Love and Beyond'
(Charles S. Singleton, 43-54), 'Guenevere, or the Uses of Courtly
Love' (Theodore Silverstein, 77-90). The book concludes with 'A
Selected Bibliography on the Theory of Courtly Love' (97-102).
B184
Painter, Sidney. *French Chivalry: Chivalric Ideas and Practices in
Mediaeval France* (Baltimore 1940)
After an introductory chapter on the social history of French
nobility, Painter combines social, intellectual, and literary history in
an analysis of three types of chivalry: feudal chivalry, religious
chivalry, and courtly love. The work concludes with a discussion of
the conflicts and compromises among these kinds of chivalry.
B185
Paris, Gaston. 'Etudes sur les romans de la Table ronde: Lancelot du
Lac, II. Le *Conte de la Charrette*,' *Romania* 12 (1883) 459-534
In section IV, 'L'esprit du poème de Chrétien,' (pp. 516-34), of this
influential article, Paris introduces to critical vocabulary the term
'amour courtois,' commonly rendered as 'courtly love' in English.
He applies the term to the love of Lancelot and Guenevere as
described in Chrétien's romance and argues that the poem reflects a
concept of love new both to 12th-century France and to all of
Europe.
B186
Reiss, Edmund. 'Chaucer's *fyn lovynge* and the Late Medieval Sense
of *fin amor*' in *Medieval Studies in Honor of Lillian Herlands
Hornstein,* ed. Jess B. Bessinger, Jr. and Robert R. Raymo (New
York 1976) 181-91

Reiss shows that *fin amor* and its cognates generally refer, in the 14th century, to legitimate married love and Christian charity.
B187
Robertson, D.W., Jr. 'The Subject of the *De amore* of Andreas Capellanus,' *MP* 50 (1952-3) 145-61
Robertson sees the work (**B173**) as a bitter satire on courtly love.
B188
Steadman, John M. ' "Courtly Love" as a Problem of Style' in Esch **CrS9**, 1-33
Steadman discusses the rhetorical background of descriptions of love in courtly poetry.
B189
Stevens, John. *Medieval Romance: Themes and Approaches* (London 1973, repr. New York 1974)
Stevens describes the genre of medieval romance in a series of topically arranged chapters discussing the characteristic conventions and motifs; most of his examples are from English and French texts.
B190
_____ *Music and Poetry in the Early Tudor Court* (London 1961)
Stevens looks for principles of continuity in court culture from 1370 to 1530; he analyses social attitudes and the related literary conventions. Two chapters are of special relevance here: 'The Game of Love' (pp. 154-212) and 'The Courtly Makers from Chaucer to Wyatt' (203-32).

CHAUCER'S ENGLISH CONTEMPORARIES

The following list of works by Chaucer's English contemporaries is highly selective; it is intended to illustrate the range of the literature being produced by his countrymen in his time and the native literary background against which his works should be set. He probably knew many of these works, but there is no direct evidence for his knowledge of them. For a list of Middle English works showing clear affinities to Chaucer, see Skeat **M43**. Chaucer's demonstrable debt to work written in English is surprisingly small and it is to writing contemporary with his own; see **M143-9**.
His extensive borrowing from work written in French and Italian

includes considerable indebtedness to his contemporaries. See listings in the section on Chaucer's sources and influences (pp. 31ff) for the following authors who were writing during Chaucer's lifetime: Eustache Deschamps, Jean Froissart, Oton de Granson, and Guillaume de Machaut, all writing in French; Giovanni Boccaccio and Francesco Petrarca, writing in Italian.

In contrast, Chaucer's indebtedness for his extensive borrowings from work written in Latin is mainly to classical authors and medieval authors of the 12th and 13th centuries. Exceptions are Pierre Bersuire (ca. 1290-1362), Robert Holkot (ob. 1349), and Nicholas of Lynn (fl. 1386).

Anthologies

B191
Bevington, David, ed. *Medieval Drama* (Boston 1975)
Bevington gives selections from liturgical drama, 12th-century church drama, the Corpus Christi cycle, saints' plays or conversion plays, morality plays, and humanist drama; he includes introductions, and, where necessary, glosses and translations.
B192
Burrow, John, ed. *English Verse, 1300-1500*. Longman Annotated Anthologies of English Verse 1, gen. ed. Alastair Fowler (London and New York 1977)
This wide-ranging anthology with excellent annotations contains the full texts of *Sir Orfeo, The Hunting of the Cheviot,* and many short lyrics and carols, as well as extracts from *Pearl, Patience, Sir Gawain, Piers Plowman, Mum and the Sothsegger,* and from the works of Chaucer, Gower, Hoccleve, Lydgate, Charles d'Orléans, Henryson, and Dunbar.
B193
Colledge, Eric, ed. *The Medieval Mystics of England* (New York 1961)
Colledge offers a representative selection, in translation, of English mystical writing from Ailred of Rievaulx to Margery Kempe.
B194
Davies, R.T., ed. *Medieval English Lyrics: A Critical Anthology* (London 1963, repr. [Chicago] 1964)
Davies includes a lengthy introduction (pp. 13-50) giving a brief

history of the medieval lyric and a discussion of various kinds of lyrics and their origin; the texts are heavily glossed and, in many cases, closely paraphrased.

B195
Ford, Boris, ed. *The Age of Chaucer.* Pelican Guide to English Literature 1 (Harmondsworth 1954, repr. 1955; rev. ed. 1959, repr. 1961)
This volume contains a well-selected anthology of Middle English verse, including all of *Sir Gawain and the Green Knight, Sir Orfeo, Robert of Sicily, Wynnere and Wastoure, The Parlement of the Thre Ages,* the York *Crucifixion,* the Towneley *First Shepherds' Play,* and extracts from Gower, Robert Mannyng's *Handlyng Synne,* and *Piers Plowman.*

B196
French, Walter Hoyt and Charles Brockway Hale, eds. *Middle English Metrical Romances.* 2 vols. (New York 1930, repr. 1964)
Each selection in this anthology includes a brief introduction, mainly linguistic, and annotations; there is also a brief general introduction to the whole and a glossary.

Anonymous Works

B197
The Floure and the Leafe and The Assembly of Ladies, ed. D.A. Pearsall. Nelson's Medieval and Renaissance Library (London and Edinburgh 1962)
These two works were included in 16th-century collected editions of Chaucer; the *Assembly* was rejected from the Chaucer canon by Tyrwhitt in his 1778 edition (**CT3**); the *Floure and the Leafe* was rejected by Skeat in his reworking of Bell's edition in 1878. This edition includes a helpful glossary, an introduction discussing the poems and their relationship to Chaucer's work, and textual notes which cite parallels to Chaucer's works.

B198
Jack Upland, Friar Daw's Reply, and Upland's Rejoinder, ed. P.L. Heyworth. Oxford English Monographs (London 1968)
Heyworth dates these alliterative poems in the early 15th century and discusses their relationship to the Lollard controversies of the period; the edition includes full textual notes.

B199

'Rolle, Richard.' *The Pricke of Conscience (Stimulus conscientiae)*,
ed. Richard Morris (Berlin 1863, repr. New York 1973)
This typical didactic treatise, wrongly attributed to Rolle, was one
of the most popular works in Middle English, judging from the
number of MSS that survive.

Clanvowe, Sir John

B200

The Works of Sir John Clanvowe, ed. and intro. V.J. Scattergood
(Cambridge 1965; repr. Totowa, N.J. 1975)
Scattergood argues that both *The Boke of Cupide* (once attributed
to Chaucer) and the *Two Ways* are by Clanvowe; he gives an edition
of each text, together with introductions, notes, and glossary.
Clanvowe was a contemporary of Chaucer, a knight, and a member
of the court of Richard II.

Gower, John

See Gower **M145-8** for his works.

Henryson, Robert

B201

Testament of Cresseid in *The Poems of Robert Henryson*, ed. Denton
Fox (Oxford 1981) 111-31
Henryson's *Testament*, a continuation of *Tr*, was included in
Thynne's 1532 edition of Chaucer and was for centuries thought to
be by Chaucer himself. Fox's introduction (especially pp. lxxxii-
xciv) discusses the relation of the *Testament* to *Tr* as in part
imitation of Chaucer's poem, in part critical commentary on it. The
edition includes notes and glossary.

Hoccleve, Thomas

B202

Hoccleve's Works. 3 vols., I and III ed. Frederick J. Furnivall, EETS

e.s. 61, 72 (London 1892 and 1897); II ed. Sir Israel Gollancz, EETS e.s. 73 (London 1925, for 1897; repr. 1937); rev. ed. of EETS e.s. 61 and 73 as 1 vol. (1970)
A contemporary and self-styled pupil of Chaucer, Hoccleve makes a number of direct references in his poetry to his admiration for his master. This edition includes poems from Phillipps MS. 8151 and Durham MS. III.9, Ashburnham MS. Additional 133, and the *Regement of Princes* from Harleian MS. 4866, together with minor poems from Egerton MS. 615; the edition includes helpful indices and glossaries, as well as an introduction discussing Hoccleve's relationship with Chaucer and Chaucer's influence on his poetry.

Langland, William

B203
The Vision of William concerning Piers the Plowman: In Three Parallel Texts, together with Richard the Redeless, ed. Walter W. Skeat. 2 vols. (London 1886, repr. 1924; repr. with bibliographical note by J.A.W. Bennett 1954, 1961)
This edition prints all three texts of the poem on facing pages, and includes an introduction, notes, and glossary. The poem called here 'Richard the Redeless,' no longer thought to be by Langland, is now believed to be part of a poem called *Mum and the Sothsegger.*
B204
Langland, William. *The Vision of Piers Plowman,* ed. A.V.C. Schmidt. Everyman's University Library (U.K.), Everyman's Library (U.S.) (London and New York 1978)
This critical edition of the B-text is based on Cambridge, Trinity College, MS. B 15. 17, with selected variant readings; it includes an introduction, side glosses, and a textual and literary commentary.

Lydgate, John

B205
The Minor Poems of John Lydgate, ed. Henry Noble MacCracken. 2 vols. I: *Part I. 1. The Lydgate Canon, 2. Religious Poems,* EETS e.s. 107 (London 1911, for 1910; repr. 1961); II, with Miriam Sherwood: *Part II. Secular Poems,* EETS o.s. 192 (London 1934, for 1933)

Lydgate acknowledges his admiration for Chaucer and, particularly in his secular poems like the *Complaint of the Black Knight,* seeks to imitate him.

B206

Lydgate's *Siege of Thebes.* 2 vols. I, ed. Axel Erdmann, EETS e.s. 108 (London 1911); II, ed. Axel Erdmann and Eilert Ekwall, EETS e.s. 125 (London 1930, for 1920)

Lydgate's Introduction is an attempt to continue *CT.* It is noteworthy for Lydgate's comments on Chaucer's pilgrims and their tales; the *Siege,* in consequence, is often found in MSS with *CT.* This edition has an introduction discussing Lydgate's imitation of Chaucer and treatment of his other sources.

The *Pearl*-Poet

B207

Cleanness, ed. J.J. Anderson. Old and Middle English Texts, gen. ed. G.L. Brook (Manchester and New York 1977)

This conservatively-edited text of *Cleanness,* or *Purity,* as it is sometimes called, includes notes and a glossary.

B208

Patience, ed. J.J. Anderson. Old and Middle English Texts, gen. ed. G.L. Brook (Manchester and New York 1969)

A special feature of this edition is the appendix listing the Vulgate passages which parallel the poem.

B209

Pearl, ed. E.V. Gordon (London 1953, repr. 1966)

This edition has full notes, a good glossary, and appendices on metre, spelling, phonology, the Scandinavian element, the French element, and accidence.

B210

Sir Gawain and the Green Knight, ed. J.R.R. Tolkien and E.V. Gordon (Oxford 1925; 2nd ed. rev. Norman Davis, London 1967)

This edition includes an appendix with very full treatment of the language and metre; the introduction discusses the relationship of the poem to its sources and analogues. The very full notes to the text add further details about language and sources. The glossary, originally a separate publication, is the work of Tolkien.

SCIENTIFIC BACKGROUND

General Studies

See Curry **CrS35** and Aiken **CT364** for studies of Chaucer's use of scientific materials; see Gallacher **CT366** and Ussery **CT89** for his use of medical lore.

B211
Crombie, A.C. *Augustine to Galileo: The History of Science A.D. 400-1650* (London 1952; repr. Cambridge, Mass. 1953); rev. ed. *Medieval and Early Modern Science*, 2 vols. (Garden City, N.Y. 1959; repr. Harmondsworth 1969)
Crombie ranges widely over a variety of fields, such as astronomy, optics, mechanics, geology, chemistry, and biology, covering developments both in scientific theory and in technology; his underlying theme is the essential continuity of scientific thought in the Latin civilization of the West from Greek times to the 17th century. Illustrations, bibliographies, and indices make his work valuable for reference.

B212
Dictionary of Scientific Biography, ed. in chief Charles Coulston Gillispie. 16 vols. (New York 1970-80)
This encyclopedia includes many up-to-date biographies of medieval scientific figures, together with selected bibliographies.

B213
Duhem, Pierre M. *Le Système du monde: Histoire des doctrines cosmologiques de Platon à Copernic.* 10 vols. (Paris 1913-59, repr. 1956-73)
Duhem's history of ancient and medieval cosmological theory was the first important comprehensive history of medieval science; his underlying thesis is that medieval science anticipated many of the achievements of Galileo and other early modern scientists. The first two volumes deal with Greek cosmology; subsequent volumes deal with medieval Latin astronomy (III-IV), the influence of Aristotelianism (V-VI), physical theories in Paris in the 14th century (VII-IX), and cosmology in 15th-century Paris (X). A disadvantage of his thesis is that it tends to lead to an approach based on precursors; see **B217** for other approaches.

B214
Gimpel, Jean. *La Révolution industrielle du moyen âge* (Paris 1975); trans. as *The Medieval Machine: The Industrial Revolution of the Middle Ages* (New York 1976, repr. London 1977)
Gimpel argues that the Middle Ages was one of the great inventive eras and he offers evidence from a variety of fields of technology: production of energy, agriculture, mining, medieval industries, architecture, the mechanical clock, and experimental science. Throughout the work he speculates on the relation between technology and social and economic history.
B215
Grant, Edward, ed. *A Source Book in Medieval Science.* Source Books in the History of the Sciences (Cambridge, Mass. 1974)
This anthology is the single most useful collection of readings in medieval science available; it includes 190 selections from eighty-five authors, nearly half of them translated (by various hands) for the first time. The main emphasis is on mathematical, physical, and biological sciences in the Latin West, with some selections from alchemy, astrology, logic, and theology as well. Each section includes an introduction and critical commentary by an expert in the field, with annotations and selected bibliographies. The volume includes a comprehensive index of subjects and names.
B216
Kohl, Stephan. *Wissenschaft und Dichtung bei Chaucer: Dargestellt hauptsächlich am Beispiel der Medizin.* Studien zur Anglistik (Frankfurt am Main 1973)
Focussing primarily on medicine, Kohl examines Chaucer's attitude towards science together with the artistic use of science in his poetry, particularly *BD, HF, PF,* the love-sickness in *Tr* and *KnT,* and the portraits in *GenProl.* He argues that, unlike his references to astronomy and astrology, Chaucer's references to medicine show no expert or specialized knowledge of the field.
B217
Lindberg, David C., ed. *Science in the Middle Ages.* Chicago History of Science and Medicine (Chicago and London 1978)
This volume is a collaborative history, divided among sixteen authors writing on their specialities: science and technology in the early Middle Ages, the transmission of Greek and Arabic learning, philosophical background of science, the universities and science,

mathematics, the science of weights, the science of motion, cosmology, astronomy, optics, the science of matter (alchemy and chemistry), medicine, natural history, the classification of the sciences, and science and magic. Each essay is designed as an introductory account and includes notes and suggestions for further reading. The underlying approach of all the essays is to understand medieval science on its own terms, not as a precursor to modern science, and to suggest connections between the history of medieval science and social and intellectual history.

B218

Manzalaoui, Mahmoud. 'Chaucer and Science' in Brewer **B8**, 224-62

Manzaloui provides an introductory account of the nature and extent of Chaucer's use of scientific and pseudo-scientific material; a large part of the discussion deals with astronomy and astrology.

B219

Sarton, George. *Introduction to the History of Science.* Carnegie Institution of Washington, Publication 376. 3 vols., II and III in 2 pts. (Baltimore 1927-48)

The primary focus of this encyclopedic work is on western Europe, but Sarton includes substantial material on Islam, India, and the Far East. Its scope and learning are a remarkable achievement for one scholar; like most encyclopedists, however, Sarton is overly credulous and occasionally treats conjectures, some of them fanciful, as if they were established fact. Consequently, the work is to be used with caution. The scope of Sarton's inquiry can be seen in the plan of vol. III, pt. II, 'Science and Learning in the Fourteenth Century' (pp. 1019-2155). The opening chapter (1019-1333) is called 'Survey of Science and Intellectual Progress in the Second Half of the Fourteenth Century.' It has 14 sub-parts as follows: General Background; Religious Background; The Translators; Education; Philosophic and Cultural Background; Mathematics and Astronomy; Physics, Technology, and Music; Chemistry; Geography; Natural History; Medicine; Historiography; Law and Sociology; Philology. All but the first of these sub-parts are expanded subsequently into full chapters on their own. Such a summary scarcely prepares the reader for the light touches in the work; in the midst of his main account of Chaucer (pp. 1417-27), for example, Sarton has a section (1422-33) called 'A note about cats in

early English literature.'
B220
Talbot, C.H. *Medicine in Medieval England.* Oldburne History of
Science Library (London 1967)
Talbot's survey is addressed to the general reader and includes no
notes or scholarly apparatus; it combines topical and chronological
arrangement and begins with Anglo-Saxon medicine. Most directly
relevant here are the chapters on anatomy (pp. 116-24), the ordinary
medieval practitioner (125-33), and medical ethics and etiquette
(134-7).
B221
Thorndike, Lynn. *A History of Magic and Experimental Science
during the First Thirteen Centuries of Our Era.* 8 vols. (New York and
London 1923-58)
Thorndike surveys medieval science and magic, concentrating
mainly on empirical rather than theoretical aspects, and
summarizing and analysing a very large number of texts, many still
in MS. For the most part, the work is chronologically arranged,
according to individual thinkers; the first four volumes deal with the
13th and 14th centuries.
B222
White, Lynn, Jr. *Medieval Technology and Social Change* (London,
Oxford, New York 1962; repr. 1963, 1964, 1968)
White combines the history of technology with socio-cultural
history in a series of essays illustrating the variety of their
interrelationships; most directly relevant here is the chapter 'Stirrup,
Mounted Shock Combat, Feudalism, and Chivalry' (pp. 1-38).
B223
Winny, James. 'Chaucer's Science' in Hussey et al. **CrS45**, 153-84
Winny provides an introduction to medieval science for beginning
students of Chaucer and reflects on the fundamental habits of mind
behind the medieval scientific outlook.

Alchemy

See the section on *CYT* (**CT388-401**) for studies of alchemy that
relate directly to Chaucer's tale.

B224
Holmyard, E.J. *Alchemy* (Harmondsworth and Baltimore 1957, repr. 1968)
Despite the absence of critical apparatus, this well-illustrated popular introduction to alchemy, written by an eminent historian of science, provides a useful sketch of the subject.
B225
Hopkins, Arthur John. *Alchemy, Child of Greek Philosophy* (New York 1934)
Hopkins examines the philosophical roots of early alchemy and the role of the idea of colour change in the development of alchemy.
B226
Read, John. 'Alchemy and Alchemists,' *Folk-Lore* 44 (1933) 251-78
Read provides an excellent short introduction to alchemy.
B227
_____ *Prelude to Chemistry: An Outline of Alchemy, its Literature and Relationships* (London 1936, many reprints)
Read's introductory study emphasizes the mystical and literary side of alchemy and provides much information on alchemical emblems and late Renaissance alchemical treatises.
B228
Taylor, F. Sherwood. *The Alchemists: Founders of Modern Chemistry* (New York 1949, repr. 1974)
Taylor gives a clear, concise historical outline of the development of alchemy, starting with the earliest Greek and Chinese MSS and ending with the 18th century; the emphasis is on the scientific aspects of alchemy.

Astronomy and Astrology

See the sections on *Astr* and *Eq* for studies of the astronomical background and sources of those works. The notes in Skeat **M31** remain a valuable guide to specific astronomical references in Chaucer's works. See also Curry **CrS35** for some of Chaucer's astrological references, and Wood **CrS73** for a detailed study of Chaucer's poetic use of astrological imagery.

B229
Grimm, Florence M. *Astronomical Lore in Chaucer.* University of Nebraska Studies in Language, Literature, and Criticism 2 (Lincoln 1919, repr. New York 1970)
Grimm gives a brief account of Ptolemaic astronomy together with other basic cosmological ideas, then canvasses Chaucer's references to cosmology and astronomy, classifying them according to subject.
B230
Hartner, Willy. 'The Principle and Use of the Astrolabe' in *A Survey of Persian Art from Prehistoric Times to the Present,* ed. Arthur Upham Pope (London and New York 1939) VI, 2530-54
Hartner gives a clear explanation of the nature and use of an astrolabe.
B231
North, J.D. 'Kalenderes enlumyned ben they: Some Astronomical Themes in Chaucer,' *RES* n.s. 20 (1969) 129-54, 257-83, 418-44
North points out some errors in Curry **CrS35** and discusses Chaucer's astronomical references in detail.
B232
Orr, M.A. *Dante and the Early Astronomers* (London 1913)
Orr includes a survey of early and medieval astronomy, as well as a detailed discussion of Dante's astronomy.
B233
Pedersen, Olaf. *A Survey of the 'Almagest.'* Acta historica scientiarum naturalium et medicinalium 30 (Odense 1974)
Pedersen summarizes and discusses the significance of the main points of Ptolemy's authoritative work on astronomy. Although there were several Latin translations of the *Almagest* available in the later Middle Ages, including a version by Gerard of Cremona which Chaucer may have known (see **CT187**), Pedersen notes that the most popular vehicle for the planetary theory of Ptolemy was an anonymous handbook (sometimes wrongly attributed to Gerard of Cremona) called *Theorica planetarum* (ca. 1250-1300), extant in more than 200 MSS. The *Theorica* remains untranslated and unedited; the best English version of the *Almagest* is *Ptolemy's Almagest,* trans. and annotated by G.J. Toomer (London 1984), who also wrote the article on Ptolemy in the *Dictionary of Scientific Biography* (**B212**). A concluding chapter summarizes and discusses

the significance of the *Tetrabiblos,* Ptolemy's influential account of astrological predictions.

B234

Pedersen, Olaf and Mogens Pihl. *Early Physics and Astronomy: A Historical Introduction* (London and New York 1974)
The main emphasis of this study is on the mathematical description of nature as it gradually emerged in astronomy and also, to a lesser extent, in mechanics and physics; it includes a dictionary of scientists and authors of texts mentioned, together with bibliographies of modern studies of their work, which forms an excellent supplement in this field to the *Dictionary of Scientific Biography* **B212**.

B235

Saxl, Fritz, Hans Meier, and Patrick McGurk. *Verzeichnis astrologischer und mythologischer illustrierter Handschriften des lateinischen Mittelalters.* 4 vols.
- I. Fritz Saxl. *Die Handschriften in römischen Bibliotheken.* Sitzungsberichte der Heidelberger Akademie der Wissenschaften, philosophisch-historische Klasse, 6-7. Abhandlung 1915 (Heidelberg 1915);
- II. Fritz Saxl, *Die Handschriften der National-Bibliothek in Wien.* Sitzungsberichte ... 2. Abhandlung 1925-6 (Heidelberg 1927);
- III. Fritz Saxl and Hans Meier, *Handschriften in englischen Bibliotheken,* ed. Harry Bober. 2 pts. (London 1953);
- IV. Patrick McGurk, *Astrological Manuscripts in Italian Libraries (other than Rome)* (London 1966)

These excellent catalogues of MSS containing astrological and mythological illuminations include large numbers of plates and line drawings. In an introduction to vol. III (pt. I, pp. xii-xxxiv), Saxl outlines the development of illustrations of the constellations in medieval England. Vol. III (pt. II) includes indices compiled by Elisabeth Rosenbaum of MSS, incipits, persons, and subjects; it also includes many illuminations of the Troy story, among them two from Oxford, Bodleian Library, MS. Douce 331, a handsomely illuminated 15th-century MS of Boccaccio's *Il filostrato.*

B236

Smyser, Hamilton M. 'A View of Chaucer's Astronomy,' *Speculum* 45 (1970) 359-73

Smyser questions some of the conclusions of North **B231** about Chaucer's use of astrological references in *PF*, and discusses Chaucer's use of astrological references in general.

B237

Wedel, Theodore Otto. *The Mediaeval Attitude towards Astrology, particularly in England.* Yale Studies in English 60 (New Haven 1920)

Wedel traces the development of medieval thought on the value and proper use of astrology from Augustine to the 15th century, and he interprets references to astrology in medieval English literature. A special section on astrologers includes discussion of astrology in Gower and Chaucer (pp. 142-56).

B238

Wood, Chauncey. 'Chaucer and Astrology' in Rowland **CrS13**, 202-20

Wood discusses some of the basic sources for further work on Chaucer's uses of astrology and discusses research on some important astrological references in Chaucer's works; he includes an extensive bibliography. See also Wood **CrS73**.

Index

The index includes all ancient, medieval, and modern authors mentioned in this book. Letter-number references are to entries; page references indicate that the author in question is discussed in headnotes there. The references for ancient and medieval authors will be found under the *National Union Catalogue* spelling of their names.

Toronto Medieval Bibliographies

Editor: John Leyerle
Centre for Medieval Studies, University of Toronto

1 Hans Bekker-Nielsen, *Old Norse-Icelandic Studies* (1967) o/p

2 Fred C. Robinson, *Old English Literature* (1970) o/p

3 James J. Murphy, *Medieval Rhetoric* (1971)

4 Andrew Hughes, *Medieval Music: The Sixth Liberal Art* (1973)

5 Rachel Bromwich, *Medieval Celtic Literature* (1974)

6 Giles Constable, *Medieval Monasticism* (1976)

7 Robert A. Taylor, *La Littérature occitane du moyen âge* (1977)

8 Leonard E. Boyle, O.P., *Medieval Latin Palaeography* (1984)

9 Richard W. Pfaff, *Medieval Latin Liturgy* (1982)

10 John Leyerle and Anne Quick, *Chaucer* (1986)